MERCY

MERCY

The ESSENCE *of the* GOSPEL *and the* KEY *to* CHRISTIAN LIFE

CARDINAL WALTER KASPER
TRANSLATED BY WILLIAM MADGES

Paulist Press
New York / Mahwah, NJ

Jacket photos courtesy of the author.
Dust jacket design by Amy C. King
Book design by Lynn Else

Library of Congress Control Number: 2014930852

ISBN 978-0-8091-0609-7 (hardcover)
ISBN 978-1-58768-365-7 (e-book)

Published by Paulist Press
997 Macarthur Boulevard
Mahwah, New Jersey 07430

www.paulistpress.com

Printed and bound in the
United States of America

CONTENTS

CONTENTS

TRANSLATOR'S PREFACE

CARDINAL WALTER KASPER'S book, *Barmherzigkeit*, was published in Germany in 2012, one year before the election of Jorge Mario Bergoglio to succeed the retired Pope Benedict XVI. In many ways, the central themes of this book prefigure key elements in Pope Francis's vision of the church's mission and his own pontificate. From the very beginning of his papacy, Pope Francis has emphasized mercy and compassion. In the homily he gave at the inauguration of his Petrine ministry, on the feast of Saint Joseph (March 19, 2013), Pope Francis used the example of Joseph, as the protector of Mary and Jesus, to exhort Christians and all others to be protectors of one another and the environment. The vocation of protector, he said, "means protecting people, showing loving concern for each and every person, especially children, the elderly, those in need, who are often the last we think about." He continued:

> Here I would add one more thing: caring, protecting, demands goodness, it calls for a certain tenderness. In the Gospels, Saint Joseph appears as a strong and courageous man, a working man, yet in his heart we see great tenderness, which is not the virtue of the weak but rather a sign of strength of spirit and a capacity for concern, for compassion, for genuine openness to others, for love. We must not be afraid of goodness, of tenderness!

A half year after his election, he gave an interview published in *America* magazine (September 30, 2013), in which he laid stress on the service of mercy as central to the church's mission. "I see clearly," Pope Francis said, "that the thing the church needs most today is the ability to heal wounds and to warm the hearts of the faithful; it needs nearness, proximity." Calling upon the church's leaders to be "ministers of mercy above all," he laid out this vision for the church: "I dream of a church that is a mother and shepherdess. The church's ministers must be merciful, take responsibility for the people and accompany them like the good Samaritan, who washes, cleans and raises up his neighbor. This is pure Gospel."

Reproposing the gospel to those who had left the church or who were experiencing a crisis of faith was a special concern of Pope Benedict XVI. He had advocated, therefore, a "new evangelization." Pope Francis has continued this mission, making mercy one of its important components. In his address to participants in the plenary of the Pontifical Council for Promoting the New Evangelization (October 14, 2013), Pope Francis declared:

> We need Christians who make God's mercy and tenderness for every creature visible to the men of our day. We all know that the crisis of modern man is not superficial but profound. That is why the New Evangelization, while it calls us to have the courage to swim against the tide and to be converted from idols to the true God, cannot but use a language of mercy, which is expressed in gestures and attitudes even before words.

In his first apostolic exhortation, "The Joy of the Gospel" (November 24, 2013), Pope Francis reiterated this point: "The Church must be a place of mercy freely given, where everyone can feel welcomed, loved, forgiven and encouraged to live the good life of the Gospel" (*Evangelii Gaudium*, 114).

For Pope Francis, the new evangelization entails renewed focus upon Jesus as the embodiment of God's love and the exemplar of divine mercy. Jesus provides the example all Christians are to follow: "To get diverted by many secondary or superfluous things does not help; what helps is to focus on the fundamental reality, which is the encounter with Christ, with his mercy and with his love, and to love our brothers and sisters as he has loved us."

In this book, *Mercy: The Essence of the Gospel and the Key to Christian Life*, Cardinal Kasper explores in depth the meaning of mercy and the role it must play in the life of the church and the world. He calls for rethinking the Christian understanding of God. Rather than understanding God primarily in metaphysical terms (Being Itself; all-knowing, all-powerful, etc.), as has been the case for most of the history of the church, Cardinal Kasper, drawing upon deep biblical roots, identifies mercy as God's fundamental and defining attribute. He then describes the consequences for the praxis of the church and for the life of individual Christians entailed by this theological reorientation.

Beginning with a description of the pressing need for mercy in our contemporary world, Cardinal Kasper reviews how mercy is understood and articulated in philosophy, the Bible, and contemporary theology. The book explores the relationship between mercy and justice and describes the value and necessity of the spiritual and corporal works of mercy for church and society.

In translating, I have striven for accuracy, staying very close to Cardinal Kasper's German text, while also trying to make the translation as intelligible and readable as possible. Every translation, however, is also an interpretation. As other translators have acknowledged, it is sometimes very difficult to translate key terms the same way every time because the range of meanings of German words does not exactly match the range of meanings of the relevant cognate English words. The translator has to make choices based on his or her understanding of the author's intended meaning and the context.

It might prove helpful to the reader to offer here a few notes concerning some of the more important German terms, my translation of them, and their shades of meaning. German terms referring to the human attitudes and actions of mercy, pity, sympathy, and empathy occur regularly throughout *Mercy: The Essence of the Gospel and the Key to Christian Life*. Among the most frequent of these terms are *Barmherzigkeit* and *Erbarmen*. Virtually without exception, I have rendered both of those terms as "mercy," although each could also be translated as "compassion." *Mitleid* is another frequently recurring term, which I have usually rendered as "compassion," although it could also be translated as "mercy," "pity," or "sympathy." I have generally maintained consistency in translating *Barmherzigkeit*, *Erbarmen*, and *Mitleid* the same way in different contexts in order to accurately communicate the distinctive phenomenon Cardinal Kasper intended to describe in the respective contexts. "Mercy," "pity," "sympathy," and "compassion" are closely related terms. For this reason, I have inserted the German word in brackets where I thought it would make clearer the specific meaning Cardinal Kasper intended.

It may also be beneficial for the reader to know that *Barmherzigkeit* and *Erbarmen*, the words most frequently used by Cardinal Kasper to describe "merciful" attitudes and actions, have a depth of meaning that goes beyond an affective disposition. These terms can connote physical tenderness and concrete care. The stem *barm*, which appears in both German words, has been connected with a Teutonic word *barm*, meaning bosom. "Hence, *erbarmen* means literally 'to cherish in one's bosom, press to one's heart.'"[1] The other root in *Barmherzigkeit* is *Herz*, the word for "heart." Thus, *Barmherzigkeit* can trace roots that go back to the Latin *misericordia*, which, according to its original meaning, suggests that one has his or her heart (Latin, *cor*; German, *Herz*) with those who are poor or in distress (Latin, *miseri*; German, *arm*).[2] Cardinal Kasper draws out this connection in his exploration of the biblical roots of mercy.

The roots of the English word "mercy" are somewhat different. Rather than specifying the actual disposition of the person who exemplifies mercy, the word originally referred to the recompense accruing to the merciful person. Although deriving directly from the French (*merci*), "mercy" has roots going back to the Latin word *merces*, meaning reward or fee. "The post-classical uses of *merces* are developed from the specific application of the word to the reward in heaven which is earned by kindness to those who have no claim, and from whom no requital can be expected."[3]

Another related word that appears in Cardinal Kasper's text, although far less frequently, is *Mitgefühl*, which literally means "feeling with." I have generally translated *Mitgefühl* as "sympathy," to distinguish it from *Mitleid* ("compassion" or "pity"), which is the German equivalent of the Latin word *compassio* and the Greek συμπάθεια. In English and in German, "compassion" (*Mitleid*) and "sympathy" (*Mitgefühl*), although related terms, have developed slightly different shades of meaning. Although both involve a degree of mental or emotional participation in the suffering or distress of another, "compassion" has stronger "fellow feeling" and includes the impulse or desire to help or comfort the one who is in distress.

It is also necessary to say a few words about references to God in Cardinal Kasper's text. The German word for God is masculine and Cardinal Kasper consistently uses the masculine pronoun to refer to God. In general, I have kept these masculine references, but substituted gender-neutral language wherever that was possible without making the translation stilted or awkward.

In a few places, I have provided a footnote to further elucidate a term or to clarify Cardinal Kasper's reference to a historical, social, or cultural element in European or German history, with which English speakers may not be familiar. I have followed the American convention of citation for Cardinal Kasper's endnotes, providing English titles and citations, where available.

I am grateful to several colleagues who have provided valuable assistance in helping me to understand the specific context of a few of Cardinal Kasper's references or in resolving particular linguistic challenges: George Augustin, Thomas Buckley, Christopher Close, and Erik Huneke. In particular, I would like to single out Paul F. Knitter for his perspicacious linguistic suggestions and insightful theological comments. My gratitude also extends to Trace Murphy, my editor at Paulist Press. Of course, full responsibility for the translation ultimately rests with me. My hope is that this translation will provide appropriate and accurate access to Cardinal Kasper's thoughts on mercy and its implications for contemporary life.

Finally, I would like to acknowledge that having the opportunity to translate this important book has been immensely satisfying. It completes a circle in my relationship to Cardinal Kasper, whom I first met while attending his lectures on the doctrine of God at the University of Tübingen in the early 1980s. Many years later, work on a project dealing with Pope John Paul II's contributions to Jewish-Catholic relations provided another occasion to meet with him. In January 2011, it was then my pleasure to represent Saint Joseph's University (Philadelphia) in awarding Cardinal Kasper an honorary doctorate for his "exemplary work as a bishop-theologian who has promoted ecumenism among Christians and strengthened the relationship between the Catholic Church and the Jewish people."

With this book, Cardinal Kasper demonstrates the continuing vitality of his theological contributions and, by calling on his readers to reimagine our understanding of God and to engage in the service of mercy, he has defined an urgent task for church and society in the twenty-first century.

William Madges
Philadelphia
Advent 2013

FOREWORD

THE PRESENT SMALL volume originated in a plan to offer
a series of lectures for a retreat. But the lecture on the mercy of God
just didn't want to click. Every theological investigation into the
topic was no help. In the following years, I took up the theme again
and again. Thinking about and investigating this issue led me to fundamental questions about the doctrine of God and God's attributes
as well as to fundamental questions about Christian existence. I
determined that mercy, which is so central in the Bible, has by and
large been forgotten or is given very little attention in systematic theology. Christian spirituality and mysticism is way ahead of academic
theology in this question, as in other questions. Therefore, the present text attempts to connect theological reflection with spiritual, pastoral, and also social considerations concerning a culture of mercy.

Much is only beginning to be thought out. I dare to hope, however, that what I say can stimulate a younger generation of theologians to pick up the thread in order to think through anew the
Christian doctrine of God and the practical consequences that derive
from it, thereby giving shape to the necessary theocentric turn in theology and in the life of the church. In the process, overcoming the
alienation between academic and pastoral theology must be an
important concern.

I express my thanks to the Cardinal Walter Kasper Institute in
Vallendar, Professor Dr. George Augustin, Mr. Stefan Ley, and Mr.
Michael Wieninger for carefully reading and editing the manuscript.

I also thank the Herder Publishing Company for its careful supervision of this project.

Cardinal Walter Kasper
Rome
Lent 2012

I

MERCY
A Crucially Relevant,
but Forgotten Topic

1. The Cry for Mercy

THE TWENTIETH CENTURY that lies behind us was a horrible century in many respects, and the twenty-first century, which is still young and which began ominously and sensationally on September 11, 2001, with a terror attack on the World Trade Center in New York, promises as yet to be no better. In the twentieth century we had two brutal, totalitarian regimes; two world wars, with fifty to seventy million dead in the Second World War alone; as well as the genocide and mass murder of millions, concentration camps, and gulags. In the twenty-first century we live with the threat of ruthless terrorism, outrageous injustice, abused and starving children, millions of people in flight, increasing persecution of Christians, and—in addition—devastating natural catastrophes in the form of earthquakes, volcanic eruptions, tsunamis, floods, and droughts. All of that and much more are the "signs of the time."

In light of this situation, it is difficult for many people to speak of an all-powerful God who is simultaneously just and merciful. Where was he when all of this happened? Where is he when all of this is happening? Why does God permit all of this? Why doesn't he intervene? People ask, isn't all of this unjust suffering the strongest argument against belief in a God who is omnipotent and merciful?[1] In fact, in the modern era the suffering of the innocent became the bedrock of atheism (Georg Büchner). The only excuse for God, it was said, is that he does not exist (Stendhal). In light of this really diabolical outbreak of evil, isn't one obliged to deny God for the sake of God's greater honor (Odo Marquard)?[2]

Often enough, speaking of God is also difficult for those who believe in God. Even they find themselves often in a dark night of faith, in which speech fails them in light of the unending misfortune and unjust suffering in the world; in light of the heavy blows of fate and painful, incurable illnesses; in light of the horror of wars and violence. Fyodor Mikhailovich Dostoevsky, who, like others, experienced much suffering in his own life, writes in his novel, *The Brothers Karamazov*, about a child whom a squire has torn to pieces by his pack of dogs in front of his mother's very eyes. He states that such appalling injustice and the suffering of a child cannot be offset by some future happy ending. For this reason, he returns his entry ticket to heaven.[3] Romano Guardini, a deeply devout, but also deeply melancholy human being—when he was already marked for death—has said that "he would not only let himself be questioned at the Last Judgment, but that he too would ask questions." He hopes then to get an answer "to the question that no book, not even Scripture, and no dogma and no teaching office of the church could answer: Why, O God, these awful roundabout ways to salvation, why the suffering of the innocent, why so much wrong?"[4]

Suffering in the world is clearly modern atheism's weightiest argument. There are other arguments as well, such as the incompatibility of the traditional Christian worldview with the contemporary scientific and naturalistic worldview, which has been shaped, for instance, by the theory of evolution or recent brain research.[5] All of these arguments have had their effect. They have led to the fact that for many people today God no longer exists. At least many live their lives as if God does not exist. Most of them appear, in fact, to be able to live quite well, at least no worse than most Christians. That has changed the kind of question asked about God. For if God does not exist for many people or if he has become unimportant to them, then the protest against God no longer makes sense. The questions— "Why all this suffering?" and "Why must I suffer?"—more likely subside and fall silent. The question about a gracious God, which so very much troubled the young Martin Luther, is no longer asked by many today. The question leaves them indifferent and cold.

Resignation in the face of the question about meaning, and its accompanying defeatism, is found not only among people whom we often far too quickly dismiss disparagingly as superficial; it is also found today—as Jürgen Habermas has shown—among those who are highly reflective and philosophical.[6] However, a feeling of what is missing remains with many thoughtful people.[7] Besides the diverse physical adversities that are difficult enough to bear, there is also spiritual poverty, the loss of orientation, and the experiences of meaninglessness. "When the utopian oases dry up, a desert of banality and helplessness spreads."[8] Just because the old answers are surrendered, does not mean that persuasive new answers are automatically discovered as a result. A void arises.

Many can bravely endure this situation and get through it. They deserve our respect. The situation, however, drives others to despair. In light of a world that is experienced as absurd, they ask themselves: Would it be better not to have been born? For Albert Camus, suicide was the only philosophical problem that needs to be taken seriously.[9] But with the negation of God, human beings negate not only God, they also negate themselves. For yet others, anxiety about always-different, new, and anonymous specters takes the place of the deities and fear of a judgmental God.[10]

Many thoughtful human beings feel the seriousness of the situation and begin the search anew. There are more people who are seekers and more unrecognized, anonymous pilgrims than we usually imagine. When the question of meaning is no longer asked, they feel that this implies, in the final analysis, the abdication of the person as a human being and the loss of his or her true dignity. Without the question about meaning and without hope, we revert back to being resourceful animals, which can find enjoyment only in material things. But then everything becomes dreary and banal. No longer to pose at all the question about meaning means giving up the hope that there will once again be justice. In that case, however, the violent criminal would be in the right and the murderer would have triumphed over his innocent victim.

For this reason, it is not only devout Christians, but also many other thoughtful and attentive human beings who recognize that the proclamation of the death of God—completely differently from what Nietzsche had hoped—does not in fact entail the liberation of the human person.[11] Where faith in God evaporates, it leaves behind—as even Nietzsche knew—a void and an unending coldness.[12] Without God we are completely and hopelessly handed over to worldly fate, chance, and the impulses of history. Without God there is no longer an authority to which one can appeal. Without God there is no longer any hope for ultimate meaning and final justice.

The death of God in the souls of many people (Friedrich Nietzsche), the "absence of God" (Martin Heidegger),[13] the "eclipse of God" (Martin Buber)[14] all represent the deepest kind of authentic deprivation. It belongs to the "signs of the times" and to "the most serious problems of this age."[15] The quotation from Max Horkheimer is well known: "To save an unconditioned sense of meaning without God is vain."[16] Theodor W. Adorno spoke of the "inconceivability [*Unausdenkbarkeit*] of despair"[17] and wrote: "The only philosophy which can be responsibly practiced in face of despair is the attempt to contemplate all things as they would present themselves from the standpoint of redemption. Knowledge has no light but that shed on the world by redemption: all else is reconstruction, mere technique."[18] We can speak of a Kantian postulate in this sense: if humanity should have absolute dignity, then it is only on condition that God exists and that he is a God of mercy and grace.[19]

Such a postulate was not a proof of God's existence according to Kant. Kant's postulate rests, indeed, on the supposition that human life should entail happiness. To abandon this presupposition can lead to nihilism, and from nihilism very quickly end in the cynicism of lethal violence and even murder. So Kant's postulate is not a proof, but a clear indication at least that the question about God has not been settled. With this question about God, the meaning or meaninglessness of human existence is determined. That is the reason why the rumor of God can so stubbornly linger despite all enlightened and all pseudoenlightened arguments to the contrary.[20] It is not belief in God that has been shown to be foolish, but rather the theories of those who have prophesied the inexorable advance of secularization and the gradual extinction of religion. Those who thought that the death knell for faith in God is already ringing have made fools of themselves.[21]

One cannot be a supporter of the problematic thesis that religion is making a comeback because atheism is also experiencing a resurgence.[22] But one may extend the invitation to engage in reflections about God anew. In this process, it is not only a matter of asking, Does God exist?—as important as this question really is. It is a matter of the existence of a gracious God, the God who is "rich in mercy" (Eph 2:4), who consoles us so that we too can console others (2 Cor 1:3f.). For in the face of the vicious circle of evil, there can be hope of a new beginning only if we can hope in a gracious, merciful, and simultaneously all-powerful God, who alone can establish a new beginning, who alone can give us the courage to hope against all hope, and who can grant us the strength for a new beginning. It is a question of the living God, who gives life to the dead and who, in the end, wipes away every tear and makes everything new (Rev 21:4f.).

Augustine, the great church father of the West, according to his own testimony, experienced in his life the mercy and nearness of God, particularly when he knew he was the farthest from him. In his *Confessions*, he wrote: "Praise be to Thee, glory to Thee, O fountain of mercies. I became more wretched and Thou more close to me."[23] And he added: "Let him praise You not who does not realize Your mercies, which my soul's depths confess to You."[24] In fact, we must be silent about God if we don't know how to speak anew the message of God's mercy to the people who are in so much physical and spiritual distress. The question about God's mercy and about merciful human beings is, after all of the terrible experiences of the twentieth as well as the still-young twenty-first century, more pressing today than ever.

2. Mercy: A Fundamental Issue for the Twenty-First Century

Two popes in the second half of the twentieth century have clearly recognized the "signs of the time" and have urged that the question about mercy be moved anew into the center of the church's proclamation and praxis. John XXIII, "the good pope"—as the Italians lovingly called him—was the first to take up the challenge. His spiritual diary contains many profound reflections concerning God's mercy. For him, mercy is the most beautiful name and the most beautiful way to address God. Our wretchedness is the throne of divine mercy.[25] Pope John cites Psalm 89:2: "I declare that your steadfast love is established forever."[26]

Therefore, it was in keeping with John XXIII's inner conviction that had matured long before, and in keeping with his deep personal concern that, in his revolutionary speech for the opening of the Second Vatican Council on October 11, 1962, he said that the point of the Council is not only to repeat the traditional teaching of the church. The church's teaching—so he said—is well-known and stands firm. The church has opposed "the errors of every age. Frequently she has condemned them with the greatest severity. Nowadays, however, the Spouse of Christ prefers to make use of the medicine of mercy rather than that of severity."[27]

With this statement, the pope sounded a new tone, which caused many to sit up and take notice. Its effect was not lacking throughout the further course of the council. For all of the sixteen conciliar documents intended to surrender or change the traditional teaching of the church just as little as did the pope himself. They did not want a break with the previous tradition of the church. But they sounded a new tone and advocated a new style in the proclamation and life of the church. Like the pope himself, these documents recognized the connection between mercy and truth.[28] John XXIII characterized this new style by speaking of the pastoral purpose of the council.

During the council as well as after it, there were many discussions and also many misunderstandings about what the concept "pastoral" means.[29] Without getting into the technical discussion here, one can say: The new pastoral style, which John XXIII intended, has much to do with what he said during his opening speech, when he spoke about the medicine of mercy. Since that time, the theme of mercy has become fundamental not only for the council, but also for the entire pastoral praxis of the postconciliar church.

Pope John Paul II continued and deepened what John XXIII had started. The issue of mercy did not occur to him while sitting at the desk in his study. This pope—as few others—knew the history of suffering of the time and he experienced it concretely in his very person. He grew up in the vicinity of Auschwitz. In his youth, in his early years as a priest, and in his time as Bishop of Cracow, he lived through the horrors of two world wars and two brutal, totalitarian regimes. He also experienced much suffering in his own people and suffered much in his own life. His pontificate was marked by the consequences of the attempted assassination and, in his last years, by personal suffering. The witness of his suffering was a more powerful sermon than his many homilies and numerous writings. In this way, he made the message of mercy the leading theme of his long pontificate. He made the church of the twenty-first century take note of it.[30]

The very second encyclical of his pontificate, *Dives in Misericordia* (1980), was dedicated to the issue of mercy. The German translation of the encyclical was given the title *The Endangered Human Being and the Power of Mercy*.[31] In this encyclical, the pope reminded us that justice alone is not sufficient, for *summa iustitia* can also be *summa iniustitia*. The first canonization in the new third millennium, on April 30, 2000, dealt intentionally and programmatically with the issue of mercy. For on that day, he canonized the Polish sister and mystic Faustina Kowalska († 1938), who up to that point in time was not well-known. In her notes, this simple sister went beyond the neoscholastic academic theology and its purely abstract metaphysical doctrine of divine attributes. She described God's mercy, completely in tune with the Bible, as the greatest and highest of the divine attributes and she emphasized mercy as divine perfection pure and simple.[32] Faustina stands, therefore, in the great tradition of female mysticism. In this context, one needs to be reminded only of St. Catherine of Siena and St. Thérèse of Lisieux.

During his visit in Lagiewniki, a suburb of Cracow where Sister Faustina had lived, the pope said on June 7, 1997, that, by means of the tragic experience of the Second World War, history has inscribed the issue of mercy as a specific aid and inexhaustible source of hope. This message, in a certain way, shaped the picture of John Paul II's pontificate. In his homily on the occasion of Sister Faustina's canonization, he said this message should be like a ray of sunshine, illuminating humanity's path in the third millennium. During his last visit to his Polish homeland, on August 17, 2002, in Lagiewniki, he solemnly dedicated the world to divine mercy. On this occasion, he charged the church with the task of transmitting the fire of mercy to the world. Inspired by Sister Faustina, he declared the Sunday after Easter—"Low Sunday"—to be the Sunday of Mercy.

Many understood it as a sign of divine providence that this pope was called home to his Father's house on the evening before the Sunday of Mercy, on April 2, 2005. Pope Benedict XVI endorsed this interpretation on the occasion of declaring Pope John Paul II Blessed on the Sunday of Mercy, May 1, 2011. Already at the funeral Mass in St. Peter's Square on April 8, 2005, the then Cardinal Ratzinger, as cardinal deacon, emphasized mercy as the special concern of his predecessor and he adopted this concern as his own personal obligation. He said: "He [that is, Pope John Paul II] has shown us Easter's secret as the secret of divine mercy. In his last book, he writes: The boundary that has been set for evil 'is ultimately divine mercy.'" That is a literal quotation from the book that John Paul II published only a few months before his death under the title *Memory and Identity*. It expresses his central concern once again in summary fashion.[33]

During the Mass at the beginning of the conclave on April 18, 2005, Cardinal Ratzinger said:

> Full of joy we hear the announcement of the Year of Mercy: divine mercy sets a boundary to evil, the Holy Father told us. Jesus Christ is divine mercy in person: to encounter Christ is to encounter the mercy of God. Christ's

commission has become our commission through priestly anointing. We are charged with proclaiming "the Year of the Lord's Mercy" not only with words, but also with our lives and with the effective signs of the sacraments.

It cannot, therefore, be a surprise that Pope Benedict XVI, already in his first encyclical in 2006, *Deus Caritas Est* (*God Is Love*), continued his predecessor's line of thought and further deepened it theologically. In his 2009 social encyclical *Caritas in Veritate* (*Charity in Truth*), he concretized this theme with an eye to new challenges. Different from the previous social encyclicals, he proceeded no longer from justice, but from love as the basic principle of Christian social teaching. The pope thereby chose a new starting point for the church's social teaching and gave new impetus for taking up again, in a new way, the concern for mercy in a larger context.

Three popes from the second half of the twentieth century and at the beginning of the twenty-first century have, therefore, handed on to us the issue of mercy. Truly it is no secondary theme, but rather a fundamental theme of the Old and New Testaments and a fundamental issue for the twenty-first century as an answer to the "signs of the times."

3. Mercy: Criminally Neglected

Emphasizing mercy as the central topic for theology in the twenty-first century—for speech about God that gives a rational account of faith in God—means to pursue anew the central meaning of the message of divine mercy in the testimony of the Old as well as the New Testament.[34] As soon as one tries to do this, we make the astounding, in fact shocking, realization that this topic, which is so central for the Bible and so relevant for the present experience of reality, appears at best in the margins of the lexica and handbooks of dogmatic theology. In the traditional as well as in the more recent dogmatic handbooks, God's mercy is treated only as one of God's attributes among others. Most often it is treated only briefly and then only after the attributes that derive from God's metaphysical essence. Mercy, therefore, is in no way systematically determinative.[35] In the more recent handbooks, mercy is often completely absent[36] and, if it appears at all, then more likely incidentally. Exceptions prove the rule; they cannot, however, fundamentally change this general finding.[37]

One cannot characterize these findings in any way other than as disappointing, even catastrophic. What is now required is to think through anew the entire teaching about God's attributes and, in the process, to allow mercy to assume its proper place. For these findings can do justice neither to the central meaning of mercy in the Bible, nor to the horrible experiences of the twentieth century and our anxiety about the future at the beginning of the twenty-first century. In a situation when many contemporaries have become discouraged, without hope and without orientation, the message of God's mercy must be brought to bear as a message of assurance and hope. Thus, highlighting the significance of divine mercy for the present situation presents theology with a powerful provocation.

The failure of theological reflection concerning the message of mercy, which is central to the Bible, has allowed this concept often to be downgraded, degenerating into a "soft" spirituality or a vapid pastoral concern, lacking clear definition and forced somehow to suit each individual. Such a soft praxis may be understandable to a certain degree as a reaction against a ruthlessly rigid, legalistic praxis. But mercy becomes pseudomercy when it no longer has a trace of trembling before God, who is holy, and trembling before his justice and his judgment. It becomes pseudomercy when "yes" is no longer a "yes" and "no" is no longer a "no"; when it does not exceed, but rather undercuts the demand for justice. The gospel teaches the justification of the sinner, but not the justification of the sin. For this reason, we should love the sinner, but hate the sin.

The reason for the paltry treatment of mercy becomes obvious when we see that the divine attributes that are derived from God's metaphysical essence as Subsistent Being itself (*ipsum esse subsistens*) are the focus of the handbooks: simplicity, infinity, eternity, omnipresence, omniscience, omnipotence, and other attributes. The metaphysical determination of God's essence, which has shaped the entire theological tradition since the early days of the church, should in no way be fundamentally questioned. Its legitimacy as well as its limits will be investigated in detail later.[38] Here we should merely point out that, within the parameters of the metaphysical attributes of God, there is scarcely room for a concept of mercy, which derives not from the metaphysical essence, but rather from the historical self-revelation of God. Within the parameters of the metaphysical divine attributes, there is just as little room for the holiness and wrath of God, which is to say his opposition to evil. Forgetting mercy is, therefore, not some kind of secondary marginal problem for the doctrine of God; rather, it confronts us with the fundamental problem of determining God's essence and the divine attributes in general. It makes new thinking about the doctrine of God necessary.

The traditional metaphysical starting point of the doctrine of God brings with it an additional problem for talking about divine mercy. If, namely, God is Being Itself, then the absolute perfection of God's being follows from this absolute fullness of being. Such perfection entails God's inability to suffer (¢π£θεια) because suffering must be understood as a deficiency. On the basis of its metaphysical starting point, dogmatic theology has difficulty speaking of a compassionate God.[39] It has to exclude the possibility that God suffers (*pati*) with his creatures in a passive sense; it can only speak of pity [*Mitleid*] and mercy, in the active sense that God opposes the suffering of his creatures and provides them assistance.[40] The question that remains is whether this satisfactorily corresponds to the biblical understanding of God, who suffers [*mitleidet*] with his creatures, who as *misericors* has a heart (*cor*) with the poor and for the poor (*miseri*).[41] Can a God who is conceived so apathetically be really sympathetic?

Pastorally, this conception of God is a catastrophe. For a so abstractly conceived God appears to most people to be very distant from their personal situation. Such a God appears to them to have little or nothing to do with the situation of the world, in which almost daily horrible news reports come, one after the other, and many people are deeply troubled by anxieties about the future. The wide divergence between the experience of reality and the proclamation of faith has catastrophic consequences. For the proclamation of a God who is insensitive to suffering is a reason that God has become alien and finally irrelevant to many human beings.

Within the parameters of the metaphysical understanding of God, the issue of mercy in the theological handbooks could finally be handled only in connection with the issue of divine justice, and that is, justice as it was understood in ancient philosophy, namely, as giving each his or her due (*suum cuique*). Legal justice (*iustitia legalis*), distributive justice (*iustitia distributiva*), and retributive justice (*iustitia vindicativa*) are also relevant here. On the basis of his retributive justice, God rewards the good and punishes the bad. This again must raise the question of how divine mercy is to be brought into harmony with retributive justice. If God is merciful and does not punish the sinner, how can that be compatible with divine justice? The answer was: God is merciful to those remorseful sinners who are willing to change their ways, but he punishes those who do not regret their evil deeds and who do not change their ways. This answer is reasonable if one acknowledges retributive justice as a higher point of view, to which one subordinates mercy, so to speak, as the occasion of retributive justice.

The picture of a punitive and avenging God has thrown many people into a state of anxiety about their eternal salvation. The best known example and the one with the greatest consequences in church history is young Martin Luther, for whom the question—"How do I get a gracious God?"—caused a frightening turmoil of conscience for a long time until he came to know that, according to the Bible, God's justice is not God's punitive justice, but rather God's justifying justice, which includes his mercy. The church became divided over this issue in the sixteenth century. The relation of justice and mercy thus became the fateful question of Western theology.[42]

Not until the twentieth century could we find a fundamental consensus between Lutherans and Catholics concerning the question of the justification of the sinner.[43] That was only possible because together we realized that God's justice is his mercy. Nevertheless, the implications for the doctrine of God and for a new way of speaking about a liberating and justifying God, which are entailed by our agreement concerning the doctrine of justification, have scarcely been drawn up to now. Here we face a fundamental common challenge in reference to a new evangelization.

We stand, therefore, before the task of pulling mercy out of the Cinderella existence into which it has fallen in traditional theology. This must happen without falling victim to the banal and trivializing image of a saccharine "dear God," which turns God into a good-spirited pal and no longer takes seriously God's holiness. Mercy must be understood as God's own justice and as his holiness. Only in this sense can we make the image of the good and merciful father, whom Jesus proclaimed to us, shine again. We could also say: it is necessary to draw a picture of a sympathetic God. That is doubly necessary in the face of ideological distortions of the God image.

4. Mercy under Ideological Suspicion

Mercy is not only an internal theological problem; in the analysis of modern ideology, it is also a social problem. The problem confronts us above all in Karl Marx and in Marxism. Marx characterized religion as the "foundation of consolation and justification" of the world. Religious misery was for him an expression of real misery and simultaneously a protest against real misery. "Religion is the sigh of the oppressed creature as it is the soul of soulless conditions. It is the opium of the people."[44]

This oft-quoted sentence is often interpreted in a one-sided way as critical of religion. It is, however, not only negative in reference to religion. It definitely acknowledges that religion offers a justified element of protest: religion as protest against misery, injustice, and bourgeois self-satisfaction. Marx, however, is convinced that religion's protest ideologically leads in the wrong direction, becomes mere consolation, and leads to a false flight from the world. One cannot honestly deny that such ideological misuse of religion has existed and continues to exist.

But such misuse cannot be the justification for labeling religious consolation in general as ideology. That would be a new injustice against those human beings who, in their distress, sought help in religion and found strength therein for dealing with life in this world. Religion and mercy have often been the source of protest against injustice and violence as well as the impetus for powerful action against them. The rise of Christian social movements, already during Karl Marx's time, is evidence in support of this thesis.[45]

Still, the attempt to want to do away with all misfortune and suffering by force, as undertaken by ideological and totalitarian communism, was not only unsuccessful—as we know from painful experience—but it also caused real, untold misery and suffering for millions of people. There is shocking evidence that the godless, harsh, and merciless world of Stalin's communism led to human misery and desolation. In that world, supposedly only justice counted and not mercy, which was regarded as an antiquated bourgeois disposition. Precisely in the total absence of mercy, the cry for mercy was still heard.[46]

In Friedrich Nietzsche we find a completely different kind of critique of compassion [*Mitleid*] and mercy than in Marxism. Over against rational thought, characterized by him as Apollonian, Nietzsche set the Dionysian, a creative kind of thinking, which breaks all the molds and exhibits an intoxicated feeling for life. On the basis of the Dionysian affirmation of life, Nietzsche sees sympathy as the propagation of suffering. For him, mercy is not altruism, but a refined form of egoism and self-enjoyment because the one who is merciful condescendingly wants the one who is poor to be shown and to feel the merciful person's own superiority.[47] In his major work, *Thus Spake Zarathustra*, Nietzsche proclaims a kind of countergospel to the Christian gospel of mercy: "God is dead; God died of sympathy [*Mitleiden*]—suffering with—human beings." Because of the death of God, room is created for the superman and his will to power. For this reason, Nietzsche can say in antithesis to the Sermon on the Mount: "I do not like the merciful.... But all those who create are strong."[48] Thus in the end, for Nietzsche, Dionysius stands over against Christ the Crucified.[49]

In the National Socialist (Nazi) elite schools, Nietzsche's words "Praised be whatever makes strong" mattered—whether the phrase was used in the proper sense or not may remain open.[50] Nietzsche's words about master morality[51] and the master race[52] had a bad history of effects. The consequences of the National Socialist ideology were inhuman. For this reason, no one today may even utter such words as master race. That does not mean that a lack of mercy isn't operative very often in Western societies. Unfortunately, now as before, there is hostility toward foreigners as well as arrogant attitudes toward other cultures.

In addition, there are Social Darwinist tendencies in our society. According to such tendencies, the rights of the stronger and the promotion of one's own selfish interests, without regard for others, are legal tender. Those who are unable to hold their own easily go to rack and ruin. Above all, in the wake of the globalization of the economy and the financial markets, unregulated, unchained neocapitalistic forces have become powerful. For such forces, human beings and entire peoples have become, often pitilessly, the playthings of the greed for money.[53]

It is significant that words like "mercy" and "pity" have largely gone out of fashion. In the ears of many, they sound sentimental. They have been used up and appear old and dusty. Behind this development lurks this attitude: whoever does not bend to the current game rules of the society of the strong, healthy, and successful or who doesn't feel comfortable with these rules, whoever holds firm to the beatitudes of the Sermon on the Mount, which put into question exactly this order of things and really inverts it, he or she is perceived to be naïve and out of place. They are greeted with pity and smiles like Prince Myshkin in Dostoevsky's novel *The Idiot*. The word pity [*Mitleid*] so often has a negative, almost cynical sound to it.[54] In our society it appears then that things don't look good for pity and mercy. Fortunately, there certainly are movements in the opposite direction.

5. Empathy and Compassion:
A New Approach

The cry for sympathy [*Mitgefühl*] and mercy has in no way been stifled in the present; in fact, it has strengthened. Although the words "pity" and "mercy" may, by and large, be "out," the corresponding views and attitudes are not. There was and continues to be a sense of stunned horror at the cold-bloodedness of the bureaucratically organized, National Socialist politics of extermination, just as there is horror at the widespread indifference and coldness of a world that has become individualistic. We are also horrified by outbreaks of violence among youth, in which others are beaten senseless, kicked, and tormented, even to the point of death. Natural catastrophes and starvation in catastrophic proportions unleash again and again an impressive wave of sympathy and a readiness to help. In such situations, the assistance provided by families, neighborhoods, and communities is not to be forgotten—even though it is most often unknown and publicly little recognized. Thank God, compassion [*Mitleid*] and mercy are by no means totally alien to us today; they have not disappeared.

Compassion—or as one prefers to say: empathy (the understanding that comes from feeling oneself in another's shoes)—has become a new and important paradigm in modern psychology and psychotherapy, in pedagogy, sociology, and pastoral work.[55] To be able to put oneself into the situation, into the feelings, thoughts, and existential situation of another, in order thereby to understand his or her thinking and acting, is generally regarded today as the presupposition of successful interpersonal relationships and as proof of genuine humanity. To be able to put oneself into the feelings, thoughts, and existential situation of another culture and another people is, moreover, the basic presupposition of intercultural encounter, peaceful relations, and cooperation between religions and cultures, just as it is the basic presupposition of politics and diplomacy in the service of peace.

Others prefer to speak of the neologism "compassion" rather than of empathy. Compassion is the name of a children's relief organization, which searches for sponsors for children living anywhere in the world who suffer deprivation.* The organization seeks sponsors who assist in overcoming the poverty and enabling the sponsored child to have a positive future. Meanwhile, Compassion also stands for an educational project, which aims to impart social learning, social competence, and social responsibility.[56] Finally, there is a *Charter for Compassion*, to which especially Karen Armstrong is committed.† In this way we see that the apparently antiquated concept has returned under a new name and in a new form.

Theology has taken up these concerns and has attempted to make them theologically fruitful. Johann Baptist Metz has declared compassion to be Christianity's program and policy for the world in the pluralistic age of religions and cultures.[57] Already in earlier publications, he made the God question, considered within the horizon of the experiences of injustice and suffering, the focal point and he demanded a theology that is sensitive to suffering and theodicy.[58]

Naturally, no merely sentimental pity and, so to speak, toothless mercy is thereby intended. One must understand the word *compassion* not only as compassionate behavior. Rather, we must also hear in "compassion" the word "passion." This means discerning the cry for justice as well as making a passionate response to the appalling unjust relationships existing in our world. This plea for justice is clearly heard first in the Old Testament prophets, then again in the last of the prophets—John the Baptist—and finally in Jesus himself. Moreover, one may not lose sight of the numerous

---

*Translator's note: According to the organization's website, "Compassion International exists as a Christian child advocacy ministry that releases children from spiritual, economic, social, and physical poverty and enables them to become responsible, fulfilled Christian adults. Founded by the Rev. Everett Swanson in 1952, Compassion began providing Korean War orphans with food, shelter, education, and health care, as well as Christian training." See http://www.compassion.com/about/about-us.htm.

†Translator's note: According to the Charter's website, "The Charter for Compassion is facilitated by the Compassionate Action Network International (CANI). CANI is a worldwide network whose goal is to advance the Charter and the spirit and practice of the Golden Rule, 'Do unto others as you would have them do unto you.'" See http://charterforcompassion.org/the-charter/#about_us.

harsh words of judgment in the Old and New Testaments, nor minimize them in the sense of a misunderstood mercy, nor soften the Bible's unequivocal and obligatory demands for justice.

But the Bible also knows that perfect justice is not now and never will be achievable in this world. For this reason, in the face of irrevocable unjust relationships, the Bible speaks of eschatological hope in God's justice. In this way, the call for mercy surpasses the cry for justice in the Bible. The Bible understands mercy as God's own justice. Mercy is the heart of the biblical message, not by undercutting justice, but by surpassing it. The Old Testament speaks of God as a gracious and merciful God (Exod 34:6; Ps 86:15; etc.) and the New Testament calls God "the Father of mercies and the God of all consolation" (2 Cor 1:3; cf. Eph 2:4).

Even today there are untold numbers of people who experience hopeless situations, unmerited catastrophes, ravaging earthquakes, tsunamis, or personal calamities, for whom the plea for mercy is the final consolation and final support. Time and again, one can see how even those who are not churchgoers spontaneously take refuge in prayer when they find themselves in such situations. One can think of countless human beings who suffer from serious illness or whose lives are enmeshed in a hopeless sense of guilt. For them, often the only consolation that remains is knowing that God is gracious and merciful. They hope that in the end God will uncover and bring an end to the entire awful network of fate and guilt, injustice, and lies. They hope that God, who peers into the hidden depths of the human heart and knows its hidden stirrings, will be a gracious judge. Consequently, also today, the Kyrie Eleison, heard in many church songs and at the beginning of every Mass, and the Prayer of the Heart, which is commonly used in the Orthodox tradition and is also increasingly prized in the Western church, speaks to many people: "Lord Jesus Christ, have mercy on me." Who could claim not to need this plea?

Dealing with the topic of mercy, therefore, concerns not only the ethical and social ramifications of this message. Above all, this topic concerns the message of God and his mercy, and only secondarily does it deal with the commandment for human behavior that derives from it. Speech about empathy and compassion can be a starting point for theological reflection on this topic. For pain and suffering are as old as humanity; they are universal human experiences. All religions ask, in one way or another, where suffering comes from, why it exists, and what is its meaning. They ask for deliverance from pain and suffering; they ask how we can cope with pain and suffering and where we can find the strength to endure them.[59] So compassion is a topic that is applicable not only to the present experience of pain and suffering, but also is universally pertinent to human experience. Thus compassion is suitable as a starting point for theology. For one can speak of God as the reality who determines everything, not by means of particular categories, but only with the help of universal categories. They alone are appropriate to the God question.

From the previous, still incomplete sketch of the problem, these questions arise for our subsequent reflections: What does it mean to believe in a merciful God? How are divine mercy and divine justice related? How can we speak of a sympathetic—that is, a compassionate—God? Can undeserved woe and divine mercy be brought into harmony with one another? Ethical questions also arise: How can we measure up to the standard of divine mercy in our own actions? What does the message of mercy mean for the praxis of the church, and how can we cause the central message of God's mercy to shine in the life of Christians and the church? Finally: What does this message mean for a new culture of mercy in our society? In short: What does the saying of the Sermon on the Mount mean: "Blessed are the merciful" (Matt 5:7)?

II

APPROXIMATIONS

1. Philosophical Approaches

PRELIMINARY CONSIDERATIONS CONCERNING LANGUAGE AND SUBJECT MATTER

MERCY IS A DIFFICULT word for many today. Often those who know how to assert themselves and to get their way make a bigger impression than those who are merciful. Mercy, on the other hand, counts as weakness in multiple ways. Therefore, as a first step, we have to expend some effort to disclose anew the original and thoroughly strong sense of this word. Philosophy can provide assistance in this regard and can open up new approaches to the topic.

The Christian message of a merciful God is, in fact, a message intrinsic to the Bible. Nevertheless, the theological tradition quite early on could draw on general human experiences and their philosophical interpretation in order to explicate the Bible's message of mercy.[1] Above all, the primordial human experience of compassion [*Mitleid*] with suffering people was a starting point. The two words, "compassion" and "mercy" [*Barmherzigkeit*], don't in fact mean the same thing, but in a purely linguistic sense, both concepts blend into each other, at least in Latin, which speaks of *misericordia*. This is also true—as is still to be shown—for the biblical use of the terms.[2]

The Latin word *misericordia*, according to its original literal sense, means to have one's heart (*cor*) with the poor (*miseri*) or to have a heart for the poor. The German word *Barmherzigkeit* also points in this direction. It means to have a merciful heart.[3] In this universal human sense, *Barmherzigkeit/misericordia* names an attitude that transcends one's own egoism and one's own I-centeredness and has its heart not with itself, but rather with others, especially the poor and the needy of every kind. Such self-transcendence in the direction of others and such self-forgetfulness is not weakness; it is strength. It is true freedom. For it is far more than self-love, which has fallen victim to its own ego; it is free self-determination and, as a result, self-realization. It is so free that it can also be free of itself. It can overcome itself, forget itself, and—so to speak—change its spots.

FOUNDATIONS IN THE ANCIENT WORLD AND THE MIDDLE AGES

Ancient philosophy picked up the topic of compassion [*Mitleid*] quite early. From the beginning, opinions about it were controversial. Already Plato anticipated many aspects of the later critique. He contrasted the emotion caused by compassion with behavior that is shaped by reason and justice. As an emotion, compassion for the accused can dissuade a judge from the right sentence.[4]

In contrast to him, Aristotle came to a positive view of compassion. He was indeed the first who gave a kind of definition of compassion. He explained that the experience of the undeserved suffering of others affects us because we know such evil could also befall us. Sympathy, in the original sense of the word (literally, suffering with), and solidarity are involved in the experience of compassion with someone's suffering.[5] Thus, the undeserved suffering of the other affects us existentially. Because their suffering could also befall us, we identify to a certain extent with them in compassion. In his *Poetics*, Aristotle shows how the presentation of the hero's fate in a tragedy effects compassion (ἔλεος) and fear (φόβος) in us and leads to an inner catharsis (κάθαρσις) of the observer.[6]

The matter is completely different with the Stoic philosophers. According to them, the feeling of compassion is incompatible with the ethical lead idea of the Stoa—the hegemony of reason over the emotions—and it is incompatible with autarchy and ataraxia (self-rule and peace of mind). Compassion, therefore, is for the Stoics an irrational despondency; it is weakness and a sickness of the soul. By contrast, the ideal of Stoic wisdom is to remain inwardly unmoved in the face of one's own or another's fate and to strive for an absence of passion (ἀπάθεια). The wise Stoic should be emotionless and unperturbed when confronting his or her own misfortune as well as the suffering of another. This orientation, however, did not exclude Stoics from knowing and valuing the attitude of clemency (*clementia*), philanthropy (*humanitas*), and benevolent readiness (*benignitas*) to help.[7]

On the basis of the Bible, the church fathers did not speak out in favor of this Stoic ideal. Augustine[8] and later Thomas Aquinas[9] interpreted the word *misericordia* in its linguistic sense: to have one's heart (*cor*) with the unfortunate (*miseri*), with those who, in the widest sense of the word, are poor and in distress. They defined compassion, in conjunction with Aristotle, as feeling or suffering with (*compassio*): *miserum cor habens super miseria alterius* (having an unhappy heart on account of the misery of another).[10] Such compassion and such mercy are for Augustine and Thomas not only a feeling that is elicited by the experience of another's suffering. They are not only affective, but also at the same time effective dispositions, which strive to combat and overcome the deprivation and suffering. That is important for a proper understanding of God's compassion and mercy. For God cannot be passively affected from the outside by the suffering of another. Mercy can be ascribed to God only in the secondary sense of active and effective resisting and overcoming of deprivation and suffering.[11]

Yves Congar has extensively reconstructed Thomas' train of thought.[12] He has shown that for Thomas mercy expresses God's sovereignty. God is not like a judge or a public servant, who justly applies the law established by a higher authority. God is the sovereign Lord, who is not subject to the law of another, but rather is the Lord who imparts his gifts in a sovereign way. In this process, he does not proceed in an arbitrary fashion; rather, he acts according to his own loving kindness.[13] Therefore, mercy is not opposed to justice. Mercy does not suspend justice; rather, mercy transcends it; mercy is the fulfillment of justice.[14]

Different from the Greek and Roman world, early Christianity developed a system of welfare for the poor not only on the private, but also on the municipal level. In this way, institutional care for the poor and the sick came into being quite early.[15] It was the task of bishops, who made use of deacons for this purpose. From the fourth century on, hospitals, houses for pilgrims, or—as the case may be—shelters for the poor were established; they became the models for the medieval hospitals, providing care of the poor and the sick. Distinct religious orders devoted to the care of the sick were also established. In this way, Christianity exercised a lasting influence both on European culture and on human civilization. This influence continues to be effective down to the present time, often in a secularized form. Without this Christian impulse, neither the sociocultural history of Europe nor human history can be properly understood.

The Universalization of Compassion and Its Critique in Modern Times

The modern development of welfare for the poor and the sick did not arise, as it were, out of nothing. It built upon the social culture of the ancient and medieval world, which had been shaped by the spirit of Christianity. However, modernity turned compassion, which always was directed toward concrete persons, into a general love of humankind. Above all, Jean-Jacques Rousseau played a decisive role in this development. For him, compassion is a feeling that precedes all reflection; it is the source of every social virtue. For at the root of compassion lies the ability to put oneself into another's shoes. Thus it is compassion that first enables an individual to have the capacity to put him or herself into social relation to another.[16] In this way, out of compassion, understood as care for a concrete, suffering human being, Rousseau developed a general, universal philanthropy and love of humanity.

A love of those most remote very often developed out of love for those nearest. One can ask whether such a universalization of compassion does not lead to an excessive sense of obligation.[17] This question arises today when especially television, in individual cases, can convey a sense of being there, eliciting a wave of compassion and a torrent of donations, which in itself is welcome. This immediacy, however, is impersonal because it is transmitted through media technology.

We find in Gottfried Ephraim Lessing a position similar to Rousseau's. He views compassion primarily from an aesthetic perspective. For Lessing as an Enlightenment figure, literature's central function consists in education. He counts the ability to be compassionate among the most important civic virtues. For him compassion became *the* positive human quality, pure and simple. In discussion with Aristotle, Lessing's theory of tragedy is concerned with tragedy's educational effect, because it arouses pity and fear in the observer.[18]

> The most compassionate human being is the best human being, the one most disposed to every civic virtue and to all kinds of magnanimity. Whoever, therefore, makes us compassionate, makes us better and more virtuous. And the tragedy which does that, also does this—or, it does that in order to be able to do this.[19]

Friedrich Schiller took up this thought in his theory of tragedy and developed it further. Already the title of his text, *The Theater as a Moral Institution*, makes clear that for him tragedy becomes an educational institution.[20]

Even for Hegel, again in conversation with Aristotle, compassion is not only a matter of feeling emotion. "With compassion of this sort [*Bedauern*]"—as he sarcastically observes—"provincial females are always ready." According to Hegel, what is intrinsic to compassion is not only the experience of the negative—that is, emotion aroused by the suffering of another—but also "sympathy at the same time with the sufferer's moral justification, which must be present in him." For Hegel, compassion—beyond mere emotion—expresses the recognition of dignity that is due to the suffering human being.[21]

In a completely different way, and not without stimulus from Buddhism, compassion becomes the focal point of ethics for Arthur Schopenhauer. According to Schopenhauer, compassion is a "common phenomenon." It is direct participation in the suffering of another being. Through such compassionate feeling, the previously insurmountable wall between "I" and "You" is dismantled more and more. Thus Schopenhauer could describe compassion as finding what is one's own in the other. He could make compassion the principle of all morality. Schopenhauer characterized compassion as nothing less than the mystery of ethics.[22] He has, therefore, become the true philosopher of compassion in the modern era.

Just like the entire modern history of ideas and philosophy, so too the development of the modern understanding of compassion and mercy does not run in a straight line. Just like the ancient views, the modern theories about compassion and mercy are also contradictory, depending on whether they take their bearings from natural, human feelings or from an ethics of reason.

The classic representative of an ethics of reason was Immanuel Kant, who clearly is the most important and most influential modern philosopher. He was critical of universal ethical systems that are based on feelings such as compassion. He wanted to promote a rational ethics of obligation. Not emotional motivation, but rather only comprehensible rational reasons can be compelling for the ethical behavior of each rational being. Kant's categorical imperative, therefore, states: "Act according to that maxim whose universality, as law, thou canst at the same time will."[23]

Because moral action can be grounded only on reason, and not on sensual motivating forces such as experience or feelings—not even compassion—Kant associates himself with the Stoic teaching concerning wisdom, and he rejects compassion as morally inferior. Compassion with someone whom I cannot help increases suffering, on the one hand, and, in addition, is "an insulting kind of beneficence," in that "it expresses benevolence with regard to the unworthy, called *pity*, which has no place in men's relations with one another; for men are not allowed to boast about their worthiness to be happy."[24] Kant, however, is realistic enough to add: although having compassion and also sharing another's joy is, in itself, not a duty, it is nevertheless an indirect obligation "to cultivate in ourselves" such feelings because, without such impulses, "the thought of duty alone would not be sufficient" for inspiring our active sharing in the fate of others.[25]

Kant would not have been the great philosopher that he was had he not also seen, in an entirely fundamental way, the limits of the ethics of reason. At the end of his *Critique of Practical Reason*, he advances postulates—that is, intellectual demands and presuppositions—whose validity is not to be proven, but whose acceptance, however, is necessary for the conceivability and possibility of morality. For him, most notably, the existence of God is one of these postulates.[26] For Kant, God is not the ground of the obligatory character of the moral law, but is indeed the presupposition for achieving the goal of morality, happiness. For only God can ensure the congruence of human morality with nature and therewith with happiness. Christianity knows, in addition, the idea of the kingdom of God, which alone satisfies the strongest demand of practical reason. Only religion makes possible hope for a meaningful and successful existence as a human being.[27]

In his manuscript about religion, *Religion within the Boundaries of Reason Alone*, Kant goes a step further. He sees that the world is in trouble and that every human being possesses an inclination to evil, having a heart that is corrupted and inverted. Morality, therefore, presupposes a revolution of disposition, rebirth, and change of heart.[28] No one can accomplish this completely by their own power.[29] Consequently, for Kant grace practically becomes a postulate of practical reason. For this reason, according to Kant, the Christian religion is the only moral religion. It offers a higher assistance to everyone who does what he or she can and must do, supplementing that which is not in his or her power.[30]

From a theological point of view, we have to judge such a statement as unsatisfactory because it is a Pelagian interpretation of the Christian doctrine of grace. But we have to add that we cannot at all expect from philosophy a well-developed doctrine of grace. Philosophy cannot achieve more than holding human thought open for the reality of grace and for the question of a gracious God. Kant did that and, in the process, he worked out a preliminary philosophical draft concerning grace—or better, an approach to the doctrine of grace—

that is significant. Kant thereby foreshadows similar considerations, which are found again in new contexts in the twenty-first century and which help us to show that talk about grace and divine mercy is humanly comprehensible and rationally responsible.[31]

NEW APPROACHES IN THE TWENTIETH AND TWENTY-FIRST CENTURIES

In the twentieth century, Kant's subject-oriented intellectual approach encountered firm opposition. The breakthrough came from the new phenomenological direction given philosophy by Edmund Husserl and Max Scheler. They wanted to overcome the subject as the neo-Kantian starting point. Therefore, they turned anew to objective reality, including objective interpersonal reality. In the process, they made empathy [*Einfühlungsvermögen*] the central starting point of their thought. Husserl's student Edith Stein published an early text, *On the Problem of Empathy*.[32]

Max Scheler attempted to rehabilitate material ethics on a phenomenological foundation. In *The Nature of Sympathy*, he presented a detailed phenomenology and theory concerning sympathetic feelings. According to him, compassion represents a primordial human phenomenon. Two kinds of compassion are to be distinguished: the sheer "infection" of feeling and genuine compassion. The latter, as "suffering in the suffering of another as this other," expresses a personal relationship.[33] With this point of view and others, Scheler exercised considerable influence on theology during his Catholic period. However, this remained only a brief episode, which was replaced in the second half of the twentieth century by directions of thought that have been described—more clumsily than clearly defined—as postmodern.

So-called postmodern thinking, in its criticism of modernity's subject-oriented point of view, went beyond Edmund Husserl's subject-referential phenomenology. This occurred already in the philosophy of dialogue (Martin Buber, Franz Rosenzweig, Ferdinand Ebner), which took up the older metacritical positions of Johann Georg Hamann and Johann Gottfried Herder. The philosophy of dialogue regarded human beings not as monological, but rather as dialogical beings, who essentially live in and through relationships.

Beyond the just-mentioned thinkers, this position found broad resonance and led to a new estimation of compassion. Representatives of the Frankfurt School also belong to this development, but on a completely different basis. For them, compassion has become important from the perspective of solidarity with suffering and oppressed people.[34] But thinkers of an entirely different stripe, such as Walter Schulz, are also to be mentioned. Because the modern position of subjectivity had already been surmounted, he proceeds from a dialectical worldview. In doing so, compassion becomes for him an ethical authority of great significance; in fact, it is the only authority and counterforce to cruelty, which depersonalizes the other and degrades him or her to a simple object of destructive desire. "Compassion is the very final possibility for saving the human person in his or her 'naked existence' in the face of the direct negation of this existence."[35]

Emmanuel Levinas, who stood in the line of Jewish tradition and was a philosophical descendant of Husserl and Heidegger, had great influence. He criticized the central location of the ego as a subject who can make ethical judgments and who can grasp and determine moral truths and values. He replaced the ego's central location with a prior obligation to respond to the absolute claim made by others. The human phenomena of love, compassion, and forgiveness came thereby into view anew.[36] From such presuppositions, Levinas reflected on the relation of justice and love. Admittedly, he did not arrive at a satisfactory balance in the process.[37]

Genuine postmodern philosophy (Michel Foucault, Jacques Derrida), following in the steps of Martin Heidegger, deconstructs the metaphysical tradition.[38] Their critique applies to what they regard as the authoritarian and totalitarian structures of modern thought concerning the subject and reason; their critique also applies to the disclosure of implicit power structures. This leads to criticism of the current social praxis and logic of economic exchange processes, which are built upon the idea of abstract justice. In its abstract conception of a parity that invokes reciprocity, this praxis and logic cannot do justice to the individual.

For our question, Jacques Derrida's reflections about forgiveness are relevant.[39] After a century of such unimaginable crimes and scandalous injustice as we experienced in the last century, the question of forgiveness unavoidably arises as a question about the continuing coexistence of humankind. One can, however, really forgive only that which in reality is inexcusable [*unverzeihbar*]. Murder and every appalling injustice are indeed unforgivable [*unverzeihlich*]. As a result, the question about forgiveness (*Vergebung*) confronts us with an apparently insoluble contraction. Pardoning [*Verzeihen*] contradicts pure transactional justice, which would desire retribution. The question, therefore, is: How can a God, who is to be conceived of as perfectly just, be merciful and forgive the perpetrators without doing violence to the victims, when the victims do not agree with God's act of forgiveness? The abstract concept of justice thereby appears to be in competition with the different moral claims that confront God.

In order to arrive at a balance of justice and forgiveness, Derrida reflects on the relation between justice and law. He speaks of the transcendence of justice in relation to positive law. Because justice is transcendently above positive law, we cannot determine, in an abstract and a priori way, how justice must be applied concretely, that is, in a positive law. The law's justification evades every rational reconstruction. Vis-à-vis law, justice unfolds as a performative power, which Derrida describes as mystical.

The demand for a justice without limits leads to a deconstruction of current systems of law and, at the same time, serves to do justice to the individual. In Derrida's deconstruction, the Platonic idea of the good, which, according to Plato, is located "on the other side of Being," serves as a placeholder for the impossibility of realizing perfect justice within any system of law.[40] So, justice as such also stands on the other side of law and is always in the process of becoming. The legacy of religion is therefore delineated in the concept of forgiving. Theology can take up these pointers from Derrida. Proceeding from Derrida, theology can develop a preliminary concept of God, who can show himself to be simultaneously just and merciful.[41]

Paul Ricoeur goes a step further.[42] He too criticizes modernity's thoughts about the subject. But, differently from Levinas, he accepts the concept of justice. In contrast to reciprocal and distributive justice—and transcending both—love means unconditioned solidarity with and affirmation of the other. While in everyday social life, it is always a matter of balancing competing claims, the ideal of justice that he envisages is focused on care for the other and being concerned for his or her well-being.

Such a concept of justice already approaches the idea of love, even to the point of including love of one's enemy. Love goes beyond the logic of exchange; it expresses an economy of gift—that logic of abundance—in contrast to the logic of parity and the economy of exchange and calculation. It does not abolish the Golden Rule—giving to the other what we hope that he or she will give to us—but interprets the Rule in the sense of magnanimity. One cannot make love a general norm in society. An economy of gift would endanger social cohesion; therefore, it needs a corrective through justice, which is oriented toward an economy of exchange. Accordingly, an irresolvable tension remains between the economy of exchange and the logic of gift. For Ricoeur, the resolution of this tension is an eschatological project. In this way, philosophical thought shows that it is open to theological reflections.

In a different way, Jean-Luc Marion pursues a phenomenology of gifting, following in his own distinct way the thought of Husserl, Heidegger, and Jacques Derrida. He strives to understand reality as something that we don't construct, but rather as something that shows itself to us, gives itself to us, and is revealed to us. He construes Being as *Gebung* ("donation").[43]

Giving and gifting has a dialectical structure: in giving, we not only present something; in giving, the one who gives, gives him- or herself. The gift is a sign of his or her self-giving. At the same time, the one who gifts gives away the gift irrevocably in the act of giving. The gift belongs no longer to him or her, but rather belongs to another. So in the act of giving, we distinguish ourselves from ourselves. In giving, we give ourselves and still remain ourselves. Therefore, everything that is shown and is given is more than what is shown. Marion speaks of *la croisée du visible*, of the intersecting and traversing of the visible. The German translation speaks, in a rather minimizing way, of the "opening of the visible."[44]

To summarize, we can ascertain that the last-mentioned phenomenological analyses arrive at a point where they pose questions that point beyond themselves. We can speak of the cry, *De profundis*.* For these sketches evince an insoluble predicament into which thinking falls; and they call for an answer, which thinking itself essentially cannot give. Indeed, mercy is essentially a free, nonderivable happening, which itself again can only be accepted or rejected freely. So we can, in a purely conceptual way, record the "absence of something," if there is no longer talk about mercy. In a final effort of thought, we can still formulate the postulate of mercy and thereby show that Christian speech about mercy, in its human core, is a reasonable and helpful response to the human situation—or at least a response that is worthy of discussion.

In such attempts, philosophy can arrive at the threshold of theology and can help theology to demonstrate that its message is compatible with reason. That does not mean that the relationship of philosophy and theology is to be characterized as a simple question-answer relationship, as occasionally happens. In relation to theology, philosophy can indeed have a critical function; and, vice versa, revelation likewise has a critical, purifying function for thought. Revelation reaches, moreover, into the dimension of faith, which transcends plain thinking. Thus, the word about the cross remains a stumbling block for natural reason (1 Cor 1:23).[45]

In his early work *Hearers of the Word*, which is still worth reading, Karl Rahner attempted to arrive at the threshold of faith via thought.[46] Presently, Thomas Pröpper and his students have taken this attempt up again, but in a new way and from a different perspective. In a way different from Rahner, they attempt, in connection with and in critical continuation of Johann Gottlieb Fichte's philos-

---

*Translator's note: This is a reference to the opening line of Psalm 130 in Latin: *De profundis clamavi ad te, Domine*, which means "Out of the depths I cry to you, O Lord."

ophy of freedom and its interpretation by Hermann Krings, to pose the God question again on the basis of an analysis of human freedom.[47] Here we can only point to, but cannot further explore these attempts, which are worthy of consideration. In what follows, we will show that such reflections from the philosophy of religion are not mere speculation. The cry for forgiveness and reconciliation and thereby for mercy is, in fact, omnipresent in the centuries-old and millennia-old world of religion. This cry illustrates a universal human phenomenon.

2. Exploring the History of Religions

The world today is closer together and adherents of non-Christian religions live among us. In this situation, for the sake of understanding and peaceful coexistence, it is necessary to take a look over the fence of our own cultural context into the world of religions. In the process, we ascertain that compassion and beneficence are not restricted to our cultural context, but rather are universal human and primordial religious phenomena.

As the Second Vatican Council stated, all religions want to provide an answer

> to the unsolved riddles of the human condition, which today, even as in former times, deeply stir the hearts of men: What is man? What is the meaning, the aim of our life? What is moral good, what is sin? Whence suffering and what purpose does it serve? Which is the road to true happiness? What are death, judgment, and retribution after death? What, finally, is that ultimate inexpressible mystery which encompasses our existence: whence do we come, and where are we going?[48]

Sympathy [*Mitgefühl*], which counts as one of the greatest virtues in all great religious traditions, also belongs to these commonalities.

An overview of the great religions of humanity would go beyond the scope of these reflections and would exceed my competence. Therefore, I will restrict myself to a few points.[49]

Hinduism belongs to the oldest religious traditions.[50] After Christianity and Islam, it is the third largest religion. In essence, Hinduism is an externally assigned, collective name for various schools of thought, different images of God, and different views, which have at their disposal neither a common, universally valid confession of faith nor a central institution. For this reason, even the concept *ahimsa*, the term that is used in Hindu spirituality for sympathy, is interpreted differently among Hindus. According to its fundamental meaning, it means the relinquishment of anything deleterious and the renunciation of the use of force. As a rule for behavior, we have evidence of *ahimsa*, understood in the sense that has become common in Hinduism, only in the final phase of the Vedic period. Most notably, Mahatma Gandhi renewed the old *ahimsa* ideal, in the sense of non-violence, and applied it to every sphere of life, including politics.

With the idea of nonviolent resistance, Gandhi achieved tremendous influence in the civil rights movements of the West. Albert Schweitzer also developed his concept *Reverence for Life* under the influence of the *ahimsa* idea. The Radha Krishna movement, which understands Hinduism—in the sense of a Western philosophy of religion—as the religion of humanity, also became influential in the West. And finally, the Ashram movement and meditative forms of yoga attained spiritual influence in the West. In the process, however, individual components of Hindu spirituality were often abruptly and uncritically transferred into a Western context.[51]

Whether Buddhism is a religion or rather a collection of wisdom teachings is debated, because Buddhism does not acknowledge the reality of God (in our Western sense).[52] According to legends about the Buddha, the experience of human suffering was intrinsic to the Buddha's conversion experience. For him all of life is suffering. Consequently, overcoming suffering through ethical behavior, meditative immersion, and sympathy [*Mitgefühl*] became the central concern of Buddhist teaching. On the path to this goal, loving kindness (*metta*) has role to play. It is an active, selfless form of love and it seeks the well-being of all sentient beings. It is an expression of compassion (*karuna*), that is, the sympathetic feeling of the suffering and fate of human beings and all living things. Correspondingly, it encounters all beings and all phenomena of this world with the same, all-encompassing love and readiness to help.

Ultimately, this path to enlightenment and the attainment of nirvana is a matter of experiencing the unity of all beings, in which all polar ideas and every form of resistance and antipathy, which are bound up with those polarities, are dissolved. In Amida Buddhism (and indeed only in this form of Buddhism), trust in the assistance and grace of the transcendent Buddha plays an important role.

First and foremost since the nineteenth century, Buddhism has exerted its attractiveness also in the West. The philosopher Arthur Schopenhauer described himself as the "first European Buddhist." Buddhism became well-known in the last few decades, most notably through the Dalai Lama as a representative of Tibetan Buddhism. Indeed, in its more vulgar adaptations, such as we find in New Age and esoteric circles, individual elements of Buddhism are often uncritically carried over into the Western context or, vice versa, Western views are read into Buddhism. The Japanese Kyoto School (Daisetz Teitaro Suzuki among others) attempts a serious encounter with Western thought via mysticism, specifically the mysticism and negative theology of Eckhart.

Currently in Europe, the encounter with Islam stands front and center.[53] This encounter is of a completely different type than the encounter with Hinduism and Buddhism. For Islam has roots in individual traditions of the Old and New Testaments and, together with Judaism and Christianity, it is often counted among the Abrahamic monotheistic religions. In doing so, one may not overlook fundamental differences in the understanding of God (the doctrine of the Trinity) and in Christology (Jesus' divine sonship and his crucifixion). In the different layers of the Qur'an we find diverse statements about Islam's relation to Christians.

For our context, it is significant that each of the 114 suras of the Qur'an (with one exception) begins with the words: "In the name of

God, the All Merciful, the Most Merciful." Of the ninety-nine names for God, All Merciful and Most Merciful are the most frequent names. Every Muslim is required to exhibit sympathy (*rahmah*) for prisoners, widows, and orphans and to give alms (*zakat*).

The cultural influence of Arabian Islam upon European culture in mathematics (the decimal system), astrology, medicine, and especially in philosophy as well as in poetry (Goethe's *West-Eastern Divan*, among others) is incontrovertible. The Second Vatican Council spoke of Muslims with esteem. It urges us to set aside the disputes and hostilities of the past, to strive for mutual understanding, and to stand up together for the protection and advancement of social justice, moral goods, and, last but not least, for peace and freedom for all people.[54] Whether in the future a specifically European form of Islam can develop remains an open question. It depends not least upon whether and to what extent Islam is capable of fully incorporating fundamental human rights (freedom of religion, the equality of women, etc.).

To summarize, we can say: Despite all of the far-reaching differences, there are also points of contact and bridges of understanding between the religions. They are important for the coexistence and collaboration of religions in our world, which is becoming one. Without peace between the religions, peace in the world is not possible.[55] The Second Vatican Council said: "The Catholic Church rejects nothing that is true and holy in these religions." It recognized in them often "a ray of that Truth which enlightens all men."[56] But from the perspective of the Council, Jesus Christ is the light of the world and the light of the people (John 8:12). Of course, the Council recognized the differences and deviations of other religions from that which the Council itself holds and teaches as true.

The points of contact and bridges of understanding do not justify the assumption that all religions are essentially the same, particularly in the question of sympathy [*Mitgefühls*], or that the differences are simply historically, culturally, and sociologically conditioned formulations of the essential core that they all have in common. The attempt to dissect and abstract such an essential core from the religions arises from the Enlightenment thinking of the West, but not from the religions' own respective self-understandings. What appears to be peripheral to an Enlightened mentality is most often sacred to the respective adherents of these religions. Mutual understanding and collaboration, therefore, should not lead to a least-common-denominator sameness, but rather should lead to regard for the respective otherness of the other. Only such a positive tolerance can become the basis for peaceful coexistence and beneficial collaboration.[57] How this can concretely happen shall be elucidated with the concrete example of the Golden Rule.

3. The Golden Rule: A Common Point of Reference

The references to Hinduism, Buddhism, and Islam demonstrate that, despite all of the far-reaching differences between humanity's religions, there are also common elements. Among these commonalities is the Golden Rule, which is especially important for our context.[58] It states that we should not do to another what we do not want done to ourselves. The Rule is expressed this way in everyday parlance: "What you don't want someone to do to you, don't do to anyone else." Formulated positively, the Golden Rule states: "We should do everything unto others that we ourselves expect and wish for from them in a specific situation."

The Golden Rule is found in all of the great religions. It is found both in Judaism (Tob 4:15; Sir 31:15)[59] and then again in the Sermon on the Mount in the New Testament (Matt 7:12; Luke 6:31).[60] Occasionally there has been a discussion about the meaning of the fact that this rule is found in the Old Testament only in a negative formulation, while in the New Testament it has a positive formulation. This discussion, however, has yielded little fruit and has not advanced understanding. In this respect, we cannot spot a fundamental difference between the Old and the New Testament.

According to Augustine, God wrote this rule into the heart of human beings.[61] Drawing upon Gratian, the Middle Ages as well as the modern Enlightenment acknowledged it as the embodiment of the natural law. Especially since the Parliament of World Religions' *Declaration toward a Global Ethic* (Chicago, 1993), the Golden Rule has functioned as a fundamental element in the modern dialogue between religions.[62] The rule is one of the traditions handed on by humanity and, as such, it is humankind's cultural heritage. That means: compassion [*Mitleid*], sympathy [*Mitgefühl*], reciprocal readiness to help, and beneficence constitute the wisdom of humankind. Yet there were and continue to be many—unfortunately, also bloody—conflicts between religions. The religions, in their concrete forms, are not only ambivalent, they also hold contradictory positions. Nevertheless, they also possess commonalities, especially in the Golden Rule, that show that none of humanity's great religions—provided they have not fallen into fanaticism, but rather remain true to themselves—can glorify violence or speak in favor of thoughtless self-aggrandizement. According to the basic convictions of every religion, the connection of religion with violence represents, therefore, a misunderstanding, a misuse, and an aberrant form of authentic religion.[63]

We should, of course, not overlook the fact that the Golden Rule also precipitates critical questions. Augustine was one of the first to draw our attention to the fact that what matters is that we ourselves and the other will what is good and not what is evil.[64] Kant labels the Golden Rule trivial because it does not specify the basis of obligation and because its content is indeterminate. Sarcastically, he observes, "On this basis the criminal would be able to dispute with the judges who punish him."[65] George Bernard Shaw made the ironic remark: "Don't treat others as you would want them to treat you. Their taste may not be the same." The Golden Rule, therefore, needs to be made more precise and interpreted according to the totality of the respective context.

The set of factors operative for defining the meaning of the Golden Rule is different in each of the religions. To separate it from the more general total context is possible only through a process of abstraction. That, in turn, depends on presuppositions of Western Enlightenment and the differentiation between the essence of the rule and its temporally and culturally conditioned manifestations.

However, what may be an inessential, contingent manifestation for an enlightened thinker is often essential, even sacred for the adherent of the respective religion, who does not share or who, in fact, rejects Enlightenment presuppositions. For this reason, the concept of a universal ethos on the basis of the least common denominator is well intentioned, but is nonetheless artificial. It therefore goes right past the concrete living reality of the religions.

For this reason we must watch carefully how Jesus adopts the Golden Rule. For Jesus it is tied up with the Sermon on the Mount and is thereby connected with the love commandment, which also includes the command to love one's enemies. This overall context establishes the basis for the Rule and how to interpret its content. Only on the basis of this rationale and this interpretation can the church fathers understand the Golden Rule as the sum and fulfillment of the entire law.[66]

So Christian ethics can connect with a common religious tradition. It is not a hermetically sealed unique system of morality, but is able to be presented and communicated in a generally comprehensible way. As a result, it is also open to interreligious dialogue. Nevertheless, Christian ethics is not reducible to a universal humanism. With its message of love, Christianity can interpret and qualify the content of the Golden Rule, which in itself is open and indeterminate. Thomas Aquinas spoke of a *determinatio* of natural morality by the gospel.[67] In this way, he succeeded in making Christian ethics capable of connecting to and communicating with a universally comprehensible system of ethics, without allowing it to degenerate into a universal morality of the least common denominator. His principle of determination means that common natural morality, which is open in different respects and can be interpreted in different ways, is given concrete content by the gospel and, in this sense, is made "unambiguous."[68]

The fact that compassion and mercy are universal human virtues can encourage us to engage in dialogue with other cultures and religions and to work together with them for understanding and peace in the world. Conversely, this common human tradition gives us pause to think. For it says that where compassion, beneficence, reciprocal assistance, and mutual forgiveness are lost, where egoism and apathy concerning one's fellow human beings gain ground and interpersonal relations are confined to economic exchange processes, the humaneness of a culture and a society is in danger. In order to meet this danger in the West, a danger that is not to be dismissed with a wave of the hand, we can take up the suggestions offered by other religions. However, it is more important to recall anew the potential of our own tradition of Christian mercy, whose potential has not yet been exhausted. It has shaped Western culture and, in addition, the culture of all humankind in a decisive way. Such reflection is urgently needed today. There is scarcely a more important topic than this.

III

THE MESSAGE OF
THE OLD TESTAMENT

1. The Language of the Bible

THE BIBLICAL MESSAGE concerning mercy can draw on
an extensive tradition of humankind. But it would be wrong to think
that the Bible and, with it, Christianity simply repeats in a popular
way what philosophers have discovered in their analysis of human
compassion and what scholars of religion have distilled from the different religions as a common human tradition. Christianity is not
what Nietzsche thought it was: "Platonism for the people."[1]
Christianity adopts many things from human tradition, but it also
criticizes that tradition, makes many things more precise, and deep-
ens them. That becomes clear when we note that the biblical message
speaks not only of compassion [*Mitleid*], but also speaks of mercy
[*Barmherzigkeit*]. Despite all of the common religious and philosophical points of contact, the concept of mercy has a specific meaning, to
which we must now attend.

There is a widely held opinion that the God of the Old Testament is a vengeful and angry God, while the God of the New Testament is a gracious and merciful God. Now there are, in fact, texts
in the Old Testament that can support this position. Those passages
speak of the killing and expulsion of the pagan population of entire
cities and peoples at the behest of God (Deut 7:21–24; 9:3; Josh 6:21;
8:1–29; 1 Sam 15). One can also think of the imprecatory Psalms
(above all Ps 58; 83; 109).[2] Nevertheless, this view does not do justice

---
41

to the gradual process by which the Old Testament's idea of God is critically transformed, nor does it do justice to the internal development of the Old Testament in the direction of the New Testament. Ultimately, both Testaments give witness to the same God.

This fact emerges already from some initial observations and reflections about language use in the Old as well as in the New Testament. It is characteristic of the Old Testament that it uses the expression *rachamim* for "compassion" and, for that matter, also for "mercy." This word is derived from *rechem*, which means "womb"; the term can also refer to human intestines. In both the Old and the New Testaments, the intestines are regarded as the seat of feelings. In the New Testament, intestines or guts (σπλάγχνα) also express the mercy that comes from the heart.[3] Likewise we find *oiktirmos* (οἰκτιρμός) as an expression for feeling, being grasped by pain, sympathy, and a readiness to help.[4] And finally, the word *eleos* (ἔλεος) is important. It originally expressed an affect of emotion, but later was often used to translate the genuinely Hebraic words *hesed* and *hen*, which became especially determinative for the description of mercy.

We will still have to ask how mercy is related to justice and will have to show in the process that, for the Old Testament, both concepts do not stand simply beside each other or in opposition to each other, but rather that God's mercy serves his justice and brings it to realization. Indeed, mercy is God's very own justice. Beforehand, however, we have to point to something else. We can understand mercy only when we include the biblical concept of "heart" (*leb*, *lebab*, καρδία) in our considerations.

In the Bible, "heart" does not simply describe a human organ that is important for life; it describes, anthropologically, the core of the human person, the seat of his or her feelings as well as the seat of his or her power of judgment. The Bible gives space and attention to the world of human feelings, both with regard to people and, in a figurative sense, also to God. Think of the Old Testament psalms of lament, the laments of Jeremiah, and David's sorrowful complaint at the death of his son Absalom (2 Sam 19). Jesus is full of anger and sadness at the obduracy of his opponents (Mark 3:5), and full of compassion for the people (Mark 6:34) and for the widow of Naim at the loss of her only son (Luke 7:13). At the death of his friend Lazarus, Jesus is deeply moved by sadness (John 11:38). So, in the Bible, compassion is not regarded as weakness and unmanly softness that is unworthy of a true hero. According to the Bible, human beings are allowed to show their feelings, their sadness, their emotion, their joy as well as their grief. They may also complain to God and do not need to be ashamed of their tears.

The Bible goes a step further and speaks theologically of God's heart. The Bible says that God chooses people according to his heart (1 Sam 13:14; Jer 3:15; Acts 13:22). It speaks of God's heart being deeply troubled by people and their sins (Gen 6:6); and it states that God leads his people with upright heart (Ps 78:72).[5] The apex of this manner of speaking is found in the prophet Hosea. In an incomparable and truly dramatic way, he says that God's heart recoils within him and his compassion grows warm and tender (Hos 11:8). God is animated by a truly passionate love of human beings.[6]

The most important expression for understanding mercy is *hesed*, which means unmerited loving kindness, friendliness, favor, and also divine grace and mercy.[7] *Hesed*, therefore, goes beyond mere emotion and grief at human deprivation; it means God's free and gracious turning toward the human person with care. It concerns a concept of relationship, which characterizes not only a single action, but rather an ongoing attitude and posture.[8] Applied to God, the concept expresses an unexpected and unmerited gift of God's grace—transcending every relationship of reciprocal fidelity—that exceeds all human expectations and bursts every human category. To think that God, who is all-powerful and holy, concerns himself with the distressing and self-caused situation of human beings, that God sees the wretchedness of poor and miserable people, that he hears their lament, that he bends down in condescension, that he descends to persons in their need and, despite every human infidelity, concerns himself with them again and again, and that he forgives them and gives them another chance, even though they had deserved just punishment—all of this exceeds normal human experience and expectation; all of this transcends human imagination and thought. In the message of God's *hesed*, something of the mystery of God, which is closed to human thought in and of itself, is revealed. We can have knowledge of this mystery only through God's revelation.

2. The Divine Response to Chaos and the Catastrophe of Sin

The meaning that the Bible's testimony ascribes to God's mercy does not emerge solely from how the word is used. The meaning of mercy can be ascertained only from the entirety of the biblical history of salvation. It begins after the biblical account of creation. In creation, God made everything good, in fact, very good (Gen 1:4, 10, 12, 18, 20, 25, 31). God created people in his image; as man and woman he created them. He blessed them. They should be fruitful with descendants and should populate the earth. God entrusted creation to them for its conservation and cultivation (Gen 1:27–30; 2:15). Everything was good; indeed, very good.

But the story immediately unfolds with a catastrophe. The human being wanted to be like God and to decide autocratically over good and evil (Gen 3:5). Alienation from God led to human alienation from nature and from other human beings. The earth now bears thorns and thistles and it has to be tilled with effort and the sweat of one's brow. New life can be born only in pain; husband and wife are alienated from each other (Gen 3:16–19); and Cain kills Abel (Gen 4). Evil follows evil in succession like an avalanche and all of the thinking and striving of the human heart becomes more and more evil (Gen 6:5).

Nevertheless, God does not allow the world and humanity simply to run headlong into disaster and fall into misery. Rather, from the very beginning he embraces countermeasures and repeatedly undertakes ever-new counteraction against the inbreaking chaos and catastrophe. Although the word "mercy" may not appear in the early chapters of the Book of Genesis, God's mercy is factually palpable and effective from the very beginning. With their expulsion from paradise, God gives human beings clothes with which they can protect themselves from the rigors of nature, cover their shame vis-à-vis each other, and preserve their dignity (Gen 3:20). He threatens retribution for anyone who lays a hand on Cain and places a mark on Cain's forehead in order to protect him from being murdered (Gen 4:15). Finally, God attempts a new beginning with Noah after the flood. He guarantees the continuing existence and order of the cosmos, blesses humanity anew, and places the life of human beings, who are made in his image, under his special protection (Gen 8:23; 9:1–5f.).

But this is not enough. Human hubris has no end; people build the Tower of Babylon, whose top is supposed to reach up to heaven. This hubris leads to the confusion of tongues; people no long understand each other and they are scattered throughout the entire earth (Gen 11). Again God does not abandon humankind to their fate, now divided into tribes and peoples who are alienated from and hostile to each other. God opposes chaos and catastrophe. He makes a new beginning with the calling of Abraham (Gen 12:1–3). With Abraham, so to speak, a counterhistory begins, that is, the actual history of human salvation by God. In Abraham all generations, all families of the Earth shall be blessed (Gen 12:3).[9] The Bible intends something both fundamental and entirely comprehensive with the word "blessing": well-being, peace, life in its complete fullness and in God's favor.[10] So with Abraham a new history of humanity begins, a history of blessing and, in other words, a history of salvation. In point of fact, talk of the graciousness and fidelity of God is found already scattered throughout the story of Abraham (Gen 24:12, 14, 27; 32:11).

Thus from the beginning of history, God's counteraction is at work against disaster.[11] From the very beginning, God's merciful action [Erbarmen] is powerfully effective. His mercy is how God provides resistance to evil, which is getting the upper hand. He does not do this forcibly and violently; he doesn't simply do battle; rather, in his mercy God repeatedly creates new space for life and for blessing.

3. The Revelation of God's Name as Revelation of Divine Mercy

The explicit revelation of mercy in the Old Testament is indissolubly bound up with the fundamental revelation of God in Israel's exodus and liberation from Egypt and with his revelation at Mt. Sinai and Horeb, respectively. The revelatory event occurs in a difficult, indeed hopeless situation for the people of Israel. The people are oppressed in Egypt, doing the hard work of slaves. Moses must flee from the Egyptian authorities, who seek to end his life. God is revealed to him as the God of Abraham, Isaac, and Jacob in the burning bush on Mt. Horeb. The revelation at Horeb connects, therefore, to the beginning of salvation history with Abraham. In both cases, God reveals himself as a God who calls forth and leads forth. God is a God of history. But while the story of Abraham provided an opening to all humankind and to all peoples, now it focuses on the story of his people, the people Israel.

God is a God who sees the misery of his people and hears their cries: "I have observed the misery of my people who are in Egypt; I have heard their cry on account of their taskmasters. Indeed, I know their sufferings, and I have come down to deliver them from the Egyptians." (Exod 3:7–8; cf. 9). God is no deaf and dumb God; he is a living God, who attends to human misery, who speaks, acts, and intervenes, who liberates and redeems. The formula "Yahweh who has brought us out of Egypt" becomes the fundamental statement of faith in the Old Testament (Exod 20:2; Deut 5:6; Ps 81:1; 114:1; etc.).

The revelation of God who condescends to draw near to his people has nothing to do with a false familiarity. This revelation is indissolubly bound up with the revelation of God's holiness, his superiority over everything earthly, his wonderfulness, and his sovereignty. Moses sees the thorn bush, which burns but does not burn up. Out of awe, he hides his face; he may not come closer; he must take off his shoes for the ground on which he stands is holy ground. When Moses then asks God for his name, he receives the mysterious answer: "I am who I am" (Exod 3:14).

Many different and controversial things have been written about the origin, pronunciation, and meaning of the so-called tetragrammaton, that is, the four Hebrew letters YHWH.[12] Martin Buber and Franz Rosenzweig translate it as: "I will be present as the one who will be there."[13] In this way the mysterious, inaccessible, and ultimately ineffable dimension of God's name is expressed. The tetragrammaton is so sacred for devout Jews that they may not say it aloud. Out of respect for Jewish sensibilities, the Congregation for Divine Worship in 2008 forbade God's name (YHWH) to be translated in the church's liturgies. The revelation of God's name thus expresses God's absolute transcendence. On the other hand, it shows God's personal care for his people and his commitment to be powerfully present in the history of his people. God reveals himself as the God who guides and leads in a history that cannot be tied down beforehand, a history in which he will always be present in a nondeducible, sovereign, and—yet again—unexpected way and who is again and again the ever-new future of his people. He is not a god of a particular place, but rather displays his power in every place his people encounter along their way. The universality of Yahweh, proclaimed explicitly by the prophets, is thereby firmly established from the very beginning.

The Septuagint, the Greek translation of the Hebrew Old Testament that came into being around 200 BCE, interpreted the revelation of God's name according to Hellenistic philosophical thought and translated it as "I am the one who is" (Ἐγώ εἰμι ὁ ὤν). This translation made history and shaped theological thought for many centuries. On the basis of this translation, one was convinced that what is the highest in thought—Being—and what is highest in faith—God, correlate to each other. In this conviction one saw confirmation that believing and thinking are not opposed to each other, but rather correspond to each other. This interpretation is already found in the Hellenistic Jewish philosopher Philo († 40 CE). However, Tertullian soon asked: "What does Jerusalem have to do with Athens?"[14] Most notably, Blaise Pascal, after having a mystical experience, highlighted the difference between the God of the philosophers and the God of Abraham, Isaac, and Jacob in his famous *Memorial* of 1654.[15]

Modern biblical scholarship has pointed out the differences between the Hebraic and the Greek understanding of being. For according to Hebraic thinking, being is not a quiescent, but rather a dynamic reality. In Hebraic thought, being means concrete, active, and powerfully effective existence. Accordingly, the revelation of God's name constitutes his promise: I am "the one who I am there." I am with you in your distress and I will accompany you on your way. I hear your cries and answer your pleas. Correspondingly, the revelation of God's name is immediately connected with the ratification of God's covenant with the patriarchs and with the classic formulation of the covenant: "I will take you as my people, and I will be your God" (Exod 6:7). In the revelation of his name, God thus enunciates his innermost reality: God's being is being present for his people and with his people. "God's being is Being-for-his-People; God's being as Pro-Existence is the wonderful mystery of his essence. Israel can unconditionally rely on this in its faith."[16]

The word mercy [*Erbarmen*] does not yet appear in the revelation at Horeb. Nevertheless, that which mercy actually means is already intimated in the revelation of God's name; it is then more fully disclosed in the revelation at Sinai. The situation in which this occurs is highly dramatic. God had led his people out of slavery in Egypt and, as the charter of his covenant, had given them the Ten Commandments on stone tablets (Exod 20:1–21; Deut 5:6–22). But scarcely was the covenant ratified before it was immediately broken. God's chosen people quickly became unfaithful; they apostatized, followed alien gods, and danced around the golden calf. God's anger flared up against the stiff-necked people and Moses shattered the tablets of the covenant at the foot of the mountain as a sign that the covenant was broken (Exod 32). Scarcely begun and everything already appears to be lost, over and done with.

Nevertheless, Moses intercedes and reminds God of his promise. He asks God for his grace and mercy: "Let me see your countenance." Then a second revelation of God's name occurs. God calls out his name to Moses in passing: "I will be gracious [*hen*] to whom

I will be gracious, and will show mercy [*rachamin*] on whom I will show mercy" (Exod 33:19). God's mercy is understood here not as the nearness of a close pal, but rather as the expression of God's absolute sovereignty and his irreducible freedom. Yahweh doesn't fit into any box, not even in the box of compensatory justice. In his mercy, he conforms only to himself and to the name he revealed to Moses.[17] So he commands Moses to prepare new tablets of the law. Despite their infidelity and stiff necks, he does not let his people sink into ruin and nothingness. God renews his covenant; he gives the people another chance and he does all of this out of pure freedom and pure grace.

Finally, on another morning, there is a third revelation of God's name. God descends to Moses in a cloud, as a sign of his mysterious presence, and calls out to him:

> The LORD, the LORD,
> a God merciful [*rachum*] and gracious [*henun*],
> slow to anger,
> and abounding in steadfast love [*hesed*] and faithfulness [*emet*].
>
> (Exod 34:6)

In this third revelation of his name, mercy is not only an expression of God's sovereignty and freedom; it is also an expression of his fidelity. In his mercy, God is faithful to himself and to his people, despite their infidelity. In this third revelation of God's name, we can recognize Israel's central affirmation concerning the essence of their God.[18] Correspondingly, this revelatory declaration is henceforth repeated continually in the Old Testament, especially in the psalms, in a formulaic way.[19] It became, so to speak, the credo of the Old Testament.

This credo is not the result of human reflection; just as little does it spring from a mystical vision. On the contrary, Moses is told unequivocally: "You cannot see my countenance for no one can see me and still live." Moses cannot directly see God's glory; he can only see his back when God passes over him. He can recognize God, so to speak, only a posteriori, that is, in hindsight and on the back of his passing in history. God is also recognized on the basis of his revelatory, interpretative word, that is, the calling out of his name (Exod 33:20–23). Thus, the decisive statement concerning God's gracious and merciful essence is not a speculative statement or the result of a mystical experience. Rather, it is a statement of faith on the basis of the historical self-revelation of God. In and through history, God reveals his essence, which has been hidden from human beings. We can speak of it only by way of a narrative, and not in a speculative way. In this sense, this formula is the summary of God's self-definition in the Old Testament.

4. Mercy as God's Inscrutable and Sovereign Otherness

We find the high point of the Old Testament's revelation of God's mercy in the prophet Hosea. Besides Amos, he is the first of the scriptural prophets. He lived and worked in a dramatic situation during the final days of the Northern Kingdom and its demise (722/721 BCE). The drama of his message corresponds to the drama of the situation. The people have broken the covenant; they have become dishonorable harlots. Therefore, God has also broken with his people. He has decided to show no more mercy to his unfaithful people (Hos 1:6). His people shall no longer be his people (1:9).

Thus, everything appears over and the future appears to be out of alignment. But then the dramatic turn comes. The Unity Translation* translates God's decisive statement as "My heart recoils within me" (Hos 11:8). But that translation plays down the meaning quite a bit. The original Hebrew text expresses the point much more drastically: God turns his justice upside down; he throws it out, so to speak. Instead of the people being subverted, the subversion takes place in God's very self.[20] Why? God's compassion [Mitleid] flares up

---

*Translator's note: This is a German translation of the Bible created between the 1960s and 1980 for liturgical use, and published by the Katholisches Bibelwerk.

and God decides not to execute his blazing wrath. Mercy is victorious over justice in God.

That turn of events does not indicate the arbitrariness of an angry God, who, mollifying his anger in a good-natured way, allows mildness to prevail again over right. The justification that God himself gives, according to the prophet, is much more mysterious and profound. It discloses the total profundity of the divine mystery: "For I am God and no mortal, the Holy One in your midst, and I will not come in wrath" (Hos 11:9). That is an astounding statement. It says: God's holiness, his Being Wholly Other, in contradistinction to everything human, is disclosed not in his righteous anger, not even in his inscrutable and inaccessible transcendence. God's being God is revealed in his mercy. Mercy is the expression of his divine essence.

This deeply moving passage shows that God already in the Old Testament is not an angry and righteous God, but rather a merciful God. Nor is he an apathetic God, who sits on his throne, oblivious to all the sin and distress of the world. He is a God who has a heart, which flares up in anger, but which then literally overturns itself out of mercy. With this "subversion," God shows himself, on the one hand, to be moved in a seemingly human way and, on the other, he reveals himself as being completely other than mortals. He reveals himself as the Holy One, the Wholly Other. The constitution of his essence, which fundamentally distinguishes him from human beings and elevates him above everything mortal, is his mercy. It is his sublimity and sovereignty; it is his holy essence.

God's sovereignty is demonstrated above all in forgiving and pardoning. Only the one who stands above and not under the demands of pure justice can forgive and pardon. Only this one can remit just punishment and vouchsafe a new beginning. Only God can forgive and forgiveness belongs to his essence.

For you, O Lord, are good and forgiving,
    abounding in steadfast love to all who call on you.
                                            (Ps 86:5)

"For he will abundantly pardon" (Isa 55:7) "He delights in showing clemency" (Mic 7:18; cf. Exod 34:6; Ps 130:4).

Theology, no matter how clever, falls short in dealing with God, who doesn't fit into any box. We cannot speak flippantly of an either/or: either a righteous God or a merciful God, as if that were the most obvious matter in the world. In our language, we can say: mercy is the revelation of his transcendence over everything mortal and over everything humanly calculable. In his mercy, God is revealed paradoxically as both the Wholly Other and the One Who Is So Close to Us. His transcendence is not infinite distance and his nearness is not close chumminess. Our merciful God is not simply the saccharine "dear God," who lets our negligence and malice pass. On the contrary, his salvific nearness is an expression of being different and an expression of his incomprehensible hiddenness (Isa 45:15). Precisely as the near and manifest *Deus revelatus*, he is the *Deus absconditus*. God's mercy points us toward his Being Wholly Other and toward his complete incomprehensibility, which is simultaneously the incomprehensibility and reliability of his love and graciousness.

5. The Mercy, Holiness, Justice, and Fidelity of God

In the Old Testament, God's mercy stands in an indissoluble connection with the other ways in which God is revealed. His mercy may not be extracted from this context and be treated independently. Already the revelation of God's name to Moses shows that divine mercy is, so to speak, encircled by graciousness and fidelity. God's self-revelation in the prophet Hosea shows that mercy is insolubly bound up with God's holiness and gives expression to it.

The coherence of God's mercy and his holiness is especially important. The Hebrew word holy (*qados*) originally means to cut off or to set apart. God's holiness, therefore, is his radical difference and superiority to everything worldly and everything evil.[21] God's holiness is expressed in a grand way in the prophet Isaiah's throne vision, in which Isaiah hears the seraphim singing, "Holy, holy, holy." This vision triggers a holy shiver in the prophet; it makes him conscious of his total unworthiness and sinfulness. "Woe is me! I am lost, for I am a man of unclean lips, and I live among a people of unclean lips" (Isa 6:3–5). This shows that we may not downplay God's mercy and make God a fool, who, with liberal leniency, over-looks our mistakes and malice and lets them simply run wild in us. Nietzsche ridiculed this conception of God and said that God died because of his pity.[22] One can't trifle with God; he doesn't let himself be mocked (Gal 6:7). In his compassion and mercy, God demon-strates his holiness and greatness.

Because of his holiness, God can offer only resistance to evil. The Bible calls this the wrath of God.[23] Many people may at first stum-ble over this statement and regard it as inappropriate. But God's wrath does not mean an emotionally surging rage or an angry inter-vention, but rather God's resistance to sin and injustice. Wrath is, so to speak, the active and dynamic expression of his holy essence. For this reason, the message of judgment cannot be expunged from the mes-sage of the Old or New Testament or be harmlessly interpreted away.

God's holiness conforms to his justice (*zedakah*).[24] The concept of law and justice is central for the Old Testament. For the pious people of the Old Testament, God's justice is a fundamental presup-position beyond debate. On the basis of his holiness, God can't do anything other than punish evil and reward good. For the Old Testament, that is anything but a fear-inducing truth; on the con-trary, it is an expression of hope. The pious person in the Old Testament hopes in the revelation of universal divine justice (Ps 5— 9; 67:5; 96:13; 98:9; etc.) and appeals to the evidence of God's justice (Ps 71:15, etc.). This eschatological hope is directed toward the com-ing of the righteous messiah (Isa 11:4). Evidence of justice in an unjust world is already a work of mercy for the oppressed and those whose rights have been denied.

So the message of God's mercy is not a message of cheap grace. God expects us to do what is right and just (Amos 5:7, 24; 6:12, et al.) or, according to a different formulation, to do what is right and kind

(Hos 2:21; 12:2, et al.). For this reason, mercy does not stand in opposition to the message of justice. In his mercy, God rather holds back his justified wrath; indeed, he holds himself back. He does this in order to provide people the opportunity for conversion. Divine mercy grants sinners a period of grace and desires their conversion. Mercy is ultimately grace for conversion.

Only one passage needs to be quoted to support this point. After the people have been subjected to the just punishment of the exile on account of their infidelity, God, in his mercy, gives them another chance.

> For a brief moment I abandoned you,
>   but with great compassion I will gather you.
> In overflowing wrath for a moment
>   I hid my face from you,
> but with everlasting love I will have compassion on you....
>
> For the mountains may depart
>   and the hills be removed,
> but my steadfast love shall not depart from you,
>   and my covenant of peace shall not be removed,
>   says the LORD, who has compassion on you.
>   (Isa 54:7–8, 10)[25]

Mercy is God's creative and fertile justice. Thus, it stands above the ironclad logic of guilt and punishment, but does not contradict justice. Rather, it serves justice. Thus God is not bound to an alien law that is superior to him. He is not a judge who passes judgment according to a law that was predefined for him. Still less is he a functionary who executes the injunction of another. In his sovereignty, God establishes what is right.

This sovereign freedom is no arbitrary freedom. It also is not the expression of a spontaneous, so to speak, instinctive and solicitous attention to the misery of his people. Rather, it is an expression of his fidelity (*emet*).[26] Graciousness (or mercy) and fidelity are intimated already in the revelation of God's name. In the word *emet* we find the stem *aman*, which means something like "to stand firm" and "to gain a hold." In this way, divine mercy corresponds to his fidelity. The covenant, which he granted at one time out of an act of free graciousness, is dependable; it provides firm ground on which to stand. Mercy is the expression of a free and gracious internal obligation that God has to himself and to the people whom he has chosen. In his absolute freedom, God is at the same time absolutely reliable. One can trust him; in every situation one can rely on him; there is absolute dependability in him.

The words *emet* and *aman* are found again in the biblical and liturgical formula of affirmation, "Amen." In the New Testament, *aman* is translated as πιστεύειν, that is, to believe. To believe does not mean simply accepting something as true. Rather, in the process of accepting something as true, it means to depend on God, to build on him, to attach oneself to him and in him to gain a firm place to stand. Faith is the act of confidently letting oneself submit to God's fidelity and mercy. "If you do not stand firm in faith, you shall not stand at all" (Isa 7:9). "Believe in the LORD your God and you will be established" (2 Chr 20:20). We can also say: having faith means saying "Amen" to God and, thereby, trusting in his favor, fidelity, and his boundless mercy. In faith human beings gain a firm place to stand. In faith they receive the gift of a reliable space in which to live.

6. God's Option for Life and for the Poor

The Old Testament message of mercy is not simply a purely spiritual message; it is a message about life and, therefore, has a physically concrete and social dimension that is essential to it. Humankind merited death because of sin. In his mercy, God grants humanity life and living space anew. God is indeed no dead God, but rather the living God who does not desire death, but rather life. God takes no enjoyment from the death of the sinner. Rather, he finds enjoyment when the sinner repents and continues to live (Ezek 18:23; 33:11). Jesus took up the message of the Old Testament and said, God is not a God of the dead, but rather a God of the living (Mark 12:27; Matt 22:32; Luke 29:38).

Thus, God's mercy is the power of God that sustains, protects, promotes, builds up, and creates life anew. It bursts the logic of human justice, which entails the punishment and death of the sinner. God's mercy desires life. In fidelity to the covenant with his people, God mercifully reestablishes the relationship with him that was destroyed by sin and he grants dependable living conditions anew. Mercy is God's option for life. It makes clear: God is not, as Nietzsche thought, an enemy of life.[27] God is the power (Ps 27:1) and source of life (Ps 36:10); he is life's friend (Wis 11:26).

God's special solicitous attention is directed toward the weak and the poor.[28] Memory of the fact that Israel itself was poor in Egypt (Exod 22:20; Deut 10:19; 24:22) and that God led his people out of Egypt with his mighty arm and saved them (Exod 6:6; Deut 5:15) continues to have an effect. In the promised land, God's special love and care were applied to the poor and the weak. It is especially evident in the command not to oppress or exploit aliens, widows, and orphans (Exod 22:20–26); it is also evident in the protection of the poor in court (Exod 23:6–8) and in the prohibition of usury (Exod 22:24–26). The Book of Leviticus knows a distinctive social legislation (Lev 19:11–18; 25). With God the normal social hierarchy is virtually inverted. In Hanna's song of thanksgiving, which prefigures Mary's Magnificat in the New Testament, we hear:

> He raises up the poor from the dust;
>> he lifts the needy from the ash heap,
> to make them sit with princes
>> and inherit a seat of honor.
>
> (1 Sam 2:8)

Special mention needs to be made of the Sabbath law (Exod 20:9f.; 23:12; Deut 5:12–15), which was also supposed to provide a day for slaves and aliens to catch their breath and rest. There is also the sabbatical year, which recurs every seven years, during which the fields are supposed to lie fallow to the benefit of the poor and during which slaves are to be granted freedom (Exod 23:10f.; Deut 15:1–18). Something similar occurs in the year of jubilee, in which every seven weeks of years (seven times seven years) all property is returned, the fields are not supposed to be sown, the grape vines are not to be harvested, and freedom is to be granted to everyone (Lev 25:8ff.; 27:14ff.). Even if this last prescription was scarcely ever observed, still in the background stands the idea of the solidarity of God's people, to whom the land was given for their common possession. The Book of Deuteronomy thus develops the conception of a people in which there should be neither the poor nor the marginalized (Deut 8:9; 15:4), a people that knows detailed regulations concerning widows and orphans, aliens, and slaves (Deut 14:29; 15:1–18; 16:11, 14; 24:10–22), and a people that also acknowledges the obligation to tithe for the poor—concretely for aliens, orphans, and widows (Deut 14:28f.; 26:12).[29]

The message of the prophets gives special emphasis to God's care and option for the poor. That message begins with the prophet Amos's harsh denunciation of exploitation, perversion of justice, and oppression (Amos 2:6–8; 4:1, 7–12; 8:4–7) and his criticism of the easy-living upper class (6:1–14). In the place of noisy festivals and burnt offerings, he demands righteousness and justice as true religious service (5:21–25). Similarly clear words are found in Isaiah (1:11–17; 58:5–7), Ezekiel (18:7–9), Hosea (4:1–3; 6:6; 8:13; 14:4), Micah (6:6–8), and Zechariah (7:9f.). There we also find words of encouragement for the poor, who in the God of Israel—different from what is found with the idols (Bar 6:35–37)—find a sympathetic ear, shelter, mercy, righteousness, and solace (Isa 14:32; 25:4; 41:17; 49:13; Jer 22:16).

Again and again we find in the prophets beseeching pleas for God's mercy (Isa 54:7; 57:16–19; 63:7—64:11; Jer 31:20, et al.) God's promise is made to the poor, not to the proud and the powerful (Isa 26:6; 41:17; 49:13). According to Third Isaiah, the Messiah is sent to the poor and the little ones in order to bring them the good news (Isa 61:1).

With the prophets we can safely speak of Yahweh's overriding option for the poor, the powerless, and the little ones. One would almost be tempted to speak of the utopia of a new social order.

However, the word "utopia" would be out of place. For we are not talking about a human project, but about God's salvific will for the life of humankind and his eschatological promise.

7. Praise of God in the Psalms

In many passages, the psalms express God's mercy with poetic beauty. Only a few examples can be mentioned here:

> All the paths of the LORD are steadfast love and faithfulness,
>   for those who keep his covenant and his decrees.
>
> (Ps 25:10)

> Your steadfast love, O LORD, extends to the heavens,
>   your faithfulness to the clouds.
>
> (Ps 36:5)

> The LORD is merciful and gracious,
>   slow to anger and abounding in steadfast love.
>
> (Ps 103:8; 145:8)

> As a father has compassion for his children,
>   so the LORD has compassion for those who fear him.
>
> (Ps 103:13)

As in the prophets, so too in the psalms they receive God's hearing, solace, and help (Ps 9:10, 19; 10:14, 17; 22:25; 113:4–8, et al.)

Besides praise for God's mercy, we repeatedly hear this call resounding in the psalms: "Be gracious to me, O LORD" (Ps 4:1; 6:2, et al.) Especially striking is the beginning of the famous *Miserere* psalm, which is ascribed to David's authorship after he committed adultery with Bathsheba, the wife of Uriah, and the prophet Nathan has taken him to account:

> Have mercy on me, O God,
>   according to your steadfast love;

according to your abundant mercy
    blot out my transgressions.
                  (Ps 51:1)

In the end, the earnest petition is time and again superseded by exclamations of thanksgiving and jubilation:

Praise the LORD!
    O give thanks to the LORD, for he is good;
    for his steadfast love endures forever.
                (Ps 106:1; 107:1)

Psalm 136 repeats this cry of jubilation twenty-six times. The psalms constitute a singular song of praise for God's mercy. The Book of Wisdom takes up this song of praise for mercy:

But you, our God, are kind and true,
patient, and ruling all things in mercy.
                (Wis 15:1)

In Israel's later days, the simple people (*am-haarez*) were impoverished and were despised by the influential and educated classes. There formed a group of *anawim*—the poor, the small, the disadvantaged, the oppressed, the meek, the humble—who had nothing to expect from the world and put all of their hope in God alone.[30] The Qumran community also belongs in this context. According to Third Isaiah, the Messiah knows that he is sent to these poor little ones in order to bring them good news and to heal all who have broken hearts. He will proclaim liberty to the captives and release to the prisoners, and he will comfort all who mourn (Isa 61:1–3). Simeon and Anna in the New Testament belong to the simple, pious people who await the Messiah (Luke 2:25–38). Jesus took up this expectation and connected its fulfillment to his appearance. He knew that he was sent to bring good news to the poor (Luke 4:16–21).

To summarize, we can say: the message of God's mercy permeates the entire Old Testament. Again and again God calms his righteous holy wrath and shows mercy to his errant people, despite their infidelity, in order to give them another chance for repentance and conversion. He is the protector and preserver of the poor and those without rights. The psalms above all provide compelling proof against the continually raised assertion that the God of the Old Testament is a jealous God of vengeance and wrath. Rather, the God of the Old Testament, from the Book of Exodus to the Book of Psalms, "is gracious and merciful, slow to anger and abounding in steadfast love" (Ps 145:8; cf. 86:15; 103:8; 116:5).

IV

JESUS' MESSAGE OF GOD'S MERCY

1. Lo, A Rose E'er Blooming

THE EVANGELISTS MATTHEW and Luke preface their presentation of Jesus' public appearance and his message with the so-called infancy narratives. It would be better to speak of the prehistory of Jesus' public ministry than to speak of the infancy narrative.[1] From an historical perspective, this narrative presents special problems. Indeed, it does not report an event that, like the major portion of both Gospels, derives from eyewitnesses. It is, however, also clear that the two evangelists did not freely fabricate this prehistory. They create the story out of an older tradition that was available to them; more precisely, they create it out of two different traditions, which agree in important points, such as the virgin birth and the birth of Jesus in Bethlehem. This very finding gives the prehistory a certain historical credibility. Above all, we need to take seriously Luke's assertion that he carefully researched everything for his entire Gospel, including this prehistory. He emphasizes the reliability of his report (Luke 1:2–4).

These few points make clear that one can't describe this prehistory as a historical report in the modern sense; but one also can't simply write it off as a historically worthless, edifying, pious legend. It is a question of a particular kind of history. The prehistory is narrative theology in the style of Jewish haggadah.[2] In this way, Luke emphasizes that what he is communicating as narrative theology took place in space and time, namely, in a particular place, principally in Bethlehem, and in a concrete historical and political situation, namely, under Emperor Augustus and his governor Quirinius (Luke 2:1). According to Matthew, the story unfolds during the time of King Herod (Matt 2:1).

Whatever happens in a particular place and at a particular point of time in history belongs simultaneously in the complete story of God's dealings with humankind. According to Matthew's genealogy, Jesus belongs in the entire history of salvation, which begins with Abraham (Matt 1:1–17). In this sense, the first sentence of Matthew's Gospel reads: "An account of the genealogy of Jesus the Messiah, the son of David, the son of Abraham." Luke goes back even further and places Jesus in the history of humanity that begins with Adam (Luke 3:23–38).

As much as we are dealing with a real event *in* history, this event does not come *from* history. According to both Gospels, Jesus enters the world through the working of the Holy Spirit (Matt 1:20; Luke 1:35). He appears miraculously through God's intervention; he is God's son (Luke 1:32–35). The real miracle here is not the virgin birth; that is only the physical sign and, so to speak, the divine gateway into history.[3] The miracle that is much greater and more astounding than the virgin birth is the miracle of God's coming and his incarnation. "Jesus'" name makes this point: God helps; he is Emmanuel, God with us (Matt 1:23). Thus in the prehistory, there is already mention of what must already be presupposed in Jesus' public history. It tells us who Jesus is and whence he comes.

If we look at the theological content of the story in detail, we see that all of the essential concerns, motives, and themes of Jesus' public history and his message are intimated in it, as in a prelude. This prehistory is something like the gospel in a nutshell.[4] It stands entirely under the sign of God's mercy. It understands Jesus' history as the fulfillment of the previous history of promise and salvation (Matt 1:22). It belongs to the history of God's merciful action (ἔλεος) from generation to generation (Luke 1:50). As he promised, God now attends to "his servant Israel, in remembrance of his mercy" (Luke 1:54).

> Thus he has shown the mercy promised to our ancestors,
> and has remembered his holy covenant.
>
> (Luke 1:72)

By the merciful love of God, radiant light from on high is visited upon us in order to enlighten all those who sit in darkness and in the shadow of death (Luke 1:78f.) Luke's Christmas story proclaims the birth of the savior, which has been long expected and hoped for: "To you is born this day in the city of David a Savior, who is the Messiah, the Lord" (Luke 2:11).

This messianic fulfillment becomes a reality in the midst of people who are descendants of a great lineage, from the house of Aaron (Luke 1:6) and David (Matt 1:20; Luke 1:27; 2:4), but who, like Zachary and Elizabeth (Luke 1:5), Simeon and Anna (Luke 2:25–38), are also counted among the simple, pious, quiet folk of the land who, in particular, eagerly awaited the arrival of the Messiah. This story, therefore, subverts human categories; it represents a transvaluation of the usually operative human rules: a barren woman like Elizabeth and a virgin like Mary become pregnant (Luke 1:7, 34), the powerful are toppled from their thrones and the lowly are lifted up, the hungry are filled with good gifts while the rich depart empty (Luke 1:52f.). In this way, this story is the fulfillment of the Old Testament history as Hannah, the mother of Samuel, celebrated it in her song of thanksgiving. It is a history in which God brings life and death, makes poor and rich, humbles some and elevates others (1 Sam 2:1–11). It anticipates the Sermon on the Mount, according to which and contrary to all purely human logic, the poor, the mourners, the powerless, the merciful, the peacemakers, and those who are persecuted are called blessed (Matt 5:3–11; Luke 6:20–26).

In its marvelous character, this story bursts the parameters that had been confined to the people Israel, and opens itself to the entirety of humanity. It stretches back beyond Moses to Abraham, who is to be a blessing for all the peoples of the earth (Gen 12:2f.) and, in fact, goes back to Adam, the progenitor of the human race. This universal dimension is also given expression in the story of the astrologers from the East, that is, representatives of a cosmic, pagan religiosity

(Matt 2:1–12). It anticipates the motif that we find already in the Old Testament about the eschatological pilgrimage of the people to Mount Zion (Isa 2; Mic 4:1, 3; cf. Matt 8:11).[5] With the coming of Jesus, the longed-for universal peace ("shalom") among all people on earth whom God favors begins to dawn (Luke 2:14). Finally, the aged Simeon praises God in the temple:

> For my eyes have seen your salvation,
>   which you have prepared in the presence of all peoples,
> a light for revelation to the Gentiles
>   and for glory to your people Israel.
>
> (Luke 2:30–32)

As wonderful and moving as the Christmas story is, so little is it suited for a sentimental romanticization. It indeed reports that the newborn Messiah found no place in the mainstream world, but found accommodation only with the despised shepherds. It further reports of Herod's opposition, the massacre of the innocents in Bethlehem, the flight to Egypt, and the prophecy that Jesus will become a sign of contradiction and that a sword would pierce his mother's heart (Luke 2:34f.). From the very beginning, the shadow of the cross overshadows the story that is now commencing.

So the prehistory of the Gospels is anything but an idyllic, folksy legend. This story bursts all normal notions and expectations: the birth of the savior from a virgin, not in a palace, but in the stable of a shelter in the midst of poor, despised shepherds. Something like this is not made up. This is not the language of a saga or myth. At the beginning a stable, at the end the gallows—"this is taken from historical stuff, not the golden stuff beloved of legend."[6] But precisely in this paradox and tension between the heavenly singing of angels and the brutal historical reality, a quite unique magic emanates particularly from the Christmas story, a magic that has always elevated the spirits of many and has touched their hearts.

This story is comprehensible only as something marvelous. In the period immediately following the New Testament, Ignatius of Antioch recognized the deep meaning of the Christmas story. He said that Jesus Christ originated from the silence of the Father.[7] He makes reference here to the Book of Wisdom 18:14–15:

> For while gentle silence enveloped all things,
> and night in its swift course was now half gone,
> your all-powerful word leaped from heaven.

God, who appears to be distant from mortals and whom we often believe we can adore only in silence, is awakened in the middle of the world's night and, according to God's unfathomable will, has stepped out of silence and communicated himself to us in his eternal Word made flesh, full of grace and truth (John 1:1f., 14). With Meister Eckhart, German mysticism picked this thought up and developed it further.[8]

The Christmas story has lost none of its fascination in two thousand years. In its more popular form, this story elicits believing or disbelieving wonder down to this very day. Francis of Assisi was the first to suggest setting up a crèche in order to make visible through it God's love, which is made manifest to us in an incredible way. To this very day, many people, even those who are alienated from the life of the church, visit the divine child in the crib, who is experienced as love's ray of light and hope in a dark and cold world.

An old Christmas carol from the sixteenth century gives vivid expression to the unimaginable, improbable, and marvelous character of this message: "Lo, how a rose e'er blooming…amid the cold of winter, when half spent was the night." A little rose in winter and at night, that is the fulfillment of the prophecy of the prophet Isaiah (11:1), that out of the blunt, apparently dead and worthless root stock, a shoot shall miraculously come forth. One can scarcely better express the unbelievable and fascinating novelty of the Christmas event.

2. Jesus' Gospel of the Father's Mercy

The evangelist Mark begins his Gospel in a way similar to Matthew, but in an almost more striking way: "The beginning of the good news of Jesus Christ, the Son of God." He condenses the exciting novelty and totality of the gospel (εὐαγγέλιον) in this summary: "The time is fulfilled, and the kingdom of God has come near" (Mark 1:15).[9] The time of fulfillment is a concept prevalent in early Jewish apocalyptic. Jesus picks this concept up and, at the same time, goes beyond it. For he says nothing less than: now the time has come. With his coming, the historical turning point, which had been foretold and expected, has come. Now the inbreaking of the Kingdom of God has been accomplished. But how does this happen? The following chapters of Mark's Gospel provide a clear answer. The kingdom of God breaks in through the miraculous healing of all kinds of sick people and through the exorcisms of demons, that is, those powers that harm human life.

Luke makes this point even more clearly. In his Gospel, the report about Jesus' first public appearance in the synagogue in Nazareth on the Sabbath takes the place of Mark's summary. There Jesus reads from the prophet Isaiah:

> He has annointed me
> to bring good news (εὐαγγέλειν) to the poor.
> …to proclaim the year of the Lord's favor.
> (Luke 4:18–19)

For Luke, Jesus' good news is the proclamation of a year of favor, that is, a year of liberation (Lev 25:10) for the poor. Jesus then added: "Today this scripture has been fulfilled in your hearing" (Luke 4:18, 21). Luke also binds Jesus' work to his person, this time in such a way that, in this concretizing identification, the vexing character of his message is expressed.

A similar statement is found in Matthew's Gospel. When the disciples of John came to Jesus and asked him whether he is the one who is to come, Jesus summarizes his public ministry by referring to Isaiah 61:1: "The blind receive their sight, the lame walk, the lepers are cleansed, the deaf hear, the dead are raised, and the poor have good news brought to them." For Matthew, Christ's works are the healing and helping deeds of mercy. Caring for those in need of help and for the poor, the little ones, and those who appear unimportant to mortal eyes is, accordingly, the epitome of Jesus' messianic mission.[10] Jesus again connects this ministry with his person: "And blessed is anyone who takes no offense at me" (Matt 11:5f.; Luke 7:22f.)

What the three programmatic Synoptic texts say is already expressed in the first beatitude of the Sermon on the Mount: "Blessed are the poor in spirit" (Matt 5:3; cf. Luke 6:20). By the poor, not only are the economically and socially poor meant, but rather all who have broken hearts, who are discouraged or despairing, all who stand before God as beggars.[11] Jesus turns to all who have to carry a heavy burden: "Come to me, all you that are weary and are carrying heavy burdens, and I will give you rest. Take my yoke upon you, and learn from me; for I am gentle and humble in heart" (Matt 11:28f.).

Jesus not only proclaimed the message of his Father's mercy, he lived it himself. What Jesus proclaimed, that he also lived. He ministered to the sick and those plagued by evil spirits. About himself he could say: "I am gentle and humble in heart" (Matt 11:29). He is moved by compassion (σπλαγχνισθείς) when he meets a leper (Mark 1:41) or encounters the sorrow of a mother who has lost her only son (Luke 7:13). He has compassion [*Mitleid*] for the many who are sick (Matt 14:14) and for the people who are hungry (Matt 15:32). He has compassion when he sees the two blind men, who ask him for pity [*Erbarmen*] (Matt 20:34), and he has compassion for those who are like sheep without a shepherd (Mark 6:34). At the tomb of his friend Lazarus, he is inwardly shaken and weeps (John 11:35, 38). In the grand Last Judgment speech, he identifies with the poor, the hungry, the miserable, and the persecuted (Matt 25:31–46).[12] Again and again he meets people who cry out, "Have mercy on me" or "Have mercy on us" (Matt 9:27; Mark 10:47f., et al.). Even on the cross, he pardoned the repentant thief and prayed for those who had brought him to the cross (Luke 23:34–43).

What is new in Jesus' message and distinguishes it from the Old Testament is that he proclaims God's mercy for all in an ultimate way. Jesus opens up access to God not just for a few righteous people, but for all. There is room for all in God's kingdom; no one is excluded. God has finally taken back his wrath and has given full scope to his love and mercy.[13]

Sinners were Jesus' addressees in a special way; they are the spiritually poor. Unlike the scribes and Pharisees, Jesus does not keep his distance from them. He eats and has dinner with them (Mark 2:13–17, et al.). He is counted as a friend of the tax collectors and sinners (Luke 7:34). In the house of Simon the Pharisee, he shows mercy to a prostitute, who was well-known in the city (Luke 7:3–50). A similar thing happens with the tax collector Zacchaeus, whose house Jesus visits (Luke 19:1–10). When the Pharisees take offense, he replies to them: "I have come to call not the righteous but sinners to repentance" (Luke 5:32; cf. 19:10). Jesus tells them the parable of the Pharisee and the tax collector, who together go to the temple to pray. It is not the Pharisee, who boasts of his good deeds, who goes home justified, but rather the tax collector, who beats his breast and prays, "God, be merciful to me, a sinner" (Luke 18:9–14).

The message about God as our Father occupies the center of Jesus' message.[14] Jesus' way of addressing God as "Abba, Father," indeed as his Father (Mark 14:36), was imprinted on early Christianity. That this form of address was transmitted to the Greek context in the Aramaic idiom (Rom 8:15; Gal 4:6) demonstrates that, at a very early date, this way of addressing God was regarded as characteristic for Jesus and for Christians. Therefore, the Our Father, which Jesus taught us to pray in response to the request of his disciples (Matt 6:9; Luke 11:2), has rightly become the best known and most widely disseminated Christian prayer. It expresses the innermost core of our understanding of God and of our relationship to God. It tells us that we stand in a personal relationship to a divine thou, who knows us, hears us, bears us up, and loves us.

Jesus added that we do not have to use big words when we pray because the Father knows what we need (Matt 6:8). We may cast our cares upon him. Just as he knows how to care for the birds of heaven and for the flowers and grass in the field, so does he all the more know what we human beings need (Matt 6:25–34). He himself cares for the sparrows; he has even counted the hairs of our head (Matt 10:2f.). He is our Father and he is the Father of all human beings. All are his children, all are his sons and daughters. He lets his sun shine on the bad and the good and he lets the rain fall on the just and the unjust (Matt 5:45). Our Father in heaven (Matt 5:16; 18:10, 14, 32f.) is not distant from us; he is the Father of both heaven and earth (Matt 11:25; cf. 6:10). Our life on earth is directed by our one Father in heaven. We may detect the Father's hand in everything, we know ourselves are secure with him in every situation, and we may call on him as our Father in our every need. Thus, we don't live in a boundless, unfeeling, and fatherless cosmos. We are not the product of an accident or the product of a meaningless and directionless evolution.

The evangelist Luke puts Jesus' message altogether in a nutshell. Where Matthew speaks of the perfection of God (Matt 5:48), Luke speaks of God's mercy (Luke 6:36). So for Luke, mercy is *the* perfection of God's essence. God does not condemn; rather, he pardons, he provides and gives gifts in a good, compendious, full, and overflowing measure. God's mercy is, so to speak, superproportional. It exceeds every measure.[15]

3. A Merciful Father in the Parables

Jesus expounds for us the message of the Father's mercy most beautifully in his parables.[16] This is true above all in the parable of the Good Samaritan (Luke 10:25–37) and in the parable of the prodigal son (Luke 15:11–32).[17] These parables have been burned into the memory of humankind and have become downright proverbial.

In the parable of the Good Samaritan, it is significant that Jesus presents us with a Samaritan, of all things, as a model of mercy. The Samaritans were not regarded by Jews of that time as orthodox Jews, but were despised as half heathens. Likewise, it must have provoked Jesus' hearers that first a priest and a Levite walk by the victim lying on the side of the road, without giving it a second thought, while precisely the Samaritan attends to him. He is the one who doesn't thoughtlessly pass by the man lying helplessly on the side of the road, a man who had been brutally beaten by robbers. When he sees the victim, the Samaritan is moved with compassion; he forgets the business matters for which he was underway, bends down in the dirt, provides first aid, and tends to the victim's wounds. In the end, he generously pays the innkeeper in advance for any further expenses and necessary assistance.

Jesus tells this parable as a response to the question: Who then is my neighbor? His answer is: not someone at a distance, but rather the one for whom you become the neighbor; the one whom you tangibly encounter and who needs your help in this particular situation. Jesus doesn't preach love of those farthest away, but love of those nearest. This love is not confined to family bonds, friendship, religious or ethnic membership. This love is gauged according to the concrete suffering and needy person who meets us on the way.

Jesus goes a step further in the Lucan parables of the prodigal son. With these parables, Jesus is reacting to the grumbling and outrage of the Pharisees and scribes, who are upset that Jesus spends time with sinners and eats with them (Luke 15:2). According to them, by doing so, Jesus transgresses the righteousness prescribed by the law. But with his parable, Jesus gives the grumblers a lesson. His behavior expresses the greater and higher righteousness of his heavenly Father. To wit, in this parable Jesus says: how he behaves is also how God himself behaves in relation to sinners or those who were then regarded as such.

That is eminently expressed in the parable of the prodigal son, which is more appropriately described as the parable of the merciful Father (Luke 15:11–32). Admittedly, the words "justice" and "mercy" do not occur in the parable. But the entire drama is described there, the drama that plays out between the father's love and the waywardness of the son, who squandered his father's inheritance through dissolute and debauched living, thereby losing his rights as a son. He can no longer make any justified claims on his father.

Nonetheless, the father is a father and remains the son's father, just as the son is a son and remains his son. So the father remains faithful to himself and thereby also faithful to his son. When he sees his son at a distance returning home, the father is moved with compassion (Luke 15, 20). The son admittedly has squandered his father's estate, has forfeited his rights as a son, and damaged his dignity as a son, but he has not lost them. So the father does not wait for his son, but goes toward him, puts his arms around him, and kisses him. By putting on him his best robe and placing a ring on his hand, the father reinstates him as his son. The father returns to him his rights as a son and acknowledges anew his dignity as a son. He thereby bestows on the son not only life-giving relationships, just as the son had hoped; the father's mercy exceeds every anticipated measure. His mercy takes its bearings not from the fair allocation of material goods, but rather from the dignity of the son. It is the measuring stick of the father's love.

In no other parable has Jesus described so masterfully God's mercy as in this one. For in this parable Jesus wants to say: Just as I act, so too does the Father act. The Father's mercy in this parable is the higher form of justice. We can also say: mercy is the most perfect realization of justice. Divine mercy [*Barmherzigkeit*] leads human beings to "a return to the truth about themselves." God's mercy [*Erbarmen*] does not humiliate the person. "The relationship of mercy is based on the common experience of that good which is man, on the common experience of the dignity that is proper to him."[18]

The parable of the good Samaritan as well as the parable of the prodigal son have become proverbial. Talk of the compassionate Samaritan has, in fact, transcended the Christian and ecclesial realm and has become a name for diverse aid organizations and emergency services (Samariter-Notdienst, Arbeiter-Samariter-Bund, Internationales Hilfswerk Samariterdienst u. a.).* This shows that the biblical message of compassion, sympathy, and mercy has deeply impressed itself upon human consciousness and also lives on in secularized forms.

It would be wrong, however, to construe the message of the parables in terms of a universal humanism. The parables serve to elucidate Jesus' own behavior as an expression of the behavior of the Father in heaven. He wants to say: just as I act, so too does God

---

*Translator's note: In 1994 the Arbeiter-Samariter-Bund Deutshcland e.V. joined three other organizations from Austria, France, and Denmark to form Samaritan International e.V., an organization that consists of sixteen member associations in fifteen countries. See http://www.samaritan-international.eu/about-us-en/what-we-want/mission-or-guiding-principles-2/.

himself act. Who sees him, sees the Father (John 14:7, 9). In him the goodness and loving kindness of God our savior appear (Titus 3:4). In him we have a high priest, who can empathize with our weakness, who in every respect has been tested as we are, but has not sinned (Heb 4:15). Jesus also wants to say to us: your story is told in the story of the prodigal son. You yourself are this prodigal son; you too must repent. But have no fear. God himself comes to meet you and takes you in his arms. He does not humiliate you; rather, he gives you back your dignity as a son.

4. Jesus' Existence for Others

Jesus' entry into public life and his message initially aroused an enthusiastic response. Masses of people flocked to him. But soon there was a reversal. His opponents criticized him for doing good on the Sabbath (Mark 3:6; Matt 12:14; Luke 6:11) and for daring to forgive sins. How can a mortal say and do such things (Mark 2:6f.; Matt 9:2f.; Luke 5:20–22)? More than anything, it was his message and his deeds of mercy that aroused opposition; they were regarded as scandalous and ultimately brought him to the cross. Jesus responded with stern words of judgment. For God's rule is the last, definitive opportunity for human wholeness; whoever rejects his rule is ultimately excluded from salvation. Therefore, we should not hide or suppress Jesus' speeches about judgment out of a false understanding of his message about divine mercy.[19] The words of judgment are concerned with a repeated and urgent call to conversion; they offer a last chance, made possible by God's mercy.

Conscious of his message's rejection and his imminent, violent death, Jesus goes to Jerusalem with his disciples.[20] Like the prophets before him, he knows that he will be killed there (Luke 13:34). Above all, he keeps the fate of the Baptist in mind (Mark 6:14–29; 9:13). He is quite clear about what awaits him. In obedience to the will of his Father and his mission, Jesus has decided to enter upon the path of salvation for his people and for the world, even to the very end. In an instruction to his disciples, he speaks of his imminent suffering and dying. To explain, he harks back to a thought that is found in the Book of Second Isaiah (53:10–12). There we find talk of God's servant, who bears the sins of many (53:12).

In the Old Testament context, this had remained a riddle that was difficult to interpret. With Jesus it now finds its ultimate interpretation and fulfillment. In connection with this statement (i.e., about the suffering servant), he says that he, as the Son of Man, has not come to be served, but to serve and to give his life as a ransom for many (ἀντὶ πολλῶν) (Mark 10:45).[21] He understands his path as a "must" (δεῖ) which, in the language of the Bible, means something willed by God, which he obediently accepts.[22] So, after his message has been rejected, he has decided to walk, in place of his people, the path of suffering, which is God's truly final offer of mercy. When Simon Peter rejects the thought of Jesus' suffering and death, Jesus, for his part, harshly rebukes the apostle. The words "you Satan" express with unsurpassable sharpness that Peter does not will what God wills and that he, therefore, wants to derail Jesus' work (Mark 8:31–33; Matt 16:21–23; Luke 9:22).

On the evening before his suffering and death, Jesus takes this thought up again in his words at the Last Supper. This thought is, so to speak, Jesus' last will and testament. Although the transmitted words of the Last Supper are different, we can nonetheless ascertain that the words "for you" (Luke 22:19f.; 1 Cor 11:24) or "for many" (Matt 26:28; Mark 14:24) play a central role in all of the different versions.[23] In Luke's and Paul's version, this being "for you" is interpreted, in the sense of the second Servant Song, as a substitutionary surrender of life and death. Thus, all the reports of the Last Supper express in summary fashion what was the core of his existence, namely, Jesus' "being for us and for all," that is, his pro-existence. The *pro nobis* ["for us"] is the meaning of his existence and his surrender unto death. As such it is the meaningful and indispensable core of all New Testament theology.[24]

This is not the place to go into all of the diverse problems posed by the words of the Last Supper in their different versions. Here what matters most of all is to understand correctly the idea of proxy and substitutionary atonement [*Stellvertretungsgedanken*]. That is not easy, especially for us today. For the idea of a proxy appears to contradict a person's responsibility for his or her own actions. How, it is asked, is another supposed to be able to act as a proxy for us, unless we have explicitly commissioned him for this purpose? It appears completely incomprehensible—in fact, it amounts to a serious offense—that, according to this view, God wanted to sacrifice his own son for the redemption of the world. What kind of God is that, it is further asked, who walks over a corpse, over the corpse of his own son? For many people today these questions count as a moral reproach and a fundamental argument against Christianity.

For this reason, liberal theology attempted to interpret the idea of substitutionary atonement in terms of the idea of Jesus' solidarity with humanity, especially his partisanship on behalf of the oppressed and disadvantaged; and it sought to replace the former idea with the latter. Some representatives of more recent Catholic theology have also taken this path.[25] This "soft" interpretation, however, does not do justice to the profundity and force of the biblical statements. The potency and intensity of the biblical testimony is revealed only when one considers the full depth and gravity of not only the social, but also the metaphysical misery—and, concomitantly, the total alienation and complete loss of well-being—into which we humans have fallen through sin.

According to the biblical understanding, sinners have forfeited their life and deserve death by virtue of their sin. The wages of sin is death (Rom 6:23). According to the Bible's communal or "corporate" understanding of the human race, this wretchedness affects not only individuals, but also the people or all of humankind. By his or her misdeed, the individual "contaminates" all of the people; thus, all have become subject to death. The idea of substitutionary atonement can be understood only in the context of this corporate understanding.[26] On the basis of this common entanglement in sin and common subjection to death, no individual can brag about being able to pull him- or herself out of the morass with his or her own two hands. First and foremost, as mere mortals we are not able to restore life by our own power. We can only be freed from sin and death when God, who is Lord over life and death, wills, in his mercy, not death, but rather life, when he again gives life a chance and makes life possible anew. No human being, but God alone, can deliver us from our deepest adversity, the affliction of death.

But God cannot simply ignore evil in history and treat it as something inconsequential and meaningless. That would be cheap grace and not authentic mercy, which takes human beings and their actions seriously. In his mercy, God also wants to serve justice.[27] Therefore, Jesus—taking our place [*stellvertretend*]—willingly takes the sins of all upon himself; yes, he even becomes sin (2 Cor 5:21). But because he is God's son, death cannot conquer him; rather, he himself conquers death. His death is the death of death. In this way, he has become for us the place where life breaks in. In him God has once again and definitively proved to be a God full of mercy (Eph 2:4f.), who makes possible for us a new beginning and gives us a new birth by his great mercy (1 Pet 1:3).

With the idea of substitutionary atonement, it is not—as a prevalent misunderstanding suggests—a matter of a vengeful God needing a victim so that his wrath can be assuaged. On the contrary, by willing the death of his son on account of his mercy, God takes back his wrath and provides space for his mercy and thereby also for life. By taking our place in and through his son, he takes the life-destroying effects of sin upon himself in order to bestow upon us life anew. "So if anyone is in Christ, there is a new creation; everything old has passed away; see, everything has become new!" (2 Cor 5:17). It is not we who can reconcile God with us. He is the one who has reconciled himself with us (2 Cor 5:18).

Substitutionary atonement [*Stellvertretung*] is, of course, not an act of replacement [*Ersatzhandlung*], in which God in Jesus Christ effects our salvation without our involvement. God reconciles us with himself to such an extent that he reestablishes the covenantal relationship. Augustine says very clearly: the one who created us without us does not want to redeem us without us.[28] The act of redemption enables us to say "yes" anew in faith or to withhold our assent. As much as the act of redemptions is exclusively christological, it is at the same time inclusive and it involves us.[29]

With the statement that God has reconciled the world with himself, the question arises of how to interpret the formula about the blood poured out "for many" (ὑπὲρ πολλῶν), which is found in the words of the Last Supper (Mark 14:24; Matt 26:28; cf. Mark 10:45). According to a widely disseminated, if not uncontested conviction, "for many" corresponds to the meaning "for all" in Hebraic linguistic usage.[30] This, however, does not signify "for all individuals," but rather means "for the totality of humanity," or alternatively "for the countless multitude."[31] In the New Testament, this totality means not simply the totality of Israel, but rather the totality of Jews and Gentiles, the totality of humankind. The words in 1 Timothy 2:6 are understood in this sense, where they clearly and unambiguously mean: "who gave himself a ransom for all [ὑπὲρ πάντων]." This universality is confirmed by the New Testament tradition as a whole (John 6:51; Rom 5:18; 2 Cor 5:15; Heb 2:9). Therefore, there can be no doubt about God's universal salvific will and the universal intention of giving his life for all.[32]

From Jesus' intention to lay down his life "for the totality [*Gesamtheit*]" of humanity, one cannot establish the theory of universal salvation and conclude that factually every last individual is saved.[33] Jesus' substitutionary atonement is exclusive insofar as he is the one and only mediator of salvation; on the other hand, his substitutionary atonement is inclusive insofar as it includes us in his self-sacrifice. Substitutionary atonement is not an action that replaces what we ourselves can do and must do. It does not replace the individual responsibility of each person, but rather sets it really free again. It reestablishes responsibility after it was squandered because of sin; it enables responsibility anew and challenges it anew. Jesus' substitutionary atonement liberates us for a new life and makes us a new creation. Therefore, in faith we may say with certainty that Jesus laid down his life for all, and thus also for me, in a totally personal way. This is how Paul understands it when he says that he lives by faith in the son of God "who loved me and gave himself for me" (Gal 2:20).[34]

This conviction of faith has not remained an abstract doctrine and, in fact, could not remain so. It has existential meaning for every individual and for his or her personal relation to Jesus. We find such a personally internalized Christ-centered piety and Christ-centered mysticism, first and foremost, in Bernard of Clairvaux. He is often pictured with Christ very personally bending down from the cross toward him and embracing him. Bernard expressed the meaning of this event in the sentence: "In becoming conformed to Christ who lays down his life, we are transformed" (*transformamur cum conformamur*).[35] This spirituality was picked up in the mysticism of Henry Suso and then in Thomas à Kempis's *Imitation of Christ*, which became a classic of spirituality. For modern spirituality, the *Spiritual Exercises* of Ignatius of Loyola became authoritative. In his exercises, Ignatius has soliloquies with the Crucified One. We encounter the same deep personally felt piety again in the well-known song by Paul Gerhard, *O Sacred Head, Now Wounded*:

> Thy grief and bitter passion
> were all for sinners' gain;
> mine, mine was the transgression,
> but thine the deadly pain....
> What language shall I borrow
> to thank Thee, dearest friend,
> For this thy dying sorrow,
> thy pity without end?"[36]

5. God's Mercy—God's Justice—Our Life

What Jesus said about God the Father and what he vividly and concretely described in his parables, what he clearly stated in prophecies about his suffering and in the words of institution at the Last Supper, all of this Paul reflects on in their entire unfathomable depths. In doing so, the cross stands in the center of the apostle's proclamation. Paul wants to know nothing except Christ and him crucified (1 Cor 2:2). Paul's theology is a theology of the cross. But in the apostle's proclamation, it is not to be separated from the message of Jesus' resurrection. Paul takes over both elements from the pre-Pauline tradition (1 Cor 15:3–5). Right there he discovered the confession that Jesus, in accordance with scripture—that is, in accord with God's preordained salvific will—died for our sins (ὑπὲρ τῶν ἁμαρτιῶν ἡμῶν) (1 Cor 15:3; cf. 11, 24).

Without the resurrection, Christ's cross would be the seal on his failure. But because of the resurrection, it is a sign of victory (1 Cor 15:54f.) and the foundation of faith, without which everything else would begin to waver and would become meaningless (1 Cor 15:14–17). The church of the first few centuries, therefore, represented the cross not as a stake to which a suffering Christ was affixed, but as a gem-studded sign of victory.[37] It is a sign of victory that says to us that love conquers over hate, life conquers over death, and that, in the end, mercy triumphs over judgment (Jas 2:13).[38]

In light of the Easter message, Paul reflected more deeply on the event of the cross and the idea of substitutionary atonement, which he discovered already in a confessional form in the tradition of his communities. In his letters, this formula is found repeatedly: Jesus died for us (Rom 8:3; 2 Cor 5:21; Gal 3:13). In this way, Paul wants to say that Jesus has taken upon himself the demand and the curse of sin and the law, according to which the sinner deserves death. Indeed, Paul formulates this thought with ultimate radicality and says that Jesus was made sin for our sake (2 Cor 5:21). He who was innocent has voluntarily discharged the requirement of justice in our place and for our benefit (Rom 8:3; Gal 3:13).

This understanding of the death and resurrection of Christ is fundamental for Paul's understanding of God's righteousness (δικαιοσύνη θεοῦ).[39] According to human logic, righteousness would have meant a death sentence for us as sinners. But now righteousness means acquittal for the sake of life. The law's demand is not thereby rescinded; rather, Jesus Christ has discharged the requirement of justice for us and in our place. He has removed from us the requirement of self-justification; he himself has become our righteousness (1 Cor 1:30). So the divine justice revealed in Jesus Christ is not a condemnatory and punitive justice, but a justice that makes righteous. It justifies us before God out of pure grace, without merit on our part; indeed, despite our demerits. It is bestowed on us, not on account of our works, but on account of our faith (Rom 1:17; 3:21f., 28; 9:32; Gal 2:16; 3:11). It is a justice that justifies a person and makes him or her righteous.

In this way, God's mercy, which is decisively revealed on the cross, allows us, who have deserved judgment and death, to revive and to live anew, without having earned it. It bestows on us a hope against all hope (Rom 4:18). It creates a space for life and for human freedom. It neither eliminates human freedom nor suppresses it. On the contrary, this new righteousness restores our freedom anew so that it can be fruitful in works of justice and in our engagement on behalf of justice in the world (2 Cor 9:10; Col 1:10). Thus the message of the new righteousness, which has been bestowed through faith, establishes Christian freedom (Gal 5:1, 13).[40]

The insight that God's justice is not a punitive justice, but rather a justice that justifies the sinner, counts as the great Reformation discovery of Martin Luther, a discovery that also liberated him personally from anxiety about sin and from a troubled conscience. Luther's discovery is fundamentally a rediscovery. It has older roots in the common tradition of the early church. We find these roots in Augustine,[41] for whom Luther had high esteem, and in Bernard of Clairvaux, who enjoyed a renaissance immediately before Luther's time and whom Luther knew well.[42] Regrettably, the debates about justification in the sixteenth century became a focal point of controversy and, in the centuries afterward, led to a long history of misunderstandings and polemic, which divided Western Christianity and caused much woe among the people of Europe. Only in the twentieth century was a fundamental agreement between Lutherans and Catholics achieved.[43] Today, thank God, Lutherans and Catholics can testify jointly to an anxious world, which is desperately concerned about itself: Have no fear! God's righteousness is his mercy and his mercy is his righteousness. It liberates you from every existential anxiety and frees you for new life, new hope, and a life lived out of love and for love.

Paul explains in detail both what the new freedom of the Christian means and what it doesn't mean. Freedom is not to be confused with arbitrariness, which says: everything is lawful for me

(1 Cor 6:12; 10:23). Freedom liberates from the weight of the law, through the fulfillment of which we thought we could justify ourselves, but which we could never fully satisfy and which incessantly demanded too much of us. It also liberates us from the burden of sin, which we lug around with us and from which we cannot free ourselves by our own power. It liberates from the anxious and the never-successful attempts at self-justification by means of success, money, power, prestige, pleasure, or sex appeal. It liberates us from enslavement to these earthly goods that tyrannize us. It liberates us from fear about the meaninglessness of existence and from the fear of death. As "freedom from," it is, however, also "freedom for," namely, freedom for God and for others. It is efficacious in love (Gal 5:6). Love is so free that it is free from its own ego and can change fundamentally. Love is the fulfillment of the entire law (Rom 13:10).

Paul conceptualized his understanding of righteousness with the image of an exchange. "For our sake he [God] made him to be sin who knew no sin, so that in him we might become the righteousness of God" (2 Cor 5:21). "Though he was rich, yet for your sakes he became poor, so that by his poverty you might become rich" (2 Cor 8:9). It is not we who reconcile ourselves with God; God reconciles himself with us through Jesus Christ. But he does that so that we, as a result, become a new creation in Christ (2 Cor 5:17–19).

This idea of a sacred exchange (*sacrum commercium*) was often taken up by the church fathers and found a resonant echo in them. They say repeatedly: The just one dies for the unjust in order to make the unjust just. He died so that we could live. The church fathers go a step further and say: God became human so that we would be divinized.[44] In the third Christmas preface, we read: "For through him the holy exchange that restores our life has shone forth today in splendor: when our frailty is assumed by your word, not only does human mortality receive unending honor but by this wondrous union we, too, are made eternal."* The idea of exchange

*Translator's note: This is the English translation of the prayer from the Roman Missal of 2011. The German text cited by Cardinal Kasper reads: "For you have performed a marvelous exchange: your divine Word became a mortal man, and we mortals receive in Christ your divine life."

received its most intense emphasis in Martin Luther, who speaks in many places of the happy change and exchange.[45]

The theology of the cross is found in a complete form in the ancient song about Christ in the letter to the Philippians (2:6–11).[46] There the idea of divine *kenosis* is found. Paul speaks of the self-emptying (κένωσις) of the one who, being in the form of God (μορφῇ θεοῦ), took on the form of a slave (μορφῇ δούλου). According to many exegetes, Paul has interpolated the following at this place in the song, which he had discovered in the community: "emptying to the point of death on a cross." Jesus willingly subjected himself to slavery at the hands of the world's fateful powers and was obedient to the point of death on a cross. But God did not leave him in death, but elevated and appointed him as the new Lord of the world (κύριος). His service as a slave in our place has thereby become a new law for the world. A change in sovereignty has been completed; a new world order has come into being. The hymn in the letter to the Colossians has picked up this idea: "He is the beginning, the firstborn from the dead....For in him all the fullness of God was pleased to dwell, and through him God was pleased to reconcile to himself all things, whether on earth or in heaven, by making peace through the blood of his cross" (Col 1:18–20).

In the *kenosis* of the one who was in the form of God, a thought, which we already met in the Old Testament, is brought to its conclusion: God withdraws, so to speak, in order to make room for his mercy and thereby also for life. The New Testament makes this thought more radical: God actually enters into the opposite of himself, he takes death upon himself and subjects himself to the power of death. God himself is dead.[47] But death could not hold God, who is immortal. Death itself, so to speak, petered out on the cross. Jesus' death on the cross, therefore, is the death of death and the victory of life. Thus Paul can sneer:

> "Death has been swallowed up in victory."
> "Where, O death, is your victory?
>   Where, O death, is your sting?"
>   (1 Cor 15:54f.)

Thus, on the cross God's mercy and, with it, life have ultimately been victorious. It was God who through Christ has reconciled the world with himself (2 Cor 5:18). God is the God of mercy (2 Cor 1:3), who is rich in compassion (Eph 2:4). By his mercy we have been rescued from death (Eph 4:24) and reborn to a living hope (1 Pet 1:3; Titus 3:5). For this reason, Paul can say: nothing can separate us from his love, not hardship, or distress, or persecution, or famine, or nakedness, or peril, or sword (Rom 8:35f.). In every situation, no matter how hopeless, in life as in death, we are accepted, held, and loved by God.

The first letter of John expresses this message again: God is greater than our hearts (1 John 3:20). He is greater than our petty calculating, greater even than our anxiety. God has called us and established us into his fellowship and into fellowship with Jesus Christ (1:3). Therefore, the first letter of John can summarize: "God is love" (4:8, 16). Mercy, as the effluence of divine love, is thus the sum of the gospel.

Many today cannot bear to look at the cross and the crucified one. They regard displays of the cross in public to be no longer appropriate and they want to remove them. But such attitudes of advanced secularization in a pluralistic society must be questioned: Has suffering no longer a place in a world of wellness? Do we push suffering away and suppress it? What would our world be missing, especially what would the many who suffer be missing if this sign of love and mercy for all were no longer permitted to be publicly visible? Should we no longer be reminded that: "By his wounds we are healed" (Isa 53:5; 1 Pet 2:24)? To believe in the crucified son is to believe that love is present in the world and that it is more powerful than hate and violence, more powerful than all the evil in which human beings are entangled. "Believing in this love means believing in mercy."[48]

To believe in love and to make it the embodiment and sum of our understanding of existence has far-reaching, indeed revolutionary consequences for our image of God, for our self-understanding and for our life praxis, for ecclesial praxis and for our conduct in the world. Love, which is proven in mercy, can and must become the foundation of a new culture for our lives, the church, and for society. That shall be our next topic, following this presentation of the biblical foundations.

V

SYSTEMATIC REFLECTIONS

1. Mercy as God's Defining Attribute

AS IT COULD NOT HELP but do, the biblical message of God's infinite mercy found a powerful echo in the theology of the early church. As early as Clement of Rome, we see that he could write to the Corinthians: "The Father, who is merciful and kind in all things, has compassion for those who fear him; willingly and joyfully he bestows gracious favor on those who come to him with simple hearts."[1] Irenaeus of Lyons described mercy as the special attribute of God.[2] To cite all of the relevant evidence in detail would take us too far afield. It is more important to note that the message of mercy in the early church did not remain an ineffective statement. When the question arose whether Christians, who have committed serious wrong after their baptism, thereby breaking their baptismal promises, could receive a second chance, reference to the infinite mercy of God was decisive and led to the introduction of the ancient church's penitential praxis.[3]

A fundamental discussion occurred as a result of disputes with Marcion, that rich ship owner from Sinope in Pontus, who joined the Christian community in Rome around 135 CE and who, after dramatic arguments, was expelled from the Roman community in 144 CE. This was an event of fundamental significance and considerable long-term effects. For Marcion drew a distinction between the just and wrathful God of the Old Testament and the merciful God of the

New Testament. In the process, he threw into question the unity of salvation history and the cohesive bond of the old and new covenants, ultimately challenging the overall testimony of the Bible and the unity of the Old and New Testaments. Viewed at a deeper level, this issue concerned the unity of the one and the same God, who is simultaneously just and merciful. In the arguments that occurred at that time, basic questions of Christian faith were raised. Therefore, it comes as no surprise that the church fathers reacted decisively. In this dispute, the essentials had to be clarified, which are authoritative for all of Christianity until this very day: a biblical canon consisting of both the Old and the New Testament and the message of one God, who is merciful and just.[4]

The decisions at that time were foundational for the entire future history of the church and of theology. They still constitute the most important ecumenical bond between the divided churches. For all churches and ecclesial communities of Christianity, which otherwise are so variegated and colorful, appeal to the canon of scripture. The fundamental decision that was made back then certainly contains considerable explosive material. For it posed the question about how justice and mercy in God are more precisely related to each other. This question—as we have already said—became the fateful question of Western Christianity.

In order to classify this problem and to understand it correctly, we must take into consideration the basic development of the doctrine of God. The starting point of the doctrine of God was and still is the revelation of God's name to Moses in the burning bush. When Moses asked the self-revealing God for his name, he received the answer, "I am the one who is there," which, on the basis of the Greek translation, was rendered in the theological tradition as "I am who I am" (Exod 3:14).[5] Behind the difference between the original Hebrew text and the Greek translation stands the difference between the Hebraic and Greek ways of thinking. The verb "to be," which is expressed in "I am," does not mean in Hebrew—in contrast to the Greek—a quiescent, but rather a dynamic Being. It does not simply mean "to exist," but concretely means "to be present there," and, in fact, to be there with and for others. The answer that Yahweh gives to Moses thus conveys the meaning: "I am the one who is there for you, who is with you and by you." God's name, therefore, is both a commitment and a promise. When the Hebrew Old Testament was translated during the Hellenistic period around 200 BCE into Greek in Alexandria as the so-called Septuagint, the revelation of God's name was interpreted in the sense of the Greek philosophy of being. Correspondingly, the Septuagint translated God's name as "I am the one who is" (Ἐγώ εἰμι ὁ ὤν).

This translation set a precedent that shaped theological thought over many centuries down to the present day. In order to make clear that God is not a being alongside or over all other beings, God was defined not as "the one who is," but rather as "Being Itself" (*ipsum esse subsistens*). This concept became God's actual name.[6] It expresses God's immanence as well as his transcendence. For it implies that God as Being is the all-determining reality in all things, and it equally implies that God as Being Itself is above all things and is not absorbed into the world, pantheistically or panentheistically as the soul of the world.

This definition of God, moreover, expresses the fact that the highest and ultimate reality to which human thought can ascend, Being, and the highest reality in faith, God, do not clash with each other. That is a magnificent insight, which became a governing idea for the entire theological tradition. It means: thought and faith are, in fact, not the same and they cannot co-opt each other, but they are correlated and do not contradict each other. That is an idea that one will not want to give up easily.[7]

But even in theology, everything has its price. Early on Tertullian asked: What does Jerusalem have to do with Athens?[8] Most notably, Blaise Pascal, after a mystical experience at night, emphasized, in his famous *Memorial* of 1654, the difference between the God of the philosophers and the God of Abraham, Isaac, and Jacob.[9] Pascal's issue caused some disturbance, which led to further inquiry. Since the Enlightenment, there have been attempts to de-Hellenize Christianity.[10] Liberal theology, above all, made the attempt to free itself from Hellenistic metaphysics. That attempt continued to have an effect in twentieth-century Protestant theology, which otherwise wanted to distance itself from theological liberalism.[11] However, when one detaches the God of the Bible from the God of the philosophers, theology is then in danger of maneuvering itself into a self-chosen enclosure.

With such self-limitation, in the name of a supposed return to a pure origin, one fails to recognize that even in the Bible there never was a faith in Yahweh that was unadulterated and, so to speak, chemically pure. On the basis of its authentic essence, faith in Yahweh was from the very beginning inculturated into whatever the respective living reality was, and then always in new ways. The revelation of God's name at Sinai indeed makes not only a particular, but also a universal claim. God revealed himself not only as the God of this people Israel—so to speak, as an ethnic or national God—but he pledged that he will demonstrate that he is God wherever his people might be during their wandering. This promise implies a universal claim. This claim is already found with Abraham, to whom the promise had been given that he would be a blessing for all peoples (Gen 12:2f.; 18:18; etc.). With the prophets, this universal claim was later expressed explicitly (Isa 41:4; 44:6–9). The same thing happened in another way when faith in Yahweh encountered the Hellenistic world. The most comprehensive concept available in Greek thinking, the concept of being, was seized upon and related to God, who is the reality that determines everything. In this way, the universal claim of Israel's God could be expressed in a new way and, simultaneously, the presupposition was created for allowing biblical speech about God to remain universally communicable.

Nowadays, therefore, it cannot be a matter of throwing overboard the traditional determination of God's essence. Instead, we will have to think critically and constructively about the Greek metaphysics of being in terms of the modern philosophy of freedom. That is not possible in the present context.[12] What is, however, important for our context is to determine the proper relation between the philosophical understanding of being and the biblical understanding of God. The question, namely, is: Is the biblical understanding of God to be classified in terms of the philosophical understanding of being and made subordinate to it, or does the biblical view succeed in drawing upon the philosophical understanding of being, but then interpreting it more carefully from the perspective of the biblical understanding of God and making it more precise? This, therefore, involves the concern that Thomas Aquinas expressed with the term *determinatio*.[13]

The attempt to begin with the philosophical concept of God and then to delineate it more specifically from the perspective of the theological understanding of God, rooted in historical revelation, is by no means new. We find this attempt already in the patristic and scholastic tradition. In what follows, I will refer only to two weighty representatives of the theological tradition, Augustine and Bonaventure.

In the seventh book of his *Confessions*, Augustine describes his own path from the Manichaean, materialistic understanding of God to the Platonic and, finally, to the Christian understanding, which is established by the revelation of God's name to Moses: *ego sum qui sum*.[14] He repeats this assertion about God in his tractate *On the Trinity*, but emphasizes that it is not a definition, that is, it is not a kind of paraphrase of God's essence, which is incomprehensible to us mortals and therefore also not capable of being defined.[15] Augustine could never detach his understanding of God from his trinitarian conception of God, that is, from his understanding of God as love. He speaks movingly about this in the concluding, fifteenth book of his tractate *On the Trinity*, where he again summarizes, as it were, his understanding of God. He says that the Father's love is nothing other than his nature and his constitutive essence, and he adds: "As we have often said already and will not tire of repeating it often."[16] For Augustine, therefore, God is the God of Christian revelation: God who is love (1 John 4:8, 16).

Augustinian thought had formidable influence on all of Western theology. We find Augustinian thinking in High Scholasticism, above all in Bonaventure. In his *The Mind's Journey to God*, his book on the pilgrimage of the soul to God, Bonaventure emphasizes that one can rightly understand God only in the light of the Crucified One.[17] Consequently, for Bonaventure, as for Thomas, the first name of God, drawing upon the revelation of his name to Moses, was "the One who is." But then Bonaventure goes a decisive step further. He makes a connection with the response that Jesus gave to the rich young man, in which God is described as the only one who is good (Matt 19:17). He then continues: "The good is defined as that which communicates itself and bestows itself [*bonum est diffusivum sui*]."[18] God is Being Itself, but Being Itself that communicates itself and exudes itself in love. With this definition of God, the philosophical understanding of God was not given up, but it was qualified theologically, concretized, and—in the terminology of Thomas Aquinas—determined. For Bonaventure as for Augustine, that means thinking of God's essence as love and thinking about and developing the doctrine of God as a doctrine of the Trinity.[19] In modern theology, Karl Rahner has given renewed impetus to this effort with his demonstration that *theos* in the New Testament always refers to God the Father.[20]

Before we can talk more about this, we must first address the consequences of the previous reflections for the question that particularly interests us, the question concerning God's attributes. In academic theology, they were unpacked within the framework of the metaphysical determination of God's essence as Being Itself. As has already been shown, God's mercy had not found its appropriate place in this framework.[21] According to the testimony of all of scripture, the Old as well as the New Testament, God's mercy, however, is the attribute, in God's self-revelation in the history of salvation, that assumes first place. Therefore, it cannot be treated, as happens in the dogmatic handbooks, as one attribute of God alongside others. It certainly cannot be treated as an attribute that is subordinated to the attributes that derive from the metaphysical essence of God and then is mentioned almost only in the margins. Instead, mercy is the externally visible and effectively active aspect of the essence of God, who is love (1 John 4:8, 16). Mercy expresses God's essence, which graciously attends to and devotes itself to the world and to humanity in ever new ways in history. In short, mercy expresses God's own goodness and love. It is God's *caritas operativa et effectiva*.[22] Therefore, we must describe mercy as the fundamental attribute of God.

Mercy, of which we have just spoken, stands in an indissoluble inner connection with God's other attributes, especially holiness, justice, fidelity, and truth.[23] It is surrounded by a crown of other divine attributes, which are organized into a whole around mercy and which express aspects of God's mercy. Scheeben mentions: benevolence, magnanimity, favor, graciousness, friendliness to human beings, condescension, generosity, clemency, leniency, mildness, gentleness, patience, and forbearance.[24] This finding suggests that we should treat mercy not as an appendix to the exposition of God's attributes, but rather as the organizing center of God's attributes, with the other attributes grouped around it.

Because God's essence is not composed of parts, but is simple through and through, the names and attributes of God, of which the scriptures speak, are ultimately coextensive with God's essence. Making distinctions between the individual attributes is valid only for our limited, human comprehension of God. In each case, we can perceive only aspects of God's single essence, which are the result of God's relationship to the world or are the effects of his activity in the world. Only to that extent does the distinction of the divine attributes in God's self have a basis in reality.[25]

The determination of mercy as the basic attribute of God has consequences for determining the relationship of mercy to God's justice and omnipotence. If mercy is the fundamental attribute of God, then it cannot be understood as an instance of justice; on the contrary, divine justice must rather be understood from the perspective of divine mercy. Mercy, then, is the justice that is idiosyncratic to God. That was the pivotal insight that lay at the basis of the agreement between the Catholic Church and Lutherans concerning the doctrine of justification.[26] We will come back to this in more detail in what follows.[27]

The implication of the central location of mercy for the relation of divine mercy and omnipotence is also important. This issue plays an important role in theology after Auschwitz. Stunned, one wonders where was God and how he could permit this horrible crime. Drawing upon the Jewish Kabbalistic mysticism of Zimzum,[28] as well as on the Lutheran theology of *kenosis* of the sixteenth and nineteenth centuries, one often came to the answer that God emptied himself so very much that he divested himself of his omnipotence in order to be totally present with the powerless and the hopelessly oppressed. At a high conceptual level, this response is found in Hans Jonas.[29] With all due respect for its subjective seriousness and conceptual niveau, one must nevertheless say that this answer can scarcely endure. For a God who was no longer all-powerful would no longer be God. Such a God could no longer help; and then one could no longer have hope in him. His mercy would be weakness pure and simple. But according to the Bible's testimony, the situation is the reverse.[30] Accordingly, God is precisely sovereign and omnipotent in that he can completely recant; precisely by being the God who mercifully is for and with the poor and oppressed, he demonstrates his divinity and his omnipotence.[31] God's omnipotence, as it says in one of the church's prayers, is disclosed above all in sparing and pardoning.[32] It is the omnipotence of his love and mercy.

It was great and holy women who overcame a doctrine of God that was one-sidedly oriented to metaphysics and who rediscovered the full power of the biblical experience of God. St. Thérèse of Lisieux, who never wrote a theological treatise but is still rightly venerated as a doctor of the church, could say: "To me He has granted His *infinite Mercy*, and *through it* I contemplate and adore the other divine perfections! All of these perfections appear to be resplendent *with love*."[33] Sister Faustina has made mercy a fundamental feature of God and has thereby been able, through Pope John Paul II, to influence the theological thinking of the twenty-first century.[34]

Finally, Yves Congar, to whom we are indebted for his interpretation of mercy in the work of Thomas Aquinas, who clearly is the most important representative of the Scholastic tradition, has shown that understanding God as love was also near at hand for Thomas. Congar rightly urged theologians to develop an ontology of love.[35] For if God is the reality that defines everything, then what follows from the assertion "God is love" is that love is the ultimate meaning of the world. Therefore, in an ontology of love, neither can the self-contained substance—as in ancient and medieval metaphysics —nor the subject—as in the modern era—be the reality that defines everything. Rather, a communal, relational way of thinking takes their place.[36] It was developed by theology in the doctrine of the Trinity originally and in exemplary fashion for secular reality.

2. Mercy as Mirror of the Trinity

The attempt to understand divine mercy as the mirror of the trinitarian essence of God may, at first glance, appear to some to be a difficult undertaking. For the confession of faith in a triune God appears to many, not just nowadays, to be a total mystery, which they have no use for and which, therefore, provides them little help in understanding better God's mercy. Even in theology, the doctrine of the Trinity was periodically neglected. However, in the last few decades a transformation has occurred in Catholic as well as in Protestant theology, not without stimuli from Orthodox theology. This change has entailed the rediscovery of the secret of the Trinity and its recognition as the key to understanding Christian faith.[37]

Of course, the doctrine of the Trinity is not a case of "supernatural" mathematics, a kind of magic formula, so to speak. It does not intend to make the contradictory statement that one is equal to three or that one and the same reality, viewed from the same perspective, can simultaneously be one and three. Rather, the doctrine of the Trinity results from the careful exegesis of the sentence from the first letter of John, in which the New Testament summarizes its entire message again: "God is love" (1 John 4:8, 16). To be sure, the confession of faith in the Trinity cannot be deduced from this statement, but it also cannot be sublated into a truth of reason, as Hegel has attempted. For those who wish to understand it in faith, in the spirit of the axiom *fides quaerens intellectum* (faith seeking understanding), the trinitarian confession can be understood as a truth that is not in itself contradictory, but that makes sense in faith and, in this sense, is comprehensible to the believer.[38]

If God is love, then his innermost essence can be understood, in an approximate way, on the basis of the analogy of human love. But this is the case of an analogy in which the dissimilarity is always greater than every similarity. For the essence of human love entails not only giving something to the other, but communicating oneself in that gift and making oneself the gift. By bestowing ourselves in love, we simultaneously divest ourselves; we give ourselves away. By giving ourselves away in and through this gift, we nevertheless remain ourselves; in fact, we find our own fulfillment in love.[39] For love entails becoming so one with the other that, as a result, neither the beloved nor the lover is absorbed into the other. Rather, love's secret is that, in becoming one, we first find ourselves and come to our own individual fulfillment. True love is not obtrusive; it respects the other's being other; it safeguards the dignity of the other. In becoming one with the other, love creates and grants space to beloved, in which he or she can become themselves. The paradox of love is that it is a unity that includes otherness and difference.

Obviously, such human love is only a very weak image of God's love. It is an analogy, in which the dissimilarity is far greater than the similarity.[40] Nevertheless, it becomes clear through this analogy that the trinitarian confession is not nonsense or an absurd, self-contradictory assertion. It does not stand in contradiction to the monotheistic understanding of God, which is fundamental for the entire Old and New Testament. The doctrine of the Trinity is not polytheism in disguise. It firmly holds that the one and only God is no solitary and dead God, but rather that God, in himself, is life and love.

The doctrine of the Trinity is no addendum and certainly no antithesis to monotheism; it is monotheism in concrete form.[41] In the doctrine of the Trinity, the abstract philosophical definition of God, according to which God is Being Itself, is concretized and qualified. It says: as Being Itself, God is love, which communicates and bestows itself as gift to others. As we have already shown, we find approaches to such a more precise concretion in Augustine and Bonaventure. God as the Good One is defined by the fact that he communicates and bestows himself as gift (*bonum est diffusivum sui*). As self-radiating love, the one God is at the same time triune. From eternity he has a beloved and a co-beloved; he is thus God as Father, Son, and Holy Spirit. In the spirit of the New Testament, God's being must be defined more precisely as Triune Being in love.[42]

Only if God in himself is self-communicating love can he communicate himself externally as the one who he already is. Were God not intrinsically self-communication, then his external self-communication would constitute his self-becoming and his self-development. In this case God would first become who he is through his self-revelation. Theology would then be theogony, with which we are familiar from myths. Were that so, then the revelation of his mercy would no longer be a free and gracious event, but rather the necessary process of God's self-becoming. Only if God in himself is love, is his self-revelation an irreducibly free, unmerited gift of his love.

The triunity of God is, therefore, the inner presupposition of God's mercy, just as, conversely, his mercy is the revelation and mirror of his essence. In God's mercy, the eternal, self-communicating love of the Father, Son, and Holy Spirit is mirrored and revealed.[43]

We can go another step further in order to penetrate as deeply as possible into the mystery of divine mercy. Thus far we said: mercy is not the actualization of God, but rather the mirror of the inner trinitarian essence of God. Now we must add: in mercy, God's trinitarian essence is admittedly not actualized, but it does become reality for us and in us in a concrete way. How are we to understand this?

Because everything that concerns God is simply infinite, the Father can communicate his godhood to the Son and to the Spirit through the Son only by retreating in his own infinity and giving space to the other in himself. This *kenosis* (self-emptying) of God is the presupposition for the fact that God, who is infinite, can make room for creation.[44] The incarnation of God in Jesus Christ and, in a more complete way, in Jesus' cross is the unsurpassable apex of God's self-revelation in his trinitarian self-withdrawal. On the cross, God enters into death, the most extreme antithesis to God, who is life, in order to conquer death by the death of one who essentially is immortal.[45] His self-emptying is the revelation of his omnipotence in love. The cross is thereby the *id quo maius cogitari nequit*, that is, that than which nothing greater can be thought.[46] When the Old Testament says that God, in his mercy, revokes his holy wrath in order to grant us the conditions for life and living space, then this is, as it were, a prelude and an anticipatory sign of what happens on the cross in unsurpassable reality.

The inner reality of God as self-emptying and self-communicating love, which has become decisively and unsurpassably revealed on the cross, does not remain in itself, but is bestowed on us concretely in the Holy Spirit. In his mercy, God lets us not only see into his heart; he creates space for us beside his heart and in his heart through the Holy Spirit. The Second Vatican Council says: in Jesus Christ, God has, in a certain sense, united himself with every human being.[47] By revealing the Wholly Otherness of his godhead through his love, which empties itself and gives itself away as gift, God, at the very same time, bestows the greatest possible closeness to himself. In this way, the already-quoted axiom of the Fourth Lateran Council can be augmented and advanced. It is not only true that for every similarity to God there corresponds a yet greater dissimilarity; it is also true that for every dissimilarity there corresponds a yet greater similarity and nearness to God, indeed an intimacy with God and an in-being in God.[48]

All of this is no abstract speculation, far removed from life. According to John's Gospel, Jesus, raised up onto the cross and dying, exhaled his spirit (John 19:30). "Raising up" in John's Gospel has the double meaning of physically being raised onto the cross and being raised to the right hand of God. The church fathers interpreted the exhalation of Jesus' spirit as a reference to the Holy Spirit.[49] If the Spirit is emitted at the same time as the elevation, this means that the cross, resurrection, ascension, and Pentecost all coincide. In the Johannine farewell speech, Jesus himself says: "Those who love me will keep my word, and my Father will love them, and we will come to them and make our home with them" (John 14:23). John speaks of a mutual being-in-the-other in many passages: he is in us and we, in him.[50] We thus have an intimate communion with the Father and with the Son, and this communion is for us perfect joy and the fulfillment of our humanity (1 John 1:3f.). A different Christ mysticism is found in Paul. He speaks not only of being in Christ and Christ's being in us. Paul also speaks of God's Spirit dwelling in us (Rom 8:9; 1 Cor 6:19; Eph 2:22).

These New Testament statements have left long and wide tracks in the history of Christian piety in the form of Christ mysticism.[51] On this basis, theology has developed its teaching about the indwelling of the Holy Spirit in the soul of the justified and baptized.[52] Accordingly, God has a place in his heart for us because of the Holy Spirit dwelling in our hearts. In God we have a place, in which we find rest already now and where we will find final rest at a time to come.

In his exposition of Psalm 24 (25) and the famous penitential Psalm 50 (51), Thomas Aquinas beautifully defined the eschatological in-between situation in which we find ourselves. He has shown that our poverty and deprivation, to which God's mercy is directed, is not only physical poverty and deprivation. Our true poverty consists in being distant from God due to sin. Indeed, from all eternity God wants to bestow on us his nearness and his fellowship; he wants to have us close to him. The message of God's mercy means that God attends to our primordial and fundamental poverty, that he is near to us in this adversity, and, consequently, that he is a God of humankind and is our friend. Mercy, therefore, means the felicity and fulfillment of the human person. It grants us mortals the experience and the savoring of an inner blessedness; it raises us up, expands our heart, and bestows on us joy and hope. It reestablishes the original order and bestows serenity, peace, and happiness by allowing us already now to have a foretaste of eternal blessedness.[53]

Bonaventure takes up this idea in his *The Mind's Journey to God* by pointing to the Augustinian longing for peace and St. Francis's preaching of peace. He wrote this text indeed under the impact of his visit to Mt. Averna (today: La Verna), where Francis of Assisi received the stigmata,[54] a place that has great spiritual significance especially for a disciple of St. Francis. Bonaventure ends his text with a reflection on St. Francis's mystical experience on Mt. Averna, where, with the crucified Christ, he was entirely one with God and was aglow with the fire of the Holy Spirit.[55]

Trinitarian theology later became explicitly trinitarian mysticism. It seized upon the biblical statements about the indwelling of the Trinity in the soul of the justified and developed them into the teaching of the divine birth of Christ in the hearts of the faithful, as a replication and continuation of the eternal birth of the Logos from the Father and the temporal birth of Jesus from Mary.[56] Meister Eckhart, John Tauler, and Henry of Suso took up these ideas. Trinitarian mysticism is found, in a different way, in the powerful visions of Hildegard of Bingen, in medieval female mysticism (Angela of Foligno, Gertrude of Helfta, Mechthild of Magdeburg, and Mechthild of Hackeborn), and among the late medieval Friends of God.

In the nineteenth century, this trinitarian mysticism was particularly pronounced in the Carmelite, Blessed Elizabeth of the Trinity. She has left us one of the most beautiful prayers in Christianity, which she wrote down on the evening of November 21, 1904. It begins:

> O my God, O Trinity, whom I adore, help me to completely forget myself and to settle in you, motionless and peaceful, as if my soul already abided in eternity. Nothing should be able to disturb my peace; nothing should cause me to fall away from you, O my Immutable One; rather, every minute should lead me further into the depths of your mystery. Grant peace to my soul, make it your heaven, your beloved dwelling, and the place of your repose.

Hans Urs von Balthasar published a selection of her writings under the descriptive title, *Der Himmel im Glauben* [Heaven in faith].[57]

Such trinitarian mysticism has nothing to do with an intoxicated absorption into God. On the contrary, God's light is so bright that people are blinded by it and fall into darkness. Christian mystics, who have been touched by the nearness of God and who have experienced in a special way the happiness and peace of his nearness, have, therefore, always also experienced the distance separating them from God and God's transcendence. Experience of divine mercy is no cheap comfort and certainly entails no reveling in God's presence. On the contrary, mystics are repeatedly, and often for a long time, plunged into the night of experiencing Jesus' abandonment by God on the cross. In the most intimate communion with God, they also experienced God's holiness and transcendence and, in the experience of God's distance, were nonetheless certain of his nearness and his companionship.[58]

The path of mysticism is a pilgrim's path, a bearing up under the cross in the hope of resurrection and communion with God for eternity. Thus, even the life of mysticism remains a pilgrim's existence. Often it lives in the darkness of Golgotha, yet in faith, in the certitude of having a place with God in his mercy, it sees the light of Easter dawning on the horizon. Mysticism recognizes that mercy is the source and the goal of God's ways.

3. God's Mercy: Source and Goal of God's Activity

If mercy is the outwardly effective, fundamental attribute of God, it is, as it were, the portent that stands at the head of all salvation history. According to the testimony of the New Testament, creation is already designed with an eye to Jesus Christ. In him, God, the Father of our Lord Jesus Christ, has chosen us from before the creation of the world and, out of love, has destined us in advance to become his sons (Eph 1:3–5). Jesus Christ, as the lamb of God, by whose blood we are redeemed, was destined and chosen before the foundation of the world (1 Pet 1:19f.). Everything was created in him, through him, and for him. Before all of creation, he is; in him everything has existence (Col 1:16f.). Everything is created in and through the eternal Logos, who became human in time. From the beginning, he is the light and life of the world (John 1:1–4, 14). Thus from eternity, the entire world and all of salvation history stands under the sign of Jesus Christ. The mercy definitively revealed in Jesus Christ stands as a sign before and over all of reality.[59] It is the watermark of all reality. God's mercy is the primordial presupposition and ground of creation and of all of salvation history.

This is no abstract theory; it has concrete consequences for the question concerning the possibility of salvation (which does not mean, as must be said immediately, the realization of salvation) of all people. The church fathers knew that God's mercy and grace, which concretely and decisively appeared in Jesus Christ, was on display from primordial times forward and, as Augustine said, is effective "from the time of righteous Abel."[60] According to Thomas Aquinas, Jesus Christ is not only the head of the church, but also the head of all humankind.[61]

Thomas convincingly shows that mercy is already active in creation. According to him, mercy is the presupposition of justice. For justice always presupposes someone to whom one owes justice. The existence of the creature, however, is not owed, but arises solely from the goodness of God.[62] God's justice does not establish his mercy; rather, mercy is the primordial root (*prima radix*) and the prior reality, to which everything else is referred.[63] Everything ultimately depends on the goodness of God. Even God's eternal salvific decision for God's incarnation in Jesus Christ originates, as Thomas emphasizes, appealing to holy scripture and Augustine and against other interpretations,[64] from God's mercy toward humanity, which has fallen into sin and is thus at a distance from God.[65] Mercy is the eternal origin of world history as well as salvation history. Everything stands in and under its sign. Mercy is the light that shines for all creation in the darkness (see John 1:5).

Unfortunately, this positive view of all of reality in the bright light of divine mercy has been clouded over in Western theology. The cause of this overshadowing is to be sought in the doctrine of predestination, as developed by Augustine particularly in his later period.[66] This great and important church father praised divine mercy in many passages of his powerful work, as in his exposition of the psalms. According to his own testimony, he richly and gratefully experienced God's mercy in his own life.[67] But in his late period, Augustine felt challenged by the Pelagians.[68] They were moralists who were definitively shaped by monastic spirituality; they represented an intensely ethical conception of Christianity; and they emphasized the necessity of good works for human salvation. For this reason, they came into conflict with the teaching of the unmerited nature of grace. This teaching caused Augustine to oppose them. According to him, God's grace is only then truly free grace if it does not depend on the good works of people and is not conditioned upon them. That led Augustine to teach unconditional predestination, that is, predestination that is not contingent upon the good or bad deeds of human beings.

In the work of the late Augustine, this thought was brought to a head through his teaching about original sin. Because in Adam— according to Ambrosiaster's translation of Romans 5:12, which Augustine adopted—all have sinned, God must condemn all for the sake of justice. So all of humankind is a *massa damnata*.[69] In keeping with his mercy, God nevertheless makes a few exceptions and predetermines a few chosen ones for eternal blessedness. That leads Augustine to the doctrine of double predestination, that is, to a predetermination, which is not conditioned on the good or bad deeds of individuals and which determines some for salvation and the others— the great mass of human beings—to eternal damnation.

That had the serious consequence of setting the course for the entire further development of the West. Admittedly, the church did not completely adopt Augustine's teaching about predestination, but essentially softened it by condemning the teaching of absolute predestination, which is predestination without the inclusion of human freedom.[70] Still, Augustine's teaching about the *massa damnata* cast a dark shadow over the biblical message of God's mercy and, in place of the biblical understanding of the saving justice that makes one righteous (Rom 1:17; 3:21–22, 26), it places a juridical understanding of punitive justice. Already in his exegesis of Luke's Gospel, Ambrose asks: *Quae est iustitia nisi misericordia?* "What is this justice other than mercy?"[71] For Ambrose, Christ is not only the just judge; he is even more so the good judge.[72] How is Christ as judge of the world supposed to condemn nearly all of those for whom he had surrendered his life on the cross in order to save them?

Augustine bequeathed the Western tradition a weighty legacy and a huge "mortgage." For his teaching caused many people to have trepidation about salvation, conscience, and hell. The most prominent example is the young Augustinian monk Martin Luther, who in great anguish asked: "How do I get a gracious God?" The Reformation breakthrough for Luther consisted in the discovery of the original biblical sense of divine justice, which is not a punitive justice, but a free and justifying, redemptive justice.[73]

However, already in medieval theology a slow overcoming of Augustine's excessively restrictive view was being prepared. This happened, on the one hand, by emphasizing the significance of the free decision of the human person and, on the other, by attaining a deeper understanding of God's justice.

The father of medieval Scholasticism, Anselm of Canterbury, was animated by the issue: how God can be simultaneously merciful and just. For, he said, justice would require God to reward the good and to punish the bad. But how can he then, in his mercy, forgive sinners? Anselm gives the answer: In his mercy, God conforms not to our deeds, but conforms to himself and his goodness. God is just, not in reference to us and our deeds, but rather in conformity with himself and his goodness. Anselm can go so far as to say, in a formula familiar to him: God is so very just that he cannot be conceived of as being more just. His mercy is his own distinctive justice.[74]

The master of theology in the high Middle Ages, Thomas Aquinas, took up Anselm's thought. He also insisted that God is not bound to an alien law, but is himself the law and, therefore, he acts according to his goodness. His *misericordia* conforms to his *bonitas*.[75] Mercy is the primordial root (*prima radix*) and the prior element to which everything else must be traced back.[76] For this reason, Thomas asserts the original biblical motif of the priority of mercy over against modes of thinking that are one-sidedly oriented to punitive justice. Unfortunately, too little attention was paid to this fact.

A decisive change, however, first occurred in the twentieth century. It came primarily through Karl Barth. According to him, election by grace is not an abstract, eternal decree of God. Jesus Christ is the one who elects and the one who is elected; we are chosen in Jesus Christ. From all eternity and before the foundation of the world, God has elected us and predestined us in Jesus Christ to become his sons (Eph 1:4–6). Thus, election is "the eternal beginning of all of

God's ways and works in Jesus Christ."[77] In this way, predestination is no longer a dark decree of God that instills terrible fear, but rather the good news of Jesus Christ, which, in faith, makes us happy and confident in God's grace.

Karl Barth has also found significant and ongoing resonance in Catholic theology.[78] Drawing upon Karl Barth, Protestant as well as Catholic theologians nowadays no longer proceed from the abstract concepts of justice and mercy in order to bring them later into balance with each other. Rather, they proceed from the concrete historical revelation of God's eternal election in Jesus Christ. In this way, God's mercy, as the primordial presupposition and the portent of the entire history of the world and of salvation, comes into play.

Admittedly, Karl Barth's position is not free of a certain one-sidedness. Hans Urs von Balthasar notes the christological constriction and idealistic mode of thinking in Barth.[79] Karl-Heinz Menke contrasts an inclusive understanding with Karl Barth's exclusive understanding of Jesus Christ's representation [*Stellvertretung*].[80] What these critics are saying is that the reality of creation, in its relative autonomy, and the human being, in his or her freedom, must be heeded. From the very beginning, they stand under the sign of God's mercy, which was decisively revealed in Jesus Christ. But just as true humanity is not absorbed by divinity in Jesus Christ, but maintains its existence unmixed and unchanged,[81] so too the free cooperation of the human person has its place in the history of humankind and in the history of salvation. Free human cooperation is not annulled because Jesus Christ is the archetype, focal point, and goal of the entire history of humankind. Rather, by means of Jesus Christ's redemptive act, the human person is renewed in his or her creaturely dignity as a new creation and is graciously elevated.[82]

In this sense, the Second Vatican Council has many times highlighted a universal Christology explicitly and emphatically. The pastoral constitution *Gaudium et Spes*, in particular, is shaped by it. The constitution describes Jesus Christ as the key, focal point, and goal of the entire history of humankind.[83] He is the "goal of human history, the focal point of the longings of history and of civilization, the center of the human race, the joy of every heart and the answer to all its yearnings." He is the "Alpha and the Omega, the first and the last, the beginning and the end" (Rev 22:12f.).[84]

For this reason, mercy stands as a sign over the world, over history, and over every human life. In his mercy, embodied in Jesus Christ, God desires from all eternity the salvation of all people. But what does God's universal salvific will mean for the salvation of each individual human being? In the end, will all people really be, in fact, saved?

4. God's Universal Salvific Will

After overcoming the heavy baggage that Augustine bequeathed to Western theology and piety with his doctrine of predestination, we must now pose the question that, according to Kant, is the question that sums up all human questions: What may we hope?[85] That is the question whose answer decides the issue of the meaning or the meaninglessness of human existence.

The answer of Christian faith to this question cannot be that our life is extinguished in the end, just like a flower withers and a drop of water evaporates. God's love, which elected us by an act of pure mercy, called us into life, and on account of which Jesus Christ laid down his life for us on the cross, is final and cannot simply cease with death. Of course, neither can the answer be the expectation of a happy ending, in the sense of the saying, "It will all work out." Precisely in his mercy, God takes us seriously. He does not want to ambush us mortals or bypass our freedom. Our eternal destiny depends on our decision and our response to the offer of God's love. Love can court the other and wants to court the other, but it cannot and does not want to force the beloved's response. God's love, therefore, desires to be reciprocated, but people can also ignore or reject it. Because we are created for God's love, its rejection means the self-negation of the human being and, thereby, his or her total misfortune. Theologically speaking, the rejection of God's love entails the loss of one's eternal beatitude. That proves the seriousness of life and the seriousness of our freedom. Our life decision is a decision for life or for death.

Thus, the question, "What may we hope?" permits no simple answer. Even the answer we can extract from scripture and tradition is not unanimous. In scripture we find two different sets of statements, which, at first glance, appear to be irreconcilable.

On the one side stands the clear and unambiguous statement: in Jesus Christ God wants all people to be saved (1 Tim 2:3). About himself, Jesus says that he has come into the world, not to judge people, but to save them (John 12:47). And he promised: "And I, when I am lifted up from the earth, will draw all people to myself" (John 12:32). Taking up this message, Paul expressed it in the form of a hymn. Concerning the exalted Lord, he said that at the name of Jesus every knee should bend, in heaven and on earth and under the earth, and every tongue should confess that "Jesus Christ is Lord, to the glory of God the Father" (Phil 2:10f.). In him God wanted to reconcile everything in heaven and on earth (Col 1:20). Through Jesus Christ God wants to be all in all in the end (1 Cor 15:27f.; cf. Rom 11:32) and he wants to gather up and unite everything that is in heaven and on earth (Eph 1:4f., 10). Irenaeus of Lyons took up the last mentioned thought and developed it systematically. He spoke of the summing up and culmination of all of human history, indeed of the entire cosmos, under and in Jesus Christ as the head of all reality (ἀνακεφαλαίωσις).[86]

Admittedly, with its message concerning judgment, the Bible has a second and different set of statements. There is so much evidence in support of it that it is impossible to skip over it or to reinterpret it in a more appealing way.[87] In the Old Testament, the threat begins already with the retribution promised in paradise: "But of the tree of the knowledge of good and evil you shall not eat, for in the day that you eat of it you shall die" (Gen 2:17). This threat of judgment threads its way through the narrative books (expulsion from paradise, the flood, Sodom and Gomorrah, etc.). It is found very often in the psalms, where it is expressed this way, among others: "He judges the world with righteousness; he judges the peoples with equity" (Ps 9:8). The prophets speak of the "day of the LORD" as a day of judgment (Amos 5:18ff.; Isa 13; 34; 66:15f.; Ezek 7; etc.). The Wisdom literature is also full of thoughts about judgment (Wis 1—5, etc.). Jesus and the New Testament stand in this prophetic tradition. It begins with John the Baptist (Matt 3:7–12) and with Jesus himself (Matt 8:11f.; 11:21–24; 12:41f.; etc.). The clearest example is Jesus' speech about the Last Judgment, according to which those who show mercy to the poor, the needy, and the persecuted are promised the Kingdom of God, whereas those who act without mercy are subjected to eternal punishment (Matt 25:31–46). There is talk there of the eternal fire that has been prepared for the devil and his angels (Matt 25:41). Paul also speaks of the day of wrath (Rom 2:5) and of recompense for the good and the bad (2 Cor 5:10; 2 Thess 1:5–10). Finally, the apocalyptic utterances of the Old as well as the New Testament (Dan 2:28–49; 1 Cor 15:23–28; Rev 7—9; 14—18; etc.) cannot be ignored, even if they must be interpreted carefully. In all of these statements, there is no talk of the eschatological redemption of all; rather, we hear talk of eschatological judgment.

The Bible's statements about judgment had a significant, long, and also richly variegated history of effects.[88] The creed's statement is fundamental: "He will come again to judge the living and the dead."[89] One can also think about the numerous depictions of judgment and hell in Christian art. The most famous representation is indeed Michelangelo's magnificent painting of the Last Judgment in the Sistine Chapel. Reflections about hell, sermons about hell, and fear of hell played a somewhat problematic role in the history of piety. Many preachers literally sought to make people feel the heat of hell, instilling in them a fear of hell.

Nowadays such sermons on hell are rarely heard. A change in mentality in the other direction has occurred, and it is no less problematic. Fear about one's salvation, such as the fear that plagued the young Luther, has become rare. Fear about hell has often given way to a banal optimism about salvation. Many are of the opinion: "It will somehow all turn out all right." Our "dear God" in his mercy certainly cannot let people languish eternally in hell. That sentiment turns into a banal song: "All of us are coming, all are coming to heaven…" But we have to take the thought of human and Christian solidarity even more seriously. Nowadays many people think solidarity appears simply to forbid the thought of eternal suffering in hell. In the end, the theological question needs to be posed: Isn't the central biblical message about mercy factually invalidated by the message about hell? How can Jesus eternally damn those for whom he died on the cross? It simply can't be the case that God's universal salvific will encounter a limit and, in the end, God's plan for salvation fails. We have to ask: Don't we have to reject the thought of eternal damnation for the sake of God's mercy?

The transformation in mentality has entailed shifting the weight today to the first series of statements from scripture. It also means that the teaching of the *apokatastasis*, the redemption and reconciliation of all people, has again become current.[90] From a purely linguistic point of view, the word *apokatastasis* can appeal to the Acts of the Apostles 3:21. There we find mention of the time when the restoration (ἀποκατάστασις) of all reality will occur. Factually, this passage in the Acts of the Apostles certainly has little or nothing to do with the speculation that has been attached to this concept. By means of this expression, an old cosmological schema has been adopted, which speaks of the eschatological return of all reality to its holy origin and thus teaches the eschatological restoration of all reality. According to the Bible, this schema can no longer be understood in the sense of a circle, but can only be understood in a more linear sense, namely, as the eschatological fulfillment of the history of God's promise. These two meanings, however, cannot be sharply separated. In the great church fathers (Irenaeus, Origen, Gregory of Nazianzus, Gregory of Nyssa, Maximus the Confessor) both meanings are superimposed. Even Thomas Aquinas took up the *exitus-reditus* schema and recast it in terms of salvation history.[91] For a purely circular schema is alien to the Bible. For the Bible, the issue is not a circular understanding of cosmic history, but the declaration that the end time will be the surpassing consummation of original creation and thus will engender a new creation.

Talk of the *apokatastasis* has led some theologians to conclude that, in the end, all people—also the godless, and even the evil spirits—will be taken up into the beatitude of the kingdom of God, which has been perfected and fulfilled. This teaching was often attributed to the great Greek theologian Origen.[92] As such, it was condemned by Emperor Justinian in the year 543 CE.[93] However, if you read Origen's statement in context and consider the cautious—actually the hypothetical—character of his statements, then you can doubt whether this condemnation really applies to him.[94] Other church fathers, such as Gregory of Nyssa and Maximus the Confessor, have held positions similar to Origen's without ever having been condemned as a result. The doctrine of the eternal duration of the punishment of hell was definitively established in the teaching of the church, primarily due to the influence of John Chrysostom and Augustine.[95]

All the same, the doctrine of *apokatastasis* has continued to elicit great fascination. It is found in some types of mysticism, albeit in different forms. Friedrich Schleiermacher, Ernst Troeltsch, and Karl Barth at least give it serious consideration. On the basis of the current optimistic attitude concerning salvation, it often resonates today, either explicitly or implicitly, as a kind of background assumption. Johann Baptist Metz has rightly warned contemporary theology about this assumption. At bottom, he argues, this theory does not make Christianity more humane; rather, it makes Christianity superfluous.[96] A superficial understanding of God's mercy would contradict his justice and his holiness. It would have nothing more to do with the hard, cold reality of the cross. A bourgeois optimism, which downplays the seriousness of human responsibility and human guilt, excuses evildoers and commits a new injustice against victims. For them, judgment is not a message to be feared, but a message of hope. For at the court of judgment all masks will fall away, all will be equal, and justice will be meted out to everyone.

Thus, the two sets of assertions in Holy Scripture have led to two extreme positions: *massa damnata*, on the one hand, and the redemption of all, on the other. That confronts us with the question whether, and as the case may be, how we can find a way out of this predicament and find a solution that avoids both extremes.

Hans Urs von Balthasar has identified a path, which is supposed to lead us on a course between Origen and Augustine. His proposal was positively seized on by many theologians, but also harshly criticized by others.[97] His suggestion was often shortened into this formula: hell exists, but it is empty. That is a flat and banal interpretation of von Balthasar's ambitious train of thought, which removes all of the existential seriousness of the issue that, however, is his central concern. With such platitudes, his intention is perverted into its exact opposite.

According to von Balthasar, in the Bible we are dealing with two different series of assertions, both of which are to be taken seriously and which cannot be sublated into a neat, higher synthesis. According to him, we can only make progress if we take into account the literary genre of both series of statements. In both cases, we are not actually dealing with an anticipatory report of what will happen at the end of time. The assertions about universal salvation are statements of hope for all, but they are not assertions about the factual salvation of every individual. Conversely, the assertions about judgment and the statements about hell do not intend to say, about any one individual or about the majority of humankind, that factually they will be subjected to the pains of hell. Revelation has not identified the eternal damnation of any concrete individual; and the church has never taught, in a dogmatically obligatory way, that any particular human being has been subjected to eternal damnation. We cannot say that with certainty even about Judas, who, however, betrayed Jesus and then subsequently judged himself by hanging.[98]

With both assertions we are dealing with statements that transcend the realm of our mundane, space- and time-bound experience. We are dealing with limit statements, which do not make possible a concrete, realistic picture. They communicate no objective information. These statements are not concerned with making factual assertions, but rather are concerned with calling people to make a decision. On the one hand, they are concerned with encouraging people to trust in God's mercy; on the other, they are concerned with an urgent appeal to conversion. Thus, the statements about hell are words of warning, which admonish us to repent. They put hell before our eyes as a real possibility; they intend to affirm that eternal failure and completely missing the point of human existence is a real possibility.

Both assertions want to be taken seriously. Although God desires the salvation of all people, he does not will it without their involvement. "God's glory is the human person alive," we read in Irenaeus.[99] In the call to conversion and to faith, we are dealing with a decision for life or death. There is also the real possibility of eternal failure. "I have set before you today life and prosperity, death and adversity....I have set before you...blessings and curses. Choose life" (Deut 30:15, 19). Paul admonishes us to work out our salvation with fear and trembling. "For it is God who is at work in you, enabling you both to will and to work for his good pleasure" (Phil 2:12f.). Fear and trembling do not refer to anxiety about hell, but refer to the fact that God is at work in us and that we should allow him to work in and through us.

Therefore, neither a cheap optimism nor a hell-fearing pessimism about salvation does justice to the biblical statements. We can neither interpret the hopeful statements about universal salvation, in the sense of the *apokatastasis* doctrine, as factual knowledge about the actual redemption of every individual, nor can we deduce the factual eternal damnation of individual human beings or, in fact, the damnation of the majority of humankind from the threat of judgment and from the real possibility of hell. However, in the end we also can't just leave the matter in an equilibrium between a mercy that saves and a justice that rejects. The human being's "no" of refusal cannot be an equally powerful possibility alongside the unconditional "yes" that God has spoken to humankind.[100] The prior reality of divine mercy must have the first as well as the last word. Jesus Christ as judge of the living and the dead is, indeed, the one who has died for all on the cross. We may hope that he is a gracious judge.

God's mercy does not entail bypassing human freedom. God recommends, but he does not force;[101] he presses us, but does not overpower or subdue us. For, according to Augustine, the one who created you without you does not justify you without you.[102] Divine mercy appeals to human responsibility; divine mercy repeatedly courts human responsibility. With its wooing, mercy demands a decision; indeed, it first makes the decision possible. Even in the human domain, freedom is awakened in the encounter with the freedom of another. A fortiori, human freedom can decide whether to accept or reject the offer of grace only in light of God's offer of grace and its empowerment. Only vis-à-vis God's gracious offer and by means of its power are we encouraged, albeit not overpowered, to say a "yes."[103] Edith Stein (Sister Teresa of the Cross) attempted to go beyond the mere interplay of divine and human freedom and, as far as that is possible for us, to penetrate God's courtship of the human person and to describe it in depth. She even talks about how God's merciful love outwits every human person. Her reflections lead to the theoretical possibility of the salvation of all. Still, the boundary remains: we can hope for the salvation of all, but factually we cannot know that all will be saved.[104]

Both divine freedom and human freedom are a mystery. Their relation to each other is, a fortiori, an unfathomable mystery, which we cannot penetrate. The only answer open to us, on the basis of biblical testimony, is unconditional trust in the immeasurable mercy of God, who knows ways, inscrutable to us, and who never ceases to court human beings and to make their positive response attractive. In his mercy, God holds the possibility of salvation open for every human being who is fundamentally willing to be converted and who is sorry for his or her guilt, even if their guilt is ever so great and their former life ever so botched up.

The doctrine of purgatory is a sign of this infinite mercy and forbearance of God for those who have not fundamentally and decisively decided against him. In the current context, we cannot go into the history of the genesis of this doctrine.[105] It has roots ultimately in the practice of praying for the dead, of which we have evidence already in early Judaism (2 Macc 12:32–46) and in the church from its very beginning. Such prayer presupposes the possibility of a cleansing in preparation for full communion with God. Purgatory is not a place and certainly not an otherworldly concentration camp for the expiation of punishments. Ultimately, it is the condition that results from encountering our holy God and the fire of his purifying love, which we can only passively endure and through which we become altogether prepared for full communion with God.[106] It is a pure work of mercy and, in this sense, it represents, so to speak, the last chance granted to us. At the same time, it offers the community of the faithful the possibility, in solidarity, to intercede for the deceased before God.

The theme of intercession takes us once again an essential step beyond what has been previously said. The possibility of intercession implies that our hope for the salvation of others is not a hope that idly waits; it is supposed to be an actively intercessory and representative hope for all.[107] For this purpose, one can appeal to Paul. For the sake of his Jewish brothers, he was willing to be accursed and separated from Christ (Rom 9:3). This is not an isolated assertion in scripture. It takes up the words of Moses, who, with an eye to the infidelity of his people, says to God in prayer: "But now, if you will only forgive their sin—but if not, blot me out of the book that you have written" (Exod 32:32). Deuteronomy describes Moses' self-offering as an act of lying prostrate in intercession before God for forty days and nights (Deut 9:25). Moses, thus, wanted to jump into the breach in order to save his people (Ps 106:23). Similar statements are found in Jeremiah (18:20) and Ezekiel (13:5; 22:30).[108]

Paul's statement in Romans 9:3 has left long and deep tracks in theology and in mysticism. According to Thomas Aquinas, we can wish for and anticipate the eternal salvation of another if we are one with him or her through love.[109] Numerous testimonials of great saints, especially holy women like Catherine of Siena, Mechthild of Hackeborn, Angela of Foligno, Julian of Norwich, Thérèse of Lisieux, and Edith Stein, have picked up on these traces and deepened them.[110] Catherine of Siena admitted to her confessor: "If I were wholly inflamed with the fire of divine love, would I not then, with a burning heart, beseech my Creator, the truly merciful One, to show mercy to all my brethren?" She did not want to be reconciled to the fact that a single one of those whom God had created according to his image and likeness would be lost.[111] In her letters, she advocated repeatedly for leniency and mercy for those who had distanced themselves from the church.[112] Thérèse of Lisieux wanted to offer her life, in the place of others, as a sacrificial burnt offering.[113]

We find evidence like this also in modern literature. Hans Urs von Balthasar captioned the corresponding chapter in his book *The God Question and Modern Man* "Rebels and Hell" and he spoke of the sacrament of brotherhood.[114] Especially impressive is the witness of Charles Péguy, to whom Gisbert Greshake has referred in detail.[115] One can also think of Maximilian Kolbe and his substitutionary death in the hell of Auschwitz. He took the place of a father with a family and died in the starvation bunker. "No one has greater love than this, to lay down one's life for one's friends" (John 15:13).

Thus, more recent theology, on the other side of the extremes from which we began, has again established the biblical primacy of mercy and thereby God's "yes" to humankind. Mercy courts every human being to the very end; it activates the entire communion of saints on behalf of every individual, while taking human freedom with radical seriousness. Mercy is the good, comforting, uplifting, hope-granting message, on which we can rely in every situation and which we can trust and build upon, both in life and in death. Under the mantle of mercy, there is a place for everyone of good will. It is our refuge, our hope, and our consolation.

5. Jesus' Heart as the Revelation of God's Mercy

The revelation of divine mercy has its concrete locus in Jesus Christ. In him, God has chosen all of us from eternity. Whoever sees him, sees the Father (John 14:9). The letter to the Hebrews says: he had to become like us in every respect, so that he might be a merciful high priest before God (Heb 2:17). He is the throne of grace, whom we can approach, full of confidence, to find mercy and grace (Heb 4:16). As the incarnate son of God, Jesus Christ is the throne of mercy.[116]

In many centuries, veneration of the sacred heart of Jesus functioned as a special expression of faith in God's love and mercy, as revealed in Jesus Christ. Nowadays this devotion has become alien to us in many different ways. The new emphases that the liturgical movement has established for piety have contributed to this development. But the representations of the heart of Jesus, as we are familiar with them from the eighteenth and nineteenth century, have also contributed to the decline in veneration of the heart of Jesus. For these representations, which portray Jesus with a pierced heart that is often surrounded by a crown of thorns, strike us today as indiscreet, indeed, tasteless and kitschy. They are also theologically questionable because they focus on the physical heart of Jesus, rather than understanding the heart as the primordial symbol and focal point of the human person, understood holistically.[117]

A brief retrospective look into the history of piety can help to break up this restrictive focus on the physical heart of Jesus and help us to penetrate again to the core and the profound meaning of the veneration of the sacred heart of Jesus. To begin with, we need to show that the veneration of the heart of Jesus has biblical roots. We can see these roots already in the promise found in the prophet Zechariah (12:10), which the Gospel of John took up: "They will look on the one whom they have pierced" (19:37). In this prophecy, Jesus' pierced heart stands for the humanity of Christ in its totality, which has been surrendered to death for our sake. A look at the pierced heart frees our sight at the same time to see the love of God that has appeared incarnate in Jesus. In Bonaventure, we find these beautiful words: "Through the visible wounds we see the wounds of invisible love" (*per vulnus visibile vulnus amoris invisibilis vedeamus*).[118] In the heart of Jesus, we recognize that God himself has a heart (*cor*) for us, who are poor (*miseri*), in the broadest sense of the word, and that he is, therefore, merciful (*misericors*). In this way, the heart of Jesus is an emblem of God's love, which became incarnate in Jesus Christ.

These biblical roots developed gradually in the history of piety and, in the process, experienced some not-insignificant transformations. What resulted are not purely edifying statements. They have a deep dogmatic foundation in the ancient church's doctrine of Jesus Christ, which unites East and West. For the ecclesial doctrine has firmly held that Jesus Christ is, one and the same, true God and true man. In this sense, the church speaks of the one hypostasis, that is, the one person of Christ in two natures. From this assertion it followed, for the Third Ecumenical Council of Ephesus (431) and again for the Second Ecumenical Council of Constantinople (553), that in Jesus Christ only a single act of worship is due his divinity and his humanity, so that worship of his divinity is inseparable from the worship of his humanity.[119] Therefore, worship (*cultus latreiae*) is owed also to the heart of Jesus as a constitutive component and the symbolic core of Jesus' humanity.[120] In light of the dogmatic Christology of the early councils, one must understand the heart of Jesus that has endured suffering for us and for our salvation as the suffering of the son of God himself. In the heart of the incarnate son of God, the heart of the son of God himself beats and suffers. Pius XI, therefore, could describe the veneration of the heart of Jesus as the epitome of the entire religion.[121]

To understand how piety shaped the veneration of the sacred heart of Jesus in the period of the church fathers, we can have recourse to Hugo Rahner's comprehensive presentation.[122] The church fathers refer to the words of Jesus, that from his heart streams of living water will flow (John 7:38). They interpreted his assertion with an eye to the statement according to which blood and water flowed from Jesus' heart when it had been pierced by a lance (John 19:34). Blood and water were, for them, a reference to the two fundamental sacraments of the church, baptism and Eucharist. On the basis of this starting point, the veneration of the heart of Jesus in the patristic period had an objectively sacramental—more precisely, a eucharistic—character. Augustine interpreted the opening up of Jesus' heart in the following way: "There the door to life was opened, from which the sacraments of the church flowed, without which one cannot attain the life that is true living."[123]

With Bernard of Clairvaux we see a turning away from the objective Christ mysticism of the fathers toward a subjectively interiorized Christ piety. Bernard seized upon the Song of Songs and interpreted it in terms of the love of God made visible in the pierced heart of Jesus.[124] This subjective Christ piety is represented in the famous picture in which the crucified Jesus personally bends down from the cross toward Bernard. At the height of medieval Scholasticism,

Bonaventure then deepened this thought theologically. He interpreted the wound in Jesus' side as a wound of love, because whoever loves is wounded by love (Song 4:9). Thus, our pathetic and so-often dull heart can be newly ignited and catch fire time and again from the fervency of the love of Jesus' heart. Jesus' love can also wound our heart, yet we cannot help but love his heart.[125] Bonaventure can, in fact, say: Jesus' heart becomes our heart.[126]

This personal Christ mysticism was further developed in medieval female mysticism. Mystics like Gertrude of Helfta, Mechthild of Magdeburg, Mechthild of Hackeborn, and others have thus established the heart of Jesus piety, as we know it.[127] We also find it in Meister Eckhart, John Tauler, and Henry Suso. In the modern era, this kind of piety has experienced a broad dispersion, emanating from the visions of St. Marguerite Alacoque in Paray-le-Monial. In the wake of this development, the feast of the sacred heart of Jesus was gradually introduced. Popes Leo XIII, Pius XI, Pius XII, John Paul II, and finally Benedict XVI have repeatedly promoted veneration of the sacred heart of Jesus. The diaries of the Polish mystic, Sister Faustina Kowalska, gave a new impetus to this devotion. For her, mercy is the greatest and the highest of the divine attributes and represents divine perfection, pure and simple.[128] Because of the horrible experiences of the twentieth century, John Paul II understood her message as an important one for the twenty-first century.[129]

People can have different opinions about the tastefulness of the representations of Jesus' heart during the last few centuries; they can similarly hold different opinions about the representation of Jesus' heart that derives from Sister Faustina. However, such questions of taste should not divert our attention from the much more important fact that the modern veneration of the sacred heart of Jesus became pervasive in the context of the dawning Enlightenment and secularization, and in connection with the strengthening sense of the absence—indeed, the death—of God.[130] The darkness of Golgotha (Luke 23:44f.) has descended ever since upon the world as the eclipse of God. In the middle of this night of moribund faith in God and the world's increasing obtuseness and apathy toward God's love in Jesus

Christ, we may experience in the heart of Jesus God's suffering because of the world and his never-ending love for us.

In the pierced heart of his son, God shows us that he went to extremes in order to bear, through his son's voluntary suffering unto death, the immeasurable suffering of the world, our coldheartedness, and our lack of love, and sought to redeem them. By means of the water and blood streaming from Jesus' pierced heart, we are washed clean in baptism of all the dirt and muck that has accumulated in us and in the world; and in the Eucharist, we may always quench our thirst for more than the banalities that surround us and, in a figurative sense, satisfy our thirst for more than the "soft drinks" that are offered to us there. Thus with Ignatius of Loyola's prayer Anima Christi, we can say: "Blood of Christ, inebriate me. Water from the side of Christ, wash me."

Two passages in John's Gospel can provide a vivid presentation of a biblically, patristically, and dogmatically renewed understanding of the heart of Jesus piety, one that conforms to our present-day sensibilities. On the one hand, there are the medieval representations of Christ's love, which show how the beloved disciple is resting on the breast of Jesus (John 13:23). These representations can illustrate that, in the midst of unrest and turmoil in the world, there is a place where we can find inner repose and peace. The other picture originates from the scene in which "doubting Thomas" meets the risen Lord. There the skeptical Thomas only comes to have faith when he can put his finger into the wound in Jesus' side, which was glorified in the Easter event (John 20:24–29). This encounter can be significant precisely for those nowadays who have questions or are plagued by doubt. For, in a certain sense, all of us are like this "doubting Thomas." Like Thomas, often we too don't want to believe simply on the basis of the word of another. So, like Thomas, we find our way to faith only in the personal encounter with the risen Lord. Like Mary Magdalene, we can't touch him physically and put our hand physically in the still-open wound in his side. Nevertheless, spiritually the pierced heart of Jesus can become also for us a path by which we become aware of God's love that has been wounded on our account. Blaise Pascal appeared to have intuited this, when he writes:

"It seems to me that Jesus only allowed his wounds to be touched after his resurrection. *'Touch me not'*" (John 20:17).[131]

There should be no argument against such heart-of-Jesus piety, which naturally qualifies as something warmhearted, indeed, as something sentimental in the good sense. For the heart and the emotions rightly have an indispensable place in piety. Where pious emotions are banned, that disordered and downright wild emotionality, which we often find today, takes its place. We should not let emotions be taken from us and we also should not be ashamed of them. God's love, as Jesus says in the chief commandment of love, engages the entire human being with all of his or her physical, psychological, and spiritual powers (Mark 12:30 par.). Finally, piety deals with the history of love between God and us mortals, and love is always impassioned. Ultimately it is a matter of a personal dialogue with God. Cardinal Newman expressed it this way in his heraldic motto: *Cor ad cor loquitur* (Heart speaks to heart).

This personal encounter ought not to remain in the purely personal realm; it must open itself to all those who are suffering next to us and around us. In the process of looking at the pierced heart of Jesus, we truly experience that God so loved the world that he gave his only son (John 3:16). In this way, we may and we can share sympathetically in God's suffering and thus be in solidarity with all of those who suffer under the darkness and barbarity of the present world. With Jesus we can plunge into the Golgotha-night of the world, endure it with Jesus, and on the behalf of the many suffer through it to the end. The church, as the body of Christ in the Holy Spirit, collectively shares in the agony of Christ in the world. According to Pascal, Jesus' agony continues to the very end of the world.[132] Thus, as the body of Christ, the church can share representationally in the world's suffering, accompany it sympathetically, and thoroughly bear its pain. In every "night" of the world, we know with certainty, by looking at Jesus' pierced heart, that in it God's heart beats for this our world. God's heart is the heart of the world, its innermost power, and its complete and entire hope.[133] We are thus able to endure the darkness of Good Friday in the certainty of a new and eternal Easter morning. It is the certainty that nothing, neither life nor death, will be able to separate us from the love of God in Jesus Christ (Rom 8:35–39).

6. The God Who Mercifully Suffers with Us

At this most intimate of all places in the life of faith, we must pause for a moment and ask: Can God then suffer? Can God be more than a God who sympathetically scowls at suffering? Can one really speak of a God who suffers with [*mitleidenden*] us and, correspondingly, also rejoices with us? That is no purely speculative question. For the answer to this question determines whether God, in the authentic sense of the word, is a sympathetic God. For the word "sympathetic," which derives from the Greek (from συμπαθεῖν), means not only "sympathetic," but also "suffering with." Can we really speak this way about God?

Traditional Scholastic theology denied that God was capable of suffering. Even ancient philosophy was convinced of God's inability to suffer (ἀπάθεια). The theological tradition, except for a few exceptions, took over this motif.[134] And it had serious reasons for doing so. The tradition argued: talk of a God who is passively affected by our suffering is incompatible with the transcendence and the absoluteness of God, that is, with his detachment from and his superiority over the world and human beings. In addition, God's perfection, which excludes every deficiency, also excludes suffering, which is indeed a deficiency. According to this reasoning, the idea of a suffering God was thus irreconcilable with the concept of God. God cannot be, like us mortals, passively and impotently at the mercy of pain and suffering.

The idea of a God who is in the process of becoming, just like the idea of a suffering God, is incompatible with the concept of God. God cannot find his way completely to his self by first going through the world's history of suffering. Such ideas, which are found in different forms in various streams of thought, including in many forms of post-Auschwitz theology,[135] don't help us to advance in answering the question about the meaning of human suffering. Karl Rahner formulated this point in drastic form: How do I benefit if things also get messy for our dear God?[136] These ideas turn the horror of Auschwitz into a myth and an unbelievable fate, to which not only we, but also God is helplessly delivered. In that way, we can exonerate ourselves from the responsibility for such suffering and from the necessary repentance.

At the same time, the biblical understanding of God already in the Old Testament leaves no doubt that God is not an apathetic God. According to the evidence of the Bible, God has a heart for the human person. He suffers with us; he also rejoices and he grieves for us and with us.[137] The Bible does not know a God, who, in his majesty and blessedness, sits enthroned over a world full of terror and is apathetic to it. According to the New Testament, the one who was in the form of God took on the form of a slave in Jesus Christ and humbled himself (Phil 2:6f.). He can feel with us; he is like us in all things except sin (Heb 4:15). A crucified God was then and still is today, beyond a doubt, a scandal. Such a message is foolishness in the eyes of the world, but it is God's wisdom (1 Cor 1:21, 23).

The encyclical of Pope Pius XII, *Haurietis Acqua* (1956), with many quotes from the church fathers, emphasizes that, on the basis of the hypostatic union of the second divine person with humanity, the emotions and suffering of the human nature of Jesus are also the emotions and suffering of the divine person. The suffering of Jesus as a human being is, therefore, the suffering of God at the same time. Matthias Joseph Scheeben writes that God became human in Jesus Christ so that literal compassion is not absent from mercy.[138] In the humanity of Jesus, God, therefore, can suffer and wills to suffer with and for us. If God himself had not suffered for us on the cross and had not himself died for us on the cross, if Jesus' death had been nothing more than the death of a human being and if he had been unjustly executed simply as a human being—like many others before him and many more down to this very day—then his dying would have been exemplary for us, but it would not have had saving significance. Only if in him God himself, who is immortal and is

Lord over life and death, suffered and died, could he conquer death in and through death.

This teaching of scripture and the patristic tradition does not contradict the traditional teaching of Scholastic theology, which proceeds from a metaphysical understanding of God. This is so because, for the Bible, the compassionate suffering [*Mitleiden*] of God is not an expression of his imperfection, his weakness, or his powerlessness; but, on the contrary, it is an expression of his omnipotence. Because of his sovereign love, God got himself involved, so to speak, in the incarnation and lowered himself to the status of a slave. He was not overpowered by suffering. As God, who is immortal and in himself incapable of suffering, he voluntarily surrendered himself to suffering and death. Precisely in this way he could vanquish death in death because he is stronger than death. "By dying he has destroyed our death, and by rising, restored our life."[139]

In Jesus' death, God has not relinquished omnipotence, but rather has acted in an all-powerful way. With Kierkegaard, one can say: an element of omnipotence, indeed the omnipotence of love, entails allowing oneself to be affected by suffering without being under its control.[140] A God who was only merciful and not omnipotent would no longer be God. A God who was only omnipotent and not also merciful would be a despicable despot. Correlatively, the church's prayer affirms that God's power is displayed "above all in mercy and in pardoning."[141]

Therefore, it cannot be an issue of contesting God's omnipotence for the sake of God's mercy and handing a powerless God over to suffering. The concept of God would be destroyed in the process, for a powerless God would no longer really be God. Therefore, God cannot be affected and overpowered, passively and involuntarily, by pain or harm. But in his mercy, God allows himself, in sovereign freedom, to be affected by pain and suffering. In his mercy, God is shown to be masterfully free. His mercy is not induced by human need or woe. God graciously chooses to be affected and moved by the pain and suffering of humankind. Thus, many theologians today in the Catholic, Orthodox, and Protestant traditions speak of the possibility of God suffering vicariously with us.[142]

Already Origen spoke of God's suffering out of love and he made love's suffering the origin of the history of salvation. He formulated the idea this way: "*Primus passus est, deinde descendit. Quae est ista, quam pro nobis passus est, passio? Caritatis est passio.*" ("First he suffered; then he descended. What kind of suffering is that which he suffered for us? It is the suffering of love.")[143] Bernard of Clairvaux expressed his understanding of God's capacity for suffering in a pregnant formula when he said that God is incapable of suffering (*impassibilis*), but he is not incapable of sharing another's suffering (*incompassibilis*).[144] Augustine explained the spiritual sense of this idea:

> It was by no necessity of his condition, but by the good will of his compassion, that our Lord Jesus took up these feelings of human weakness, as he also took the flesh of human weakness and the death of human flesh. He did it to transform into himself his Body, the Church, whereof he has deigned to be the Head, that if ever it happened to any of his holy and faithful ones to be saddened and sorrowful in the midst of human temptations, he should not on that account fancy himself estranged from the grace of his Saviour, and should learn that such occurrences are not sins, but indications of human infirmity. Thus the Body was to take the note from the Head.[145]

Benedict XVI has expressed a similar thought:

> Man is worth so much to God that he himself became man in order to *suffer with* man...Hence in all human suffering we are joined by one who experiences and carries that suffering *with* us; hence *consolatio* is present in all suffering, the consolation of God's compassionate love— and so the star of hope rises."[146]

Those are theological and spiritual insights that first illuminate the full and unfathomable depth of divine mercy and thus delve deeply into the mystery of God. So much love can effect in people of faith only amazement and profound gratitude because God has done all of this and has suffered for us and for me. It is our guilt, it is my guilt that he has taken upon himself. Despite that, or perhaps because of that, we may pose one final question to him: Why is there then immeasurable pain and suffering of so many innocent people in the world? And to what end?

7. Hope for Mercy in the Face of Innocent Suffering

The message of God's boundless mercy crashes repeatedly into the hard realities of the world and the often tragic experience of innocent suffering in the world.[147] Here we may think not only of the atrocities for which people are responsible—wars, acts of violence, ethnic cleansing, scandalous injustice, torture, and other enmities, as well as physical and spiritual cruelties. We must also name the evil for which people are not responsible, such as devastating earthquakes and tsunamis; catastrophic droughts and floods; epidemics like the plague and cholera; AIDS; congenital, life-long severe handicaps; painful, long-lasting illnesses; serious mental illnesses; grief at the loss of a spouse or children; and tragic accidents of different kinds. The history of humanity's suffering threads its way through the entire history of humankind and it has many faces. How can God permit all of this suffering? Where was he? Where is he when all of this is happening? How can this history of suffering be reconciled with God's mercy and with his omnipotence?

Pain and suffering already became the occasion for asking religiously critical questions in the cultures of the ancient world, in ancient China, India, Iran, Babylonia, Egypt, and Israel. Early on in the ancient world, the objection was voiced: Either God is good, but not all-powerful and capable of opposing evil; but then he is not God. Or, on the other hand, he is all-powerful, but not good; he could, but chooses not to oppose evil; in that case, he is a malicious demon.[148] This objection has been seized upon repeatedly since that time down to the present day. After the Shoah, these old questions have led to post-Auschwitz theology and have raised the issue of theodicy anew.[149]

Ever since ancient times there have been repeated attempts to justify God in the face of suffering and evil in the world (theodicy). Time and again, the attempt was made to understand evil in the world as something necessary for the harmony of the cosmos. Others sought to understand it as a necessary transitional phase on the path toward a more perfect world. Neither explanation is satisfactory because they seek to instrumentalize human suffering for the sake of a greater harmony or a supposedly higher purpose. Such argumentation is cynical and commits a new injustice against victims.

The most famous theodicy is the work of Gottfried Wilhelm Leibniz, *Essais de Théodicée* (1710 CE). According to Leibniz, there is an infinite number of possible worlds. From among them, God created only one, not simply an ideal and perfect world, but "the best of all possible worlds." Leibniz argued in the following way: God's infinite wisdom allowed him to discover the best of all possible worlds; his infinite goodness let him choose the best of all possible worlds; and his omnipotence enabled him to bring this world into existence. Consequently, the world that God created must be "the best of all possible worlds," and, therefore, every form of evil is ultimately explicable and necessary.

The devastating earthquake of 1755 in Lisbon signaled the end of such rational optimism. Voltaire responded to Leibniz's attempt at theodicy with his satirical novella, *Candide or Optimism*. In 1791 Kant wrote the treatise "On the Failure of All Attempted Philosophical Theodicies." According to Kant, our human faculty of understanding is limited; metaphysical speculations concerning issues that transcend the realm of human experience are fundamentally impossible for us.[150]

Kant's treatise marked the end of discussion about theodicy up to that time. For, in fact, every attempt at theodicy failed to show proper respect for God and the inscrutable mystery of his will, as well as failed to show proper respect for the mystery of the human person and his or her suffering. A fortiori, the relation of God and the world and the relation of divine and human freedom cannot be inserted, from a higher perspective, into a meaningful and ordered context encompassing both, no matter if the context is sapiential or dialectical. With every such attempt, we elevate ourselves above God and his actions and we try to judge him from a supposedly higher vantage point. But this is arrogance and hubris. Thus, Kant's criticism of the attempts at theodicy cannot be circumvented. We must regard all of these attempts as failed.

Kant, of course, also recognized that there would be a price to pay for giving up the idea of God in the face of evil in the world. For if the dignity of the human person should remain, despite the experience of evil, that is only possible if one holds fast to the idea of God as a postulate of practical reason. Only with the presupposition of God, who encompasses human freedom and the order of nature, is hope possible for the reconciliation of human freedom and our natural fate. The idea of God preserves in itself hope for the success of human freedom.[151] To relinquish this hope would mean to abandon the human person and, ultimately, to turn away from those who suffer with a shrug of our shoulders. Jürgen Habermas follows this same line of thought when he notes that it is worth our while to tend to the embers left smoldering by questions of theodicy[152] and that we must acknowledge that to lose hope in the resurrection is to find ourselves in a perceptible void.[153] There remains a "consciousness of what is missing."[154]

The hope that Kant formulated is a postulate. Philosophy cannot formulate more than that. This postulate, for its part, depends on an option; it depends on the decision whether the human person and the dignity of the human person should have some absolute meaning, whether—in the face of injustice and woe that is irreconcilable in the course of history—one should hold open the possibility of a reconciliation or whether one wants to exclude such a reconciliation and thereby have to ultimately admit that suspicion about the meaninglessness of existence is correct. Admittedly, the question is whether and how one can live with this last-mentioned option. Thus, the theodicy question has ultimately become a question of "anthropodicy," the justification of the meaning of human existence.

What is the answer that the Bible and theology gives to the theodicy question, which has proven to be insoluble? The Bible is not familiar with the modern issue of theodicy or anthropodicy. The Bible does not proceed from a postulate; it proceeds from the primordial experience of Israel, which was also the experience of the first Christians, namely, the fidelity of God in difficult and humanly hopeless situations, a fidelity that was experienced anew in history over and over again. Toward the end of the Old Testament period, in the situation of persecution and martyrdom, Israel's basic conviction experienced its final intensification in the hope for the resurrection of the dead (2 Macc 7). In Jesus' raising from the dead, this hope was definitively sealed for the first Christians. God's pledge of fidelity grounded their hope even in the face of death, the situation that from a human perspective seems the most extremely hopeless. God's fidelity established confidence in final justice and eternal life.[155]

This message of hope in the Bible is no simple answer that makes everything add up. This fact is clearest in the Book of Job. Its repeated editorial revisions show a dramatic struggle with God and against God.[156] In the beginning, there is Job's protest. Job curses the day of his birth (Job 3:3). His life has become loathsome (10:3). He accuses God of despising humanity (7:20). His friends try everything to justify God with the help of the traditional wisdom theology. According to their cherished logic concerning a connection between deeds and consequences, happiness is the reward for good deeds and misfortune is the punishment for bad deeds. But this wisdom theology, which intends to understand and explain everything and ultimately wants to figure out God, fails. In Israel's late period, this wisdom theology falls into crisis.[157] God himself renders a fatal judgment against it in the Book of Job: "You have not spoken of me what is right." In the end, it is not Job's friends, who wanted to explain everything and figure out God's actions, but rather the plaintive Job who is given his due (Job 42:7f.).

At the end of the Book of Job, however, the perspective is reversed. Now it is no longer the complaining human being who accuses God or who seeks to justify God that holds center stage. God himself seizes the word and the human being is the one who is questioned (38–41). God's wisdom proves to be too great for fitting into some human schema. Therefore, Job covers his mouth with his hand and grows silent (40:4). He acknowledges that one cannot argue with God.

> Therefore I have uttered what I did not understand, things too wonderful for me, which I did not know…I had heard of you by the hearing of the ear, but now my eye sees you. Therefore I despise myself, and repent in dust and ashes. (42:3, 5–6)

It is impossible to argue and quarrel with God. Thus we can say in summary fashion, theodicy is not a possible undertaking, from a biblical perspective.

On the other hand, complaining to God and even struggling with God is on solid ground in biblical speech about God and with God. Although complaint erupts in the Book of Job, it arises from hope:

> For I know that my Redeemer lives,
>   and that at the last he will stand upon the earth;
> and after my skin has been thus destroyed,
>   then in my flesh I shall see God,
> whom I shall see on my side,
>   and my eyes shall behold, and not another.
> My heart faints within me!
>   (19:25–27)

The Bible contains complaints and lamentations in large number.[158] All of the psalms of lament in the Old Testament (Ps 6, 13, 22, 31, 44, 57, etc.) are uttered in great distress from the feeling of abandonment by God; they speak of great existential trauma. But they never end with despair; rather, in the end, they are filled with certitude that God is close to the supplicant precisely in his or her need. In each case, the mood in the psalms of lament changes from lament to praise. The psalms of lament don't conclude with complaint, accusation, and despair. Rather, in the end, each of them becomes a song of praise and gratitude.

Jesus stands in this Old Testament tradition. On the cross, even he experienced abandonment by God and, with Psalm 22, he called out: "My God, my God, why have you forsaken me?" (Mark 15:34). This cry is often interpreted as the expression of despair. But, in the Jewish tradition, the citation of the beginning of a psalm denotes the citation of the entire psalm. Therefore, it is important to see that Psalm 22 does indeed begin with a moving lament, but then ends with the prospect of rescue and redemption by God. Accordingly, Jesus' cry of abandonment does not express despair, but rather it expresses trust and hope, even in the most extreme sense of abandonment by God.[159] Luke already interprets Jesus' cry in this sense in that he has the dying Jesus say with Psalm 31:6: "Father, into your hands I commend my spirit" (Luke 23:46).

Encounters with the Risen One convinced the disciples that God, in fact, decisively made good on his promise of fidelity through the death and resurrection of Jesus. But the Easter hallelujah did not come easily for the disciples. The Easter stories of the New Testament confirm that the disciples had to come to this conviction by going through questioning and doubt. The Emmaus story (Luke 24:13–35) describes in a particularly impressive way the path of faith that the first disciples had to travel. It reports the disciples' disappointment and their disbelieving response to the testimony of the women until they recognize Jesus in the breaking of the bread. And then they rush to return to Jerusalem.

The path to Emmaus is a paradigm for the path that Christians, in general, have to walk. The Christian is indeed baptized into the death of Christ, and he or she lives in this world in the hope of future resurrection (Rom 6:3–6). We are redeemed in hope; hope that one sees already fulfilled, however, is not hope (Rom 8:24). Often it is a hope against all hope (Rom 5:18). Thus, Paul's assertion in Romans 8:35–39, that nothing—neither life nor death—can separate us from the love of God, stands not at the beginning, but only at the end of a long, theological passage through the experience of the hardships of the Christian at the hands of the powers of perdition in the world (Rom 7–8).

The Letter to the Hebrews takes up this thought. It tells us that Jesus Christ is like us in all things except sin. Therefore, in him we have a high priest who can empathize with our weakness. We can approach his throne full of confidence that we will find mercy and grace there (Heb 4:15; cf. 2:17; 5:2). Hardship and temptation are a part of the Christian life. But in every situation, no matter how embattled or hopeless it may seem, we may be certain that God is by us and with us and "that all things work together for good for those who love God" (Rom 8:28; cf. Heb 12:5–7; 10–11).

This certitude articulates a hope that is not realized in this world or in this life, but that is directed beyond this world toward the resurrection of the dead and eternal life. Only there will every injustice be requited and only there will everyone receive his or her due. Only then will all tears be dried and wiped from our eyes.

> "Death will be no more; mourning and crying and pain will be no more, for the first things have passed away." And the one who was seated on the throne said, "See, I am making all things new." (Rev 21:4–5)

Now we are still on the way; we still don't live in sight of what will be. Our situation, so to speak, is the situation of the Easter vigil. There the Easter candle, as a symbol of Christ's light, is brought into the still dark nave of the church, its light illumines the space, and we can also light our candle from it. But it still shines in the darkness of the church's nave. It is still the Easter vigil. The cry of *maranatha* (1 Cor 16:22)[160] from the ancient Christian liturgy of the Eucharist expresses both realities: the Lord is there and yet we still call out for his final coming.[161]

Out of this already indestructible and hopeful certainty of being definitively secure and enfolded in God's love,[162] an inner serenity arises for the believer. The believer is prepared to give up everything for the sake of Christ (Phil 3:8), to be resigned to every situation, and to endure deprivation. "In any and all circumstances I have learned the secret of being well-fed and of going hungry, of having plenty and of being in need" (Phil 4:12; cf. 2 Cor 11:23–33). Believers know that Christ's grace is enough for them and grace proves its strength in weakness (2 Cor 12:9). The Greek church fathers spoke of the disposition of apathy and ataraxia (inner peace). They didn't mean this in the sense of the Stoa, but rather meant being intensively on the lookout for and being prepared for the coming of the Lord.

The masters of German mysticism (Eckhart, John Tauler, Henry Suso) spoke often of the serenity that, contrary to our enslaving and greedy tendencies to have and hold, results from the liberating disposition of letting go, relying upon, and surrendering ourselves completely to God.[163] In his *Spiritual Exercises*, Ignatius of Loyola speaks of indifference, that is, a fundamental openness to God's will such that we don't desire health more than sickness, wealth more than poverty, honor more than dishonor, a long life more than a short one, and in all things that we long for and choose that which, in each case, helps us advance toward the goal for which we have been created.[164]

Thomas Pröpper has pointed to a sentence from Charles Péguy that he encountered early on in the discussion about theodicy and which has stuck with him: "God has come beforehand. He has begun....God has hoped in us; should that then mean that we, however, did not hope in him?"[165] Memory grounds hope, which waits for the pending promise and chafes at what it doesn't understand or what offers resistance. But the remaining question is only answered when God really brings to completion for everyone the purpose for which he created us. Until then, identity succeeds only in the mode of hope. Even in sadness, doubt, and anxiety, the strength and resistant power of hope remains. The christological confession thus gives us no theoretical or ready answer, but it opens up for us a path. Because God is faithful, we may trust that he will keep his "yes" until the end and, in his love, will save humankind and also the world.[166]

Such hopeful certainty and serenity is not theoretical, like what is found in the different proposals for a theodicy. It is an assertion and disposition of faith, of which one can speak only in the same way as the psalms, namely, as lament and plea for mercy and also as praise-exalting doxology of God's infinite mercy. That is the way in which the church too, in the Kyrie Eleison of the Mass and in the great hymn of praise *Te Deum*, speaks: "Have mercy on us, O Lord, have mercy on us. Bestow your mercy on us as we have placed our hope in you. In you, O Lord, I have placed my hope. In eternity I will not be put to shame."

Those are statements of hope, which are convincing only in faith and which will remain foreign to non-believers. Even for Christians in difficult situations, they do not trip easily over their lips. They stand not at the beginning, but rather at the end of an often long and difficult path of faith. For that journey, we need the support, the accompaniment, and the intercession of other Christians. Those who do not share the Christian faith need even more human sympathy, human intimacy, and caring assistance in such situations. We must practice mercy. That is the only persuasive answer we can give. Such practical evidence of mercy is representative hope for others. By means of our merciful action, a ray of light and warmth from God's mercy can fall in the midst of a gloomy situation. Only in this way can we make talk about God's mercy credible and persuasive; only in this way can we make it a message of hope.

Hope for the coming of the salvation that is still pending is not a vacuous longing and an empty promise. It gives light and strength here and now. We are in this world, not as if we are sitting in the waiting room of eternity, waiting only until the door to life opens. Hope is an active force and an activating power. The experience of divine mercy encourages and obliges us to become witnesses of mercy and to deploy on behalf of mercy in the world. We have to turn to this theme in detail in the following chapters by turning our attention to human mercy. It is the concrete form of divine mercy in the world.

VI

BLESSED ARE THEY WHO SHOW MERCY

THE MESSAGE OF DIVINE MERCY is not a theory that is alien to praxis and world realities, nor does it stop at the level of sentimental expressions of pity. Jesus teaches us to be merciful like God (Luke 6:36). In the Sermon on the Mount, he declares the merciful blessed (Matt 5:7). In the Letter to the Ephesians, we read: "Therefore be imitators of God, as beloved children, and live in love, as Christ loved us and gave himself up for us, a fragrant offering and sacrifice to God" (Eph 5:1–2). This motif of *imitatio Dei*, the imitation of God and his actions in Jesus Christ, is foundational for the Bible.[1] Therefore, the message of divine mercy has consequences for the life of every Christian, for the pastoral praxis of the church, and for the contributions that Christians should render to the humane, just, and merciful structuring of civil society.

1. Love: The Principal Christian Commandment

In the Old Testament, the words "merciful" and "mercy" rarely appear as characterizations of human behavior; the reality meant by those words, however, is present in the Old Testament. Psalm 15 responds to the question:

O LORD, who may abide in your tent?
Who may dwell on your holy hill?

Those who walk blamelessly, and do what is right,
and speak the truth from their heart;
who do not slander with their tongue,
and do no evil to their friends,
nor take up a reproach against their neighbors;...
who stand by their oath even to their hurt;
who do not lend money at interest,
and do not take a bribe against the innocent.
(Ps 15:1–5)

Psalm 112:5 says something similar:

It is well with those who deal generously and lend,
who conduct their affairs with justice.

We have spoken already in detail about the social order of the Old Testament, which was directed toward the protection of the weak and the poor. We have also spoken of the message of the prophets, whose critique of unjust relationships leaves nothing to be desired.[2] The prophet Micah summarizes what God expects from human beings:

He has told you, O mortal, what is good;
and what does the LORD require of you
but to do justice, and to love kindness,
and to walk humbly with your God?
(Mic 6:8; cf. Tob 12:8)

The obligation of almsgiving is particularly emphasized (Tob 4:7–11; Sir 7:10, 29). Upon this foundation, the works of love in early Judaism play an important role.[3]

Jesus stands in this Old Testament-Jewish tradition. The enumeration of the works of love in his great speech about the Last Judgment especially conforms to this Jewish tradition: feed the hungry, give drink to the thirsty, provide shelter for the homeless, clothe

the naked, and visit the sick and those in prison (Matt 25:35–39, 42–44). What is striking in this list is that, as the criterion for judgment, Jesus exclusively names works of charity rather than pious deeds. In doing this, Jesus seizes upon the words of the prophet Hosea: "I desire mercy, not sacrifice" (Matt 9:13; 12:7; cf. Hosea 6:6; Sir 35:3). Therefore, in the Sermon on the Mount, he says: "So when you are offering your gift at the altar, if you remember that your brother or sister has something against you, leave your gift there before the altar and go; first be reconciled to your brother or sister, and then come and offer your gift" (Matt 5:23–24; cf. Mark 11:25). If we were to take these words of Jesus truly seriously, we would have to ask how often we too would have to seek reconciliation before the celebration of the Eucharist and how often we would have to refrain from receiving communion.

Jesus explained his teaching by means of striking parables.[4] Jesus' parable of the good Samaritan has become downright proverbial. In those days, Samaritans were not regarded as orthodox Jews. Consequently, Jesus' precise choice of a Samaritan as the role model of proper behavior was provocative, and he warns: "Go and do likewise" (Luke 10:25–37). In the parable of the unforgiving servant, Jesus explains again that we must show mercy to those who are in our debt, just as God has shown mercy to us (Matt 18:23–35). If God treats us mercifully and forgives us, then we too must forgive and show mercy to one another. In our acts of mercy, God's mercy for our neighbor becomes concretely realized. In our acts of mercy, our neighbor experiences something of the miracle of God's royal dominion, which begins to dawn secretly. In this way, mercy connotes far more than a social security benefit or a caritative or sociopolitical organization (even though these are, of course, not excluded).

Therefore, it can scarcely surprise us that, when Jesus is asked to identify the greatest commandment, in the spirit of the Old Testament he names love of God and love of neighbor (Mark 12:29–31; Matt 22:34–40; Luke 10:25–28).[5] Both commandments are found in the Old Testament in two separate places (Deut 6:5 and Lev 19:18), but there is already a tendency of the Old Testament to find them together.[6] With Jesus they form a completely indissoluble unity.

In doing this, Jesus extended the concept of neighbor beyond those belonging to the Jewish people and applied it to all people. It is fundamentally important that both commandments are held together; there is no love of God without love of neighbor. Only when they are together do the two commandments sum up and fulfill the entire law. Together they are the quintessence, summary, and epitome of Christian existence.

Augustine beautifully expressed how the two commandments belong together:

> Let none say: "I do not know what I am to love." Let him love his brother, and he will love that same love....The object of charity's love must be something which charity makes us love; and that, if we are to start from what is nearest, is our brother....The train of thought makes it clear enough, that this same brotherly love (the love wherewith we love another) is...not only "of God," but "God."... We infer from this that the Two Commandments cannot be separated.[7]

If we take this connectedness seriously, then, of course, it cannot be acceptable to let love of God be absorbed into love of neighbor, which could only end in a one-dimensional humanism, in which love of God and a relationship to God, in general, gets lost. The radical love of neighbor that Jesus demands is not possible without the power that comes from the love of God.[8]

For Paul too, love is the fulfillment of the law (Rom 13:10; Gal 5:14) and the bond of perfection (Col 3:14). Like Jesus, Paul also seizes the message of Hosea and exhorts us "by the mercies of God" to holy and acceptable worship of God (Rom 12:1; cf. Eph 5:1f.). God's merciful and forgiving activity in Jesus Christ must be the model for Christian action: "Be kind to one another, tenderhearted, forgiving one another, as God in Christ has forgiven you" (Eph 4:32; cf. Col 3:12). Again, we are not dealing with a purely humanistic grounding, but rather with an explicitly christological grounding of the love of neighbor.

The heights and also the practical ramifications to which this christological view leads become magnificently clear, above all, in the praise of love that Paul voices in the First Letter to the Corinthians (13).[9] One will have to understand this passage, with its critical intensification and prominence, over against the enthusiasm of radicals. Against enthusiastic exuberance, Paul wants to introduce love—the one thing necessary—as a corrective. Without love, everything else— prophecy, understanding mysteries, knowledge, faith, even great works and deeds of charity—is nothing; each is worthless and without fruit. That is also true of the most rhetorically polished sermon, the most learned theology, and the most zealous commitment to orthodox faith, if it is self-righteous, dogmatic, haughty, and lacking in love. Even martyrdom as such doesn't count. Heretics, communists, and others have their martyrs too. Love alone is the distinctive characteristic of the true Christian.[10] "If I...do not have love, I am nothing" (1 Cor 13:2–3).

But one should not speak, however, of a canticle of love, because Paul's description of love's way is anything but sentimental. It is very concrete and realistic. Jesus Christ has shown us the way of love. The path by which Jesus descended to us is the only one by which we can ascend to him.[11] In the end, everything else will pass away; only love will remain. Love is the greatest of all things (13:13). If only love remains, then too the works of love will remain. They are all that will be at hand at the time of eschatological judgment and they are all that we, so to speak, can produce in the face of judgment. They perdure in the continuing existence of reality; they are an essential element in the eschatological transformation of all reality. In the craziness of love, the *eschaton* is beginning to dawn now.

John takes these thoughts further and completely plumbs their depths. According to him, we are loved by God (John 14:21) so that we can love one another (John 13:34). In light of this strictly theological foundation, John speaks of the new commandment of love as the distinguishing characteristic of Christians: "I give you a new commandment, that you love one another. Just as I have loved you, you also should love one another. By this everyone will know that you are my disciples, if you have love for one another" (John 13:34–35). In the process, he makes clear that love is the specific mark of Christian living. The measure of this love exceeds every normal human measure; it is measured by the love that Jesus himself demonstrated to us by surrendering his life. "This is my commandment, that you love one another as I have loved you. No one has greater love than this, to lay down one's life for one's friends" (John 15:12–13).

The first letter of John takes up these statements:

> Whoever loves a brother or sister lives in the light,...But whoever hates another believer is in the darkness, walks in the darkness, and does not know the way to go, because the darkness has brought on blindness."...Those who say, "I love God," and hate their brothers or sisters, are liars; for those who do not love a brother or sister whom they have seen, cannot love God whom they have not seen. The commandment we have from him is this: those who love God must love their brothers and sisters also. (1 John 2:10–12; 4:20–21; cf. 5:3; 2 John 5f.)

All of this depends on the central assertion that God himself is love (1 John 4:8, 16).

We can cite countless testimonies from the church fathers concerning the fundamental and central meaning of the love of neighbor and mercy. I will make reference only to two of the Greek church fathers. In a time of economic decline that led to dramatic deprivation for broad sectors of the population, Basil advocated decisively for the day laborers who owned no property, the slaves, the impoverished peasants, the artisans, and the tradespeople. When famine broke out, he attacked the unscrupulous profiteers and the speculators and called on them to distribute their wealth.[12] Like Jesus, Chrysostom uncovered all kinds of hypocritical piety. According to him, love of neighbor is the mother of everything good and the distinguishing characteristic of the Christian.[13] For this reason, Basil appealed powerfully to the conscience of the wealthy and told them in no uncertain terms that all of their pious deeds would be to no avail without beneficence.[14] For Chrysostom, love of neighbor is better than all other virtuous deeds or acts of penance, better even than martyrdom.[15] Without virginity, he says, one can still see God, but not without mercy.[16] In reference to external works, Thomas therefore names mercy the *summa religionis christianae*.[17]

The beatitude concerning the merciful is a concrete instantiation of the love of neighbor. In Dietrich Bonhoeffer we find an appealing interpretation of this beatitude:

> These men without possessions or power, these strangers on earth, these sinners, these followers of Jesus, have in their life with him *renounced their own dignity*, for they are merciful. As if their own needs and their own distress were not enough, they take upon themselves the distress and humiliation and sin of others. They have an irresistible love for the down-trodden, the sick, the wretched, the wronged, the outcast and all who are tortured with anxiety. They go out and seek all who are enmeshed in the toils of sin and guilt. No distress is too great, no sin too appalling for their pity. If any man falls into disgrace, the merciful will sacrifice their own honour to shield him, and take his shame upon themselves. They will be found consorting with publicans and sinners, careless of the shame they incur thereby. In order that they may be merciful they cast away the most priceless treasure of human life, their personal dignity and honour. For the only honour and dignity they know is their Lord's own mercy, to which alone they owe their very lives. He was not ashamed of his disciples, he became the brother of mankind, and bore their shame unto the death of the cross. That is how Jesus, the crucified, was merciful. His followers owe their lives entirely to that mercy.[18]

2. *"Forgive One Another" and the Commandment to Love One's Enemies*

Jesus' demand to love one's neighbor is not only central, it is also radical, so radical that it can take your breath away. In the antitheses of the Sermon on the Mount, with the demand for a more perfect righteousness (Matt 5:20), Jesus goes beyond not only the Jewish tradition, but beyond every human measure. This is evident in the demand to renounce violence: "Do not resist an evildoer." In this way, he rescinds the so-called *ius talionis*, the rule of an "eye for eye, tooth for tooth" (Exod 21:24) and establishes a different rule in its place: "But if anyone strikes you on the right cheek, turn the other also…" (Matt 5:38–42; cf. Luke 6:29f.). That transcends normal human power. It demands a human and Christian largesse and restraint that breaks up the cycle of evil and the vicious cycle of violence and counterviolence, establishing peace in their place.

For Jesus, the apex and highest expression of the mercy and love that is demanded in the Sermon on the Mount is the command to love one's enemies: "Love your enemies and pray for those who persecute you." Jesus establishes this extreme demand—extreme from a purely human perspective—on the basis of God's extreme behavior toward sinners. He says, "So that you may be children of your Father in heaven;…Be perfect, therefore, as your heavenly Father is perfect" (Matt 5:43–48; cf. Luke 6:27–29, 32–36). In the Our Father, Jesus teaches us to pray that God would forgive us our debts as we forgive our debtors (Matt 6:12; Luke 11:4). Jesus added that we should offer forgiveness not only once, not even seven times, but rather seventy-seven times (Matt 18:21–22), which means repeatedly without limit. Jesus illustrated this demand in the parable of the unforgiving servant (Matt 18:23–35). Jesus himself offered forgiveness while he was dying on the cross: "Father, forgive them; for they do not know what they are doing" (Luke 23:34). The deacon and first martyr, Stephen, expressed the same plea as he was being stoned and was dying (Acts 7:60).

In the ancient world, forgiveness, in the sense of pardoning, was regarded as the virtue of kings. It is an act of magnanimity that presupposes sovereignty. In reality only God can forgive. "Who can forgive sins but God alone?" (Luke 5:21). Therefore, forgiveness is only possible in the power and at the prompting of God's saving activity in Christ (Rom 3:25f.). It is possible only in light of the statement that God has reconciled us to himself while we were still enemies (Rom 5:10). According to God's model behavior, we too are supposed to forgive:

> Forgive us our debts,
>> as we also have forgiven our debtors.
>> (Matt 6:12; Luke 11:4)

As such, forgiveness is also necessary. Therefore: "[Forgive] one another, as God in Christ has forgiven you" (Eph 4:32). "Just as the Lord has forgiven you, so you also must forgive" (Col 3:13).

It is clear: love of one's enemy is perhaps the most humanly difficult demand of Jesus and yet it is, at the same time, one of the most central Christian commandments. It is rooted in the innermost essence of the Christian mystery and, therefore, represents the specific character of Christian behavior.[19] The church fathers believed that this commandment is an element that properly belongs to Christianity and is something new, both vis-à-vis the Old Testament and pagan philosophy.[20] The second letter of Clement says: whoever does not love the one who hates him or her is not a Christian.[21] Tertullian calls the love of one's enemy the "fundamental law";[22] for Chrysostom it is the highest instantiation of virtue.[23]

Of course, the church fathers also knew the difficulties in concretely realizing this commandment in the face of the complexities and the structures of sin in this world. In order to arrive at a solution, they developed a kind of two-tier ethics. According to Ambrose, it is an obligation not to repay evil for evil; but to repay evil with good is perfection.[24] According to Augustine, the highest form of almsgiving is to pardon those who have wronged us. Admittedly, he is realistic enough to know that the great majority of people fail to have such virtue, which is a gift of the perfect children of God. However, every believer should strive after such virtue and pray for it. At the very least, the believer should pardon those who ask for forgiveness. In this case, whoever does not forgive will also not be forgiven by our heavenly Father (Matt 6:15). Augustine speaks of this fact as an earth-shaking warning: whoever does not wake up to this reality, he or she is not merely sleeping, but is already dead.[25] A similar, graduated position is found in Thomas Aquinas: it is necessary for love to prepare its heart when, in a concrete case, it becomes necessary to love the enemy, but to love one's enemy independent of any concrete necessity, for the sake of God's love, is, on the other hand, not necessary for salvation. In that case, love of enemy belongs not to necessity, but to the perfection of love.[26] Although one can see Christian realism in such attempts at softening or downgrading the command to love one's enemy, we should, however, not make it all too easy to downplay this command. For these church fathers, the fully realized love of enemy is no longer the focus, as it was for Jesus. Rather, it is a limit situation or, alternatively, the ultimate goal of the Christian praxis of faith.[27] Love of enemy is essentially more difficult within the problematic context of war. It is not possible in wars to restrict love of enemy to the demand to conquer personal feelings of hatred, thereby confining love of enemy to a personal disposition. Jesus desires the concrete act.[28]

Not only the individual Christian, and not only countries, but also the church struggles with realizing the love of enemy. For how has Christianity behaved in the case of persecution of Jews and heretics, in the crusades, and in the wars of religion? How has the church dealt with its opponents in polemics and controversies, which very often were anything but objective and fair? And many sermons on war also leave a macabre impression. Therefore, not only individual Christians, but the church itself has very often failed to obey the command to love the enemy. Here too the ideal and the real are often far apart.

Questions arise not only concerning the issue of war and peace, but also in reference to the unfriendly neighbor, the professional rival, and the competitor in business, politics, and other spheres of life. In the economic and political spheres, there exist unavoidable situations of competition, in which one wants to degrade and bring one's political opponent and economic rival to their knees—not personally, but certainly economically and politically. And in the world, as it now concretely exists, one feels that he or she has to do this. In these situations, one cannot honestly get around making the kinds of distinctions that we found in Augustine and Thomas.

But, one can further ask, is the commandment to love one's enemies at all realistic? Isn't this commandment something utopian? Doesn't it make an excessive demand on people? How is a mother supposed to love the person who murdered her child? Can she forgive the murderer? Where does it get us if we offer no resistance to evil, if we pardon instead of demanding justice? In that case, isn't the one who acted unjustly rewarded? Heinrich Heine, Friedrich Nietzsche, Sigmund Freud, and others have posed such questions, critically and polemically. For Freud, the command to love one's enemies belongs to a *credo quia absurdum est* [I believe because it is absurd].[29]

But one can counter the question, where do we get if we renounce violence and forgive, with this question: Where do we get if there is no pardon and no forgiveness, when we repay every wrong done to us with a new wrong, taking an eye for an eye, and a tooth for a tooth? After the horrific experience of twentieth-century atrocities, the problem of forgiveness and love of enemy has acquired a sad new currency and, in broad sectors, has led to an urgently needed rethinking. It has become clear that, however much mercy, forgiveness, and pardon are superhuman acts, they are nonetheless highly sensible acts.

Only if we extend our hands anew across old ditches that divide, and ask for forgiveness as well as grant forgiveness, can bloody and traumatic conflicts be handled; a process of healing for the injuries that have been suffered be introduced; and the spiral of violence and counterviolence—as well as the vicious circle of guilt and revenge (blood feuds)—be broken. One cannot simply forget the wrong that has been done; still less is one permitted to simply try to sweep it under the table. One must honestly face up to the wrong that he or she has done and admit it. When that happens, it can lead to a reconciled recollection, in which relationships are detoxified and lose their inimical quality. By means of a reconciled memory that heals the wounds of the past, a new beginning can be made and a new, common future becomes possible.[30]

This is true not only in the realm of personal relationships, but also in the political realm. Here one can think perhaps of the Jewish-Christian, German-Israeli, German-French, or German-Polish reconciliations that took place after World War II. One can also think of the Truth Commission in South Africa, in Ireland, and elsewhere.[31] Finally, one can think of the changed ecumenical and inter-religious relationships, where—despite all the remaining objective differences—the old hostilities and thinking in terms of factions and rivals have, in large measure, been able to be overcome to the benefit of collaboration for justice and peace in the world. The love of enemy, therefore, is no *credo quia absurdum*, but rather a *credo quia rationabile* [I believe because it is sensible.].

3. The Corporal and Spiritual Works of Mercy

Corresponding to the Jewish tradition, the New Testament has catalogs of virtues, which deal with and concretely interpret the command to be merciful (1 Pet 3:8; cf. Rom 12:8, 15; 2 Cor 7:15; Phil 1:8, 2:1; Col 3:12; Heb 13:3). Such a catalog is also found in Jesus' major speech about the Last Judgment (Matt 25). On this basis in the New Testament, the Christian tradition has then fleshed out what mercy concretely means. In order to do that, it has distinguished and enumerated in detail seven corporal works and seven spiritual works of mercy.[32]

The corporal works of mercy are: feed the hungry, give drink to the thirsty, clothe the naked, shelter the homeless, visit the sick, ransom captives, and bury the dead. The spiritual works of mercy are: instruct the ignorant, counsel the doubtful, comfort the sorrow-ful, admonish the sinner, gladly forgive injuries, bear wrongs patiently, pray for the living and the dead. In his *Rule*, Benedict augmented these works or, as he called them, these instruments of good works in one respect, adding: "Never despair of God's mercy."[33]

. In the case of the corporal works and especially the spiritual works of mercy, it is interesting to note that we are not dealing with the prohibition of violations of God's explicit commandments. As in Jesus' speech about the Last Judgment, no sinners who murdered, stole, committed adultery, lied, or cheated others are condemned. Jesus' condemnation does not concern violations of God's commandments, but rather failures to do what is good. Again it is a matter of the higher righteousness (Matt 5:20). Accordingly, one can sin not only by violating God's commandments, but also by failing to do what is good, something that, unfortunately, is too-little heeded.

Thus, mercy is concerned with more than justice; it is a matter of attentiveness and sensitivity to the concrete needs we encounter. It is a matter of overcoming the focus on ourselves that makes us deaf and blind to the physical and spiritual needs of others. It is a matter of dissolving the hardening of our hearts to God's call that we hear in the encounter with the adversity of others.[34]

The differentiated enumeration of the corporal and spiritual works of mercy is thereby neither naïve nor arbitrary. It corresponds to the distinction of a fourfold poverty. The easiest to comprehend is physical or economic poverty: no roof over one's head and no food in one's pots, hunger and thirst, or no clothes and no shelter to protect one from the adversities of weather and climate. Nowadays, one would also include unemployment in this list. In addition, there are serious illnesses or disabilities that don't have the opportunity to receive appropriate medical treatment and care.

No less important than physical poverty is cultural poverty: in the extreme case, this means illiteracy; less extreme but still severe is having no chance or reduced chances for education, and, consequently, having slim prospects for the future. Cultural poverty also includes exclusion from participation in social and cultural life. The third form of poverty is the lack of relationships. As a social creature, the human person can experience various forms of poverty: loneliness and isolation, the loss of a partner, the loss of family members or friends, communication difficulties, exclusion from social intercourse—whether self-caused or forced upon a person—discrimination and marginalization, including the extreme cases of isolation because of imprisonment or exile. The final form of poverty to be mentioned is mental or spiritual poverty, which represents a serious problem in the West: lack of orientation, inner emptiness, hopelessness and desolation, despair about the meaning of one's own existence, moral and spiritual aberration to the point of neglecting one's soul.

The variety and multiple dimensions of these situations of poverty demand a multidimensional response. Without a doubt, material assistance is fundamental. For only if basic physical life and survival are first secured, can cultural, social, and spiritual poverty be remedied. Nonetheless, Christian mercy cannot and may not confine itself to addressing only physical hardships, because mercy is humane only if it doesn't place the needy in an ongoing situation of dependence, but rather provides them with assistance for helping themselves. That is only possible if the cultural, social, and spiritual situation of poverty is also remedied. Christian charity, therefore, makes a holistic approach necessary, which sees the different dimensions of poverty in their reciprocal relations and thus helps to provide not only for mere survival, but rather helps to provide for a life that is at least in some measure humanly fulfilled.

In a prayer from the year 1937, Sister Faustina expresses very beautifully how wide and how deep the delicacy of feeling for mercy goes, what it can concretely mean for a Christian, and what it can concretely accomplish:

> Help me, O Lord, that my eyes may be merciful, so that I may never suspect or judge from appearances, but look for what is beautiful in my neighbors' souls and come to their rescue.
>
> Help me, O Lord, that my ears may be merciful, so that I may give heed to my neighbors' needs and not be indifferent to their pains and moanings.
>
> Help me, O Lord, that my tongue may be merciful, so that I should never speak negatively of my neighbor, but have a word of comfort and forgiveness for all.

Help me, O Lord, that my hands may be merciful and filled with good deeds, so that I may do only good to my neighbors and take upon myself the more difficult and toilsome tasks.

Help me, O Lord, that my feet may be merciful, so that I may hurry to assist my neighbor, overcoming my own fatigue and weariness. My true rest is in the service of my neighbor.

Help me, O Lord, that my heart may be merciful so that I myself may feel all the sufferings of my neighbor. I will refuse my heart to no one. I will be sincere even with those who, I know, will abuse my kindness. And I will lock myself up in the most merciful Heart of Jesus. I will bear my own suffering in silence. May Your mercy, O Lord, rest upon me.

You Yourself command me to exercise the three degrees of mercy. The first: the act of mercy, of whatever kind. The second: the word of mercy—if I cannot carry out a work of mercy, I will assist by my words. The third: prayer—if I cannot show mercy by my deeds or words, I can always do so by prayer. My prayer reaches out even there where I cannot reach out physically.

O my Jesus, transform me into Yourself, for You can do all things.[35]

4. No Laissez-Faire Pseudomercy!

Even mercy and religion can be misused. The commandment of Christian love of neighbor, and especially the commandment to love the enemy, must indeed be realized within the conditions of the world. That can lead to mercy itself becoming ambivalent, even misunderstood and misused in the ambivalence of temporal situations. One could almost pervert mercy into its opposite and make the appeal to mercy a kind of metaphorical "fabric softener" for the Christian ethos.

A much-discussed form of such pseudomercy nowadays consists in protecting the wrongdoer more than the victim. Such indulgence can occur because of misguided friendship or collegiality. It can also happen because one wants to protect an institution—whether it be the church, the state, a religious order, or club—from the adverse consequences of uncovering and prosecuting wrongdoing. Such a mindset goes against the spirit of the gospel, which advances the preferential option for the poor and advocates for whoever is the weaker. Protection of the victim, therefore, must precede protection of the offender.

There are still other, no-less-weighty misunderstandings of mercy. Mention must be made, first of all, of a laissez-faire point of view that lets everything happen or get by. It begins when parents indulge their children in everything, out of a false sense of mercy. This abnormal attitude is exhibited when one ignores bad or sinful behavior, rather than demanding a change.

In the prophet Ezekiel, we find a powerful warning. He says if the sentinel fails to blow the ram's horn when danger is approaching and does not warn the people of the imminent danger, then he is held accountable for the blood that is spilled. Ezekiel then continues: if you do not speak to warn the wicked, telling them that they will have to die on account of their guilt, then the wicked shall die in their iniquity. "But their blood I will require at your hand." But if you warn the wicked and they do not turn from their ways, "the wicked shall die in their iniquity, but you will have saved your life" (Ezek 33:6–9).

Paul clearly states that the other person cannot be a matter of indifference to us; rather, we bear responsibility for one another out of love and mercy. Therefore, Paul does not hesitate to caution his community (Rom 12:1); and he appeals, in fact, to the highest authority for this purpose (2 Cor 5:20). Quite generally, he reminds his community of the care and responsibility that Christians have for each other: "Teach and admonish one another" (Col 3:16). Thus the New Testament speaks of fraternal correction (1 Thess 5:11, 14; 2 Thess 3:15; 2 Tim 2:25; Titus 1:13; 2:15). If such rebuke (παράκλησις) is not self-righteous, but occurs with an awareness of one's own faults and failures, then it is a work of spiritual mercy.[36] In this way, mercy can also be a necessary and bitter pill.[37] Sometimes it must hurt, just as the doctor causes pain in an operation and has to cut—not in order to harm, but rather to help and to heal.[38]

A further grave misunderstanding of mercy occurs if, in the name of mercy, we think we may ignore God's commandment of justice and understand love and mercy, not as fulfilling and surpassing justice, but rather as undercutting and abrogating it. Therefore, we cannot contravene elementary commandments of justice because of a sentimental misunderstanding of mercy. One cannot advise or provide assistance for an abortion out of a phony sense of mercy, if the birth of a child with disabilities appears to expect too much of the mother or the child. Just as little can one, out of pity for an incurably sick person, offer active assistance in committing suicide in order to "release" him or her from their pain and suffering. Such pseudomercy does not imitate God's mercy; rather, it dismisses God's commandment "Thou shall not murder" (Exod 20:13; Deut 5:17).

Not to be guilty of phony mercy does not mean dealing unsympathetically with people who, in their situation, struggle with God's commandment or who have, in fact, broken it. For the sake of mercy properly understood, one will have to set forth and explain God's commandment, but will have to do this in a compassionate way. One, however, will have to help people, in word and deed, to carry out the demands of the commandment in their often complex and difficult situation, as especially the church's counseling services are supposed to do. In cases when people have burdened themselves with guilt, which often lies heavy on their souls for their entire lives, one should respond to them pastorally, just as Jesus responded to sinners. One should not sit in coldhearted judgment over them, but rather should help them, not to suppress the guilt, but to acknowledge it and then to entrust themselves to the ever-greater mercy of God and his readiness to forgive.

The relation of mercy and truthfulness is similar. This issue becomes pertinent when one is supposed to tell seriously ill or dying persons the truth about their situation. To withhold the truth out of a false understanding of mercy or to offer them totally unrealistic expectations does not really help the affected persons, but hinders them in facing the truth and coming to terms with their situation in a humane and spiritual way. Authentic mercy will say the truth in such situations, not in an insensitively harsh way, but rather sensitively with love (Eph 4:15). Real mercy will express the truth in such a way that it helps the patient to accept the truth and to come to terms with it. To do this requires considerable ability to empathize as well as kind, pastoral tact.

5. Encountering Christ in the Poor

In his great speech about the Last Judgment, Jesus expresses the deepest dimension of mercy that has been put into action. He says: "Just as you did it to one of the least of these who are members of my family, you did it to me" (Matt 25:40; cf. 45). He who was rich became poor for our sake (2 Cor 8:9) and has taken on the form of a slave (Phil 2:7). He not only established solidarity with the poor, he identified himself with them. Therefore, we can encounter him in the poor.

Augustine repeatedly referred to the christological foundation of the love of neighbor. In his work, it has been calculated, he cites Matthew 25 more than 275 times.[39] In a sermon, he writes (in a dense Latin style, which can scarcely be translated, but is only able to be paraphrased): What else have you given but from that which you have received from me? You give something earthly; you take something heavenly. You have given from what is mine. I bestow myself upon you. Christ has given himself to you; how can we not also give Christ, who encounters us in those who are in need? Christ gives nourishment and, for your sake, he is in need. He gives and he is needy. If he gives, do you want to receive? If he, however, is in need, do you not want to give to him? Christ is needy when the poor are needy. The one who wishes to bestow eternal life on all has deigned to receive something temporal in the guise of the poor. You want to meet Christ who is enthroned in heaven. Expect to meet him when he lies under the bridges; expect him when he is hungry and shudders from the cold; expect him as the stranger.[40]

All of the great saints of Christian charity have seen this situation and lived it: Deacon Lawrence, Martin of Tours, Nicolas of Myra, Elizabeth of Thuringia, Camillus of Lellis, Vincent de Paul, Damian de Veuster. At the beginning of her journey, Mother Teresa of Calcutta had a mystical experience of Christ when she encountered a fatally ill person.[41] She expressed this christological—we could even say—this mystical dimension of the love of neighbor in a prayer:

Lord, may I see you today and every day in the person of the sick and, while caring for them, may I serve you.

Even if you hide in the inconspicuous disguise of an irascible, demanding, or intransigent person, may I recognize you and say: "Jesus, my patient, how good it is to serve you."

O Lord, give me these eyes of faith, for then my work will never be monotonous. I will always find joy in bearing the moods and fulfilling the wishes of all the poor people who are suffering.

O my beloved sick, how doubly dear you are to me when you embody Christ; and what an honor it is for me to be able to serve you.

Lord, make me to appreciate the dignity of my high calling and its great responsibility. Do not permit me ever to prove unworthy of this vocation by falling into hardheartedness, unfriendliness, or impatience. And then, O God, because you are Jesus Christ, my patient, condescend to be for me too a patient Jesus. Be lenient with my mistakes and look only upon my resolute intention to love you and to serve you in the person of each of these ailing persons. Lord, increase my faith, bless my effort and my work, now and at all times. Amen.[42]

Jesus' words and all of the saints just mentioned show us ultimately what is at stake in mercy and the Christian love of neighbor. It is a matter not only of a general love of humanity, which is not at all objectionable if it doesn't simply amount to hollow words, but becomes concrete in deed. It is also not simply a matter of compassion with the suffering, which is quite positive in comparison to hard-heartedness and egoism. It is not even a matter of ideas for making the world a better place. In this regard, the Bible is very realistic. It knows: "You always have the poor with you" (John 12:8). What ultimately is at stake in Christian mercy is the encounter with Jesus Christ himself in and through those who suffer. Therefore, mercy is principally not a matter of morality, but a matter of faith in Christ, discipleship, and an encounter with him. As the parable of the good Samaritan makes clear, the heart of the matter is the needy person, whom I encounter concretely, who is dependent on my help, and for whom I have become the neighbor (Luke 10:25–37). In this poor person, I encounter Jesus Christ himself.

This is not to question the fact that love of neighbor has social and political consequences, which extend beyond the realm of the individual. We will soon speak of those consequences in detail.[43] Social and political engagement, of course, can only be credible if it makes demands not only on others or on municipal and ecclesial institutions, but also demands that we live out, in our own lives and in our personal sphere of influence, concretely and in exemplary fashion, what it means to be a disciple of Christ and to be "pro-existence." Such witness will catch on and impel others to concrete engagement. Thus, identification with Jesus Christ in the poor extends beyond an individual encounter; it has significance for others and for the church.

6. Mercy as Christian Existence for Others

Personal connectedness with Jesus Christ means participation in his pro-existence. Consequently, the Christian form of mercy is ultimately Christian existence on behalf of others. [*Stellvertretungs-Existenz*]. That becomes evident when one pays attention to the different layers of meaning in Jesus' call to discipleship.[44] The call to discipleship means more than an invitation to walk behind Jesus and to accompany him on his journeys. Discipleship involves a fellowship of life and mission (Mark 3:14 and parallels); in the end, it means a fellowship of fate, suffering, and the cross. "If any want to become my followers, let them deny themselves and take up their cross and follow me" (Mark 8:34 and parallels). Just as Jesus made himself a servant of all, so should his disciples be. Whoever wants to be first among his disciples must be the servant of all (Mark 10:45; cf. John 13:15). Just as in the case of Jesus Christ, this "dying" with Christ can entail following Christ to the cross and surrendering one's life for his sake (Mark 8:34f. and parallels).

On the evening before his suffering, Jesus gave his disciples a concrete example. Just as he provided his disciples the most menial service of a slave, by washing their feet, so they too should do the same (John 13:14f.). His disciples should now make their lives, which had been bestowed on them by Jesus, a gift for others. That can definitely lead to extremes. For a greater love has no one than to lay down one's life for his or her friends (John 15:13; cf. John 12:25f.). Existence as a disciple, just like Jesus' own existence, is understood to mean being for others, or being pro-existence.

Participation in the representative, atoning death and resurrection of Jesus Christ through baptism (1 Cor 12:13; Gal 3:28) and through the celebration of the Eucharist (1 Cor 10:16f.) incorporates this thought in a new and deeper way after Easter. Being in Christ means being with and for others in Christ's body. "If one member suffers, all suffer together with it; if one member is honored, all rejoice together with it" (1 Cor 12:26). Thus: "Bear one another's burdens, and in this way you will fulfill the law of Christ" (Gal 6:2). Paul is willing, therefore, to become a slave to all in order to gain as many as possible. "I have become all things to all people, so that I might by any means save some" (1 Cor 9:22). He lets himself be worn down and is worn out, which he understands as a sacrificial offering in the faith of his community (Phil 2:17; cf. 2 Cor 12:15). Apostolic and pastoral service means, in the literal sense of the word, wearing oneself out and, precisely in such apostolic and pastoral suffering, letting Jesus Christ, his death, and his resurrection become present for others. Apostolic existence happens not only with words, but with and through one's entire existence. In this way, the idea of proxy or representative atonement [*Stellvertretungsgedanke*] has become a key concept of Christian existence.[45]

The idea of discipleship as representative atonement has assumed different forms in the course of history.[46] In the first instance, with the martyrs, whose blood became the seed of new Christians,[47] then with the hermits and monks, with the Irish and Scottish wandering monks in their peregrination and homelessness for the sake of Christ and their mission (*peregrination propter Christum*). With Francis of Assisi, discipleship has also taken the form of poverty and humility.

Since the time of Bernard of Clairvaux, a subjectively internalized mysticism of the cross has developed that aimed to reproduce and internalize, via sympathetic participation, the love of God revealed in the suffering of Jesus. Bernard of Clairvaux is often represented with the image of Christ bending down toward him from the cross and embracing him. He gave expression to the meaning of this event with the statement: "By taking on the form of the self-sacrificing Christ, we are transformed" (*transformamur cum conformamur*).[48] This spirituality is again found in the mysticism of Meister Eckhart, John Tauler, and Henry Suso; it is also found in the *Imitation of Christ* by Thomas à Kempis and finally, in Ignatius of Loyola's book of Spiritual Exercises, in which the attentive and empathetic following of the life and passion of Jesus provides the foundation for uniting the contemplative and active life.

This mysticism of the cross also entered art. Whereas the Byzantine and Romanesque presentations of the crucifixion showed Jesus as the victorious *pantocrator*,* Gothic art represented him as the man of sorrows. One can especially recall the late medieval plague crosses, with which afflicted persons were identified for centuries and on which they could be lifted up.† This spirituality was carried

---

*Translator's note: The *pantocrator* image depicts Jesus as all-powerful or as the ruler and sustainer of the world. Such images can be found in ancient churchs, such as the Church of the Holy Sepulchre in Jerusalem.

†Translator's note: During outbreaks of the plague, infected people visited shrines with plague crosses, where they could prayerfully identify with the suffering of the crucified Christ and metaphorically lift themselves up on the cross with him.

over into popular Christian piety in the devotional form of stations of the cross. In sympathetic and pious meditation upon the suffering and death of Jesus, believers could identify themselves with the various stations of the cross. In my home town of Wangen in the Allgäu, veneration of the imprisoned savior was popular. This devotional practice traces back to older medieval forms of piety. It was promoted in the eighteenth century by means of the visions of Crescentia Höss from Kaufbeuren, who was canonized in 2001. Who wouldn't be able to identify with the various forms of imprisonment: inmates and prisoners of war, those interned in concentration camps, political prisoners, those who are confined to bed or to a wheelchair, those entangled in sin, those forced into dire straits and hopelessness because of financial problems or other forms of confinement.

This self-identification with the suffering and death of Jesus could also lead to aberrations. Already in the *devotio moderna* and in Pietism, and then more completely in the Enlightenment, the *imitatio* Christology was released from its objective, sacramental, and ecclesial foundation and became an imitative Jesusology. Jesus became a role model worthy of emulation. What was originally grounded in the indicative of a sacramentally mediated salvific act now became the imperative of following Jesus' moral path.[49] Another danger was the reduction of the imitation of Christ to an individualistic understanding of salvation. This reduction ran the risk of forgetting that the inclusive character of Jesus' substitutionary atonement [*Stellvertretung*] means that we are actively implicated in Jesus' act of representing us. And, consequently, "representation" transcends the heartfelt, personal connection with Jesus and must become discipleship for the sake of others.

Paul declares that he is even ready to be accursed as a surrogate for his Jewish brethren (Rom 9:2). This statement has entailed a long history of effects in the mystical tradition. We know of many saints who, in the desert, in the dark night of faith, and in God's abandonment of Jesus on the cross, were able to endure, in a substitutionary way [*stellvertretend*], for those who are caught in the night of unbelief and distance from God. This idea is found above all in the Carmelite mysticism of John of the Cross.[50]

Thérèse of Lisieux gave lasting expression to this idea of Carmelite mysticism. She wants to present herself as a burnt offering to love. She understands her calling and her place in the church to be a vocation for the mystical body of Christ in love. In order to extinguish its flames, she wanted to shower the suffering church with blossoms of love from heaven; she wanted to shower the church militant* with those same blossoms so that it would be victorious.[51] Even now she prays for her brothers and sisters, the unbelievers. With this disposition, she was prepared to enter the dark tunnel, in which she passed through the terror of the modern eclipse of God as their proxy. So she prays for her unbelieving brothers and sisters that even they might catch a glimpse of the ray of faith.[52] She, a person who herself wanted to be a missionary in the worst way, intended to help missionaries by means of her prayer and sacrifice.[53] From her perspective, the zeal of a Carmelite must encompass the entire world.[54]

Edith Stein (Sister Benedicta of the Cross) also stands in this Carmelite tradition. During the persecution of Jews by the Nazis, she entered the gas chambers of Auschwitz as a substitutionary representative for the Jewish people, to whom she continued to feel bound.[55] Maximilian Kolbe was motivated by the same spirit when he voluntarily offered up his life for the sake of another prisoner, who was the father of a family. Even Mother Teresa, after initial radiant, mystical experiences, lived in a mystical darkness until the time of her death. Her statement is well-known: "If I ever become a saint, then quite certainly a 'saint of darkness.' I will perpetually be absent from heaven—in order to ignite a light for those who live in darkness on earth."[56]

One can also think of poets such as Léon Bloy, Charles Péguy, and others, who have dissolved the individualistic constriction of the idea of representation and have renewed its ecclesial and universal dimension. They have once again understood representation

---

*Translator's note: The "suffering church" or *ecclesia penitens* refers to those Christians in purgatory; hence Thérèse's reference to extinguishing its (i.e., purgatory's) flames. The church militant or *ecclesia militans* refers to Christians now living on earth, who are fighting against the forces of sin and evil.

[*Stellvertretung*] as the heart of what it means to be a Christian and they have grasped Christian existence as pro-existence, being for others. Dietrich Bonhoeffer gave good expression to this deeper sense of representation or action by a proxy. For him, the eclipse of God is the world's malady. He says the following about this form of suffering:

> Suffering has to be endured in order that it may pass away. Either the world must bear the whole burden and collapse beneath it, or it must fall on Christ to be overcome in him. He therefore suffers vicariously for the world. His is the only suffering which has redemptive efficacy. But the Church knows that the world is still seeking for someone to bear its sufferings, and so, as it follows Christ, suffering becomes the Church's lot too and bearing it, it is borne up by Christ. As it follows him beneath the cross, the Church stands before God as the representative of the world.[57]

This spirituality of standing up for others and taking their place could break up the inward-looking orientation of many communities in their current diaspora situation within a secularized world, and it could become a spiritual guidepost for both today and tomorrow. Love of neighbor, when lived in a radical way, thus points to the ecclesial dimension, a topic to which we must now turn.

VII

THE CHURCH
MEASURED BY MERCY

1. The Church: Sacrament of Love and Mercy

THE PRECEPT OF MERCY applies not only to individual Christians, but also to the church as a whole. As in the case of individual Christians, the command for the church to be merciful is grounded in the being [*Sein*] of the church as the body of Christ. The church, therefore, is not a kind of social or charitable agency; as the body of Christ, it is the sacrament of the continuing effective presence of Christ in the world. As such, the church is the sacrament of mercy. It is this sacrament as the "total Christ," that is, Christ in head and members. Thus the church encounters Christ himself in its own members and in people who are in need of help. The church is supposed to make present the gospel of mercy, which Jesus Christ is in person, through word, sacrament, its whole life in history, and the life of individual Christians. However, the church too is the object of God's mercy. As the body of Christ, it is redeemed by Jesus Christ. But the church encompasses sinners in its bosom and, therefore, must be purified time and again in order to be able to stand there, pure and holy (Eph 5:23, 26f.). Consequently, the church must self-critically ask itself repeatedly whether it actually lives up to that which it is and should be. Conversely, just as Jesus Christ did, so too we are supposed to deal with the flaws and failings of the church, not in a self-righteous, but in a merciful way. We must, however, be clear about one thing: a church without charity and without mercy would no longer be the church of Jesus Christ.

These fundamental statements concerning the essence and the mission of the church, its holiness, and its continual need for renewal cannot be justified or developed here in detail. That has to be done in a doctrine of the church, which we must presuppose in our current context.[1]

The inner connection of charity (or mercy) and the church, or more precisely, between charity/mercy and the unity of the church becomes particularly clear in a text from St. Augustine. He refers to the praise of love in 1 Corinthians 13: "If I do not have love, I am nothing." In this regard, he understands love, not only individualistically as the work of individual Christians, but ecclesially as that element that unites the church. Consequently, the works of love, almsgiving, also virginity and even martyrdom have no value outside of the love in the church and outside of the church community. Without this community in love, the bond of unity is torn and the good works are like branches cut off from the vine.[2] So Augustine repeatedly emphasizes this point, in response to the schismatic Donatists: without love and outside of the community of the church, everything else is nothing.[3] These statements are fundamentally correct: charity and mercy are not the private undertaking of individual Christians; charity and mercy in the church are also not simply acts of social service, like many others today. Rather, they have a specific ecclesial dimension; they belong essentially to the community of the church, its faith, and to the church's lived unity.

On the other hand, the statements quoted from Augustine, which derive from his debate with the schismatic Donatists, are difficult for us to say today when we think of ecumenism. We have to understand those words together with other statements that Augustine makes in the same context. There he says that many are only superficially in the church, but have their hearts outside of the church, whereas many who are outside of the church really have their hearts in it.[4] External membership is not sufficient. One has to belong to the church with his or her heart, which means, living out

of the Holy Spirit, the spirit of love. We often find such love, however, outside in people who do not belong to the visible church.

The Second Vatican Council took up these thoughts. It has
acknowledged that the Catholic Church indeed has the fullness of the
means of salvation, but that the Holy Spirit is at work in many spiritual gifts outside of its visible boundaries.[5] There are also works of
love and mercy outside of the visible church. In many respects, we can
take non-Catholics, sometimes even non-Christians, as an example in
this regard and learn from them. Conversely, those who belong to the
visible church must do everything in order to live out ecclesial love
and make it visible in acts of corporal and spiritual mercy.

The message of mercy, therefore, has consequences not only for
the life of individual Christians, but it also has far-reaching consequences for the teaching, life, and mission of the church.[6] The worst
reproach that can be leveled against the church and that, in fact,
often applies to it is that it does not do what it proclaims to others.
Indeed, many people experience the church as rigid and lacking in
mercy. For this reason, at the opening of the Second Vatican Council,
Pope John XXIII said that the church must, above all, use the medicine of mercy.[7] Pope John Paul II took up this declaration in his
encyclical *Dives in Misericordia* and devoted an entire chapter to the
topic "The Mercy of God in the Mission of the Church." He emphasized that it is the church's task to give witness to divine mercy.[8]

This can happen in a threefold way: the church must proclaim
the mercy of God; it must concretely provide people God's mercy in
the sacrament of mercy, the sacrament of reconciliation; and it must
allow God's mercy to appear and be realized in its concrete structures, its entire life, and even in its laws.

2. The Proclamation of Divine Mercy

The church's first task is to proclaim the message of mercy. In
the contemporary situation, in which many people live as if God does
not exist, the church must not allow itself to be pushed to the side or

relegated to secondary venues for proclaiming this message. It must push forward to the center of the gospel message and make the message about a merciful God its focus. It should proclaim, therefore, neither a bland, vague, or religiously general and philosophically abstract God, nor speak, in a trivializing banal way, of a saccharine "dear God," nor cause people anxiety with talk about a judgmental and vengeful God. With the psalms, the church must praise God's inexhaustible mercy and proclaim God as "the Father of mercies and the God of all consolation" (2 Cor 1:3), "who is rich in mercy" (Eph 2:4). It must recount the concrete history of God's merciful interaction with people, as attested in the old and the new covenant. It must expound upon this history, as Jesus did in his parables, and bear witness to God, who has definitively revealed his mercy in the death and resurrection of Jesus.

In its proclamation, the church must demonstrate that the history of the proofs of God's mercy will be true for us and other hearers today (cf. Luke 4:21). The story of salvation from back then becomes, in a certain sense, the story of salvation today and thus becomes our story of life today. In the Letter to the Hebrews, we find a biblical example of such a contemporary evangelization. The letter was written in a situation in which the original enthusiasm had subsided and the threat that many would fall away was real. In this situation, a situation somewhat similar to ours, the word "today" occurs repeatedly: "Today, if you hear his voice, do not harden your hearts" (Heb 3:7–8; cf. 15); "exhort one another every day, as long as it is called 'today'" (3:13). For God in his mercy grants us once again a "today" (4:7).

The message about God and his mercy coming alive today acquires relevance especially in the context of the new evangelization, which is not concerned with a cheap assimilation or currying favor with today's fashions and moods.[9] The new evangelization cannot proclaim a new gospel, but it can make the one and the same gospel contemporary in a new situation. As preachers, we will only reach the hearts of our hearers when we speak of God concretely, in light of people's hardships and woe, and help them to discover the merciful God in their own life story. In this process, it does no good only to be critical of the modern world and contemporary human beings (which we are too). We must attend to the present situation with mercy and say that, above all of the fog and frequent gloominess of our world, the merciful countenance of a Father prevails, who is patient and kind, who knows and loves each individual, and who knows what we need (Matt 6:8, 32).

The new evangelization can say to those who are alienated from God and the church that God was graciously and mercifully near to them, even when they imagined that they were far from him, and just like the father in the parable of the prodigal son, who went out to meet him, God has waited for them, in order to welcome them back to him and to reinstate them in their rights as his sons (see Luke 15:20–24). Like the good Samaritan, God picks them up, as it were, from the side of the road, bends over them, and binds their wounds (Luke 10:30–35). Like the good shepherd, he goes after them, when they go astray and are caught in whatever thicket, and he puts them on his—on our—shoulders and carries them, full of joy, back to the community of all Christians. We can assure those who are alienated and who, nevertheless, are often much closer than they themselves think, that there is more joy in heaven over a single sinner who has repented than over ninety-nine righteous people, who do not need to repent (see Luke 15:3–7).

When the church attests to the mercy of God, it not only proclaims the deepest truth about God, it also proclaims the deepest truth about us humans. For the deepest truth about God is that God is love, which bestows itself and is always ready to forgive anew (1 John 3:8, 16). The deepest truth about human beings is that God in his love has created us in a wonderful fashion, that he has not forsaken us even when we have distanced ourselves from him, and that he has mercifully reestablished us and our dignity in a still-more wonderful way.[10] He descended to us in our deepest abasement in order to raise us to himself and draw us to his heart. There we can finally find rest and peace. Augustine begins his *Confessions*, after a restless life, by saying: "You move us to delight in praising you; for you have formed us for yourself, and our hearts are restless till they find rest in you."[11]

We can only proclaim this message of the God of mercy credibly when our speech is also shaped by mercy. We should engage in debate with the opponents of the gospel, who are as many today as there were in the past, firm in our cause, but not foaming at the mouth polemically, nor should we repay evil with evil. To pay enemies back in kind, in light of the Sermon on the Mount, is not a behavior that the church can justify. Even in debates with enemies, not polemics, but rather the endeavor to speak the truth in love and to act accordingly must determine our manner of speech (Eph 4:15). We should engage in battle about the truth resolutely, but not uncharitably, says Chrysostom.[12] Therefore, the church should not reprimand its audience from above in a know-it-all manner. To see the modern world only negatively, as a decadent phenomenon, is not fair and is perceived as unfair. The church should value the legitimate concerns of modern people and the progress in humanity that has occurred in the modern era, but deal mercifully with their problems and wounds.

Mercy without truth would be a consolation that lacks authenticity; it would be a mere empty promise and, ultimately, empty prattle. Conversely, truth without mercy would be cold, dismissive, and hurtful. We cannot proclaim the truth according to the motto "sink or swim." Truth is not like a wet washcloth, with which we beat others around their ears; it is more like a warm coat, into which we help another to slip so that he or she is snug and protected against adverse weather.

In this respect, a new tone and a new dialogical style is necessary. The polemical type of debate is found in some cases already in the New Testament;[13] it is often found in the church fathers. Controversial theology* was not altogether characterized by fairness, objectivity, and a readiness to hear and understand the other. By way of contrast, the Second Vatican Council voted for a new dialogical style. That has nothing to do with relativizing the truth or with covering up the existing antitheses. A dialogue that was not concerned with the truth would not deserve the name dialogue. Dialogue, rightly understood, presupposes a listening heart and reciprocal lis-

---

*Translator's note: Controversial theology is theology that defends the church's teachings against objections.

tening to each other. It means mutually vouching for the truth and coming to an exchange, ready to understand the truth, in order, as far as possible, to arrive at a common agreement in the truth, but there, where that is not possible, to say honestly that we agree to disagree.[14] It is necessary to speak the truth in love. Only then can it be attractive and convincing; only then can it be understood and accepted as that which it is, namely, as saving truth.

3. Penance: The Sacrament of Mercy

The message of the gospel of mercy is central. In Jesus Christ, however, the word became flesh (John 1:14); so the word of the church also assumes concrete shape in the sacraments.[15] All of the sacraments are sacraments of God's mercy. The sacrament of initiation, baptism, integrates the baptized into the communion of the church, which is a community of life and love. Because baptism forgives sins (Acts 2:38; 1 Cor 6:11; Eph 1:7; Col 1:14), it is a sacrament of divine mercy. The same is true of the anointing of the sick (Jas 5:15). In the Eucharist, the sin-forgiving power of the Lord's blood, which was shed on the cross, is made present each time (Matt 26:23). Thus, the celebration of the Eucharist has the power to forgive our everyday sins. According to the well-known words of Augustine, it is the sacrament of unity and love,[16] which binds us to the deepest unity in and with Jesus Christ and with one another, and through which we are sent into the world in the service of love and mercy.[17]

The church quite early on learned that Christians who had become a new creation through baptism (2 Cor 5:17; Gal 6:15) fall back into the life and the vices of their former world. In the early church there was a harsh debate about whether a second act of penance is possible after such a relapse. The words of Jesus, according to which the church has been given full power to bind or to loose (Matt 16:19; 18:18), tipped the balance. In John's Gospel, this authority is interpreted as the power to forgive or not to forgive sins (John 20:22f.). This authority is the Easter gift of the risen Lord for his disciples. On this foundation, the early church developed a penitential practice with the sacrament of reconciliation. It understood this penitential practice as a second plank of salvation after the shipwreck of sin[18] and as a second arduous baptism, not by means of water but by means of tears.[19] So the sacrament of reconciliation is the genuine sacrament of the mercy of God, who repeatedly forgives us anew and grants us time and again a new chance and a new beginning.[20]

In the course of centuries, this sacrament has experienced many changes, which we cannot discuss here.[21] The sacrament of reconciliation, as it has evolved, is recommended in the warmest possible terms by many great saints, such as Catherine of Siena, Alphonsus Liguori, the pastor from Ars, Padre Pio, Sister Faustina, and many others. The church's teaching and pastoral offices also recommend this sacrament enthusiastically.[22] Such a long praxis, which has been repeatedly recommended by the church, cannot be an undesirable development, but rather must be of great utility for the development of the spiritual life.

Karl Rahner, who was very occupied with the history and theology of the sacrament of reconciliation, has written an impressive essay on the praxis of penance and the meaning of frequent confession of devotion.[23] One ought not interpret its significance exclusively or even primarily from the perspective of spiritual direction and conscience formation, which can be obtained outside of confession and are to be commended. There are other means, especially the Eucharist, for gaining strength to meet daily challenges. Furthermore, the sacrament of reconciliation is a genuine and essential manifestation of the church's life. For mundane sins are still stains and wrinkles on the bride of Christ that diminish its power to shine and, by and large, weighs on the life of the church. To this extent, every confession is also a visible act of orientation to the visible body of Christ, which is the church.

Presently, one must speak of a serious crisis concerning this sacrament. In most parishes, the sacrament has largely fallen out of use and many Christians, even those who regularly participate in the Sunday Eucharist, do so without the sacramental praxis of penance. This fact is one of the deep wounds of the present church; this must be an occasion for us to seriously examine our personal and our pastoral conscience. For the future of the church, it is essential to come to a reinvigorated penitential order and a renewal of the sacrament of reconciliation.

The reasons for the current crisis are diverse. Many no longer experience the sacrament of reconciliation as an Easter gift of liberation. On the contrary, it is often understood as a coercive instrument of control that attempts to regulate people's conscience and deprive them of the right to make their own decisions. For some older adults, many a downright traumatic experience is bound up with the sacrament of reconciliation. But most people today know of such negative experiences only from hearsay. While the older generation has reservations because they had bad experiences, today many younger Christians have reservations because they have absolutely no more experiences that require confession. In addition, many contemporaries have a virtually pathological delusion of innocence.[24] Only others or "the system" are guilty. A grandiose mechanism of exculpation is at work, which finally puts into question personal responsibility and, consequently, human dignity. Meanwhile, it appears that the page is slowly being turned to something better. Especially at pilgrimage sites, spiritual centers, and world youth days, the sacrament of reconciliation is again being sought and is experienced anew by many as a gift of grace.

The sacrament of reconciliation is a true refuge for sinners, which all of us are. Here the burdens that we carry around with us, are taken from us. Nowhere else do we encounter the mercy of God so immediately, so directly, and so concretely as when we are told in the name of Jesus: "Your sins are forgiven!" Certainly no one finds it easy to humbly confess his or her sins and, often enough, to confess the same sins over and over again. But everyone who does that and then is told "I absolve you," not generally and anonymously, but concretely and personally, knows of the inner freedom, inner peace, and joy that this sacrament bestows. When Jesus speaks of the joy in heaven over the repentance of one sinner (Luke 15:7, 10), then whoever receives this sacrament may experience the fact that this joy is not only in heaven, but also echoes in his or her own heart. Therefore, it is necessary to discover this sacrament again. That is especially true for priests. For the commission to remit sins is the commission the risen Lord gave to the apostles. It is for every priest, therefore, a duty and a work of mercy to be ready to administer this sacrament.

Certainly, there are various forms of penance: prayer, works of mercy, fraternal correction, voluntary fasting, and others. Every celebration of the Eucharist begins with an act of penitence and an intercessory prayer of absolution. All of these forms of penance have their value and meaning; they should prepare for the sacrament of reconciliation, accompany it, and follow it up, but they don't intend to replace nor can they replace the sacrament of reconciliation. Spiritual direction and psychological counseling also have their value, but they too cannot take the place of the sacrament of reconciliation. Counselors and psychologists can help us to better understand ourselves and our often most messed-up situations; they can help us to recondition what is uneven in our lives, to accept ourselves and others, and they can give good advice for these situations. As pastors we will often have to appeal to their professional competence and human experience. But no psychologist or counselor can say: "Your sins are forgiven" or "Go in peace."

This sacrament corresponds today, just as in previous times, to a deep need, and it still has its relevance. It is a work of mercy, both for the individual and for the church community. It could help to overcome aggression and the formation of camps in the church; it could assist in giving Christian humility a new lease on life, establishing more merciful dealings with one another in the church and thereby helping the church to become more merciful.

4. Ecclesial Praxis and the Culture of Mercy

Of course, it is not sufficient for the church simply to utter the word mercy; it is necessary to do the truth (John 3:21). Especially today, the church is judged more by its deeds than by its words. The church's message, therefore, must have an effect on its concrete praxis and result in a culture of mercy in the entire life of the church.[25]

In the Greek and Roman world, there was indeed beneficence and philanthropy, which was not directed towards the poor, but rather to citizens (distribution of food, health services, etc.). By contrast, ecclesial life from the very beginning was characterized by a lively charitable praxis. It drew upon Jewish praxis, but, on the basis of Jesus' message, it also went its own way. From the very beginning, a distinguishing mark of this praxis was that it was not left to private piety, but rather was lived out by the community in an institutionalized form.

Thus, from the very beginning, gathering together for the Lord's Supper was connected with an *agape* meal (a filling meal celebrated as a love feast). The Acts of the Apostles reports that serving the tables, already in the original Jerusalem community, assumed such a large scale that the apostles could no longer handle it, so that seven individuals, later called deacons, were appointed for this service (Acts 6:1–4). In fact, Paul insisted upon a clear differentiation of the Lord's Supper from an actual meal because of grievances dividing the community. He didn't want the two intermingled, but the fact that the two belong together was beyond question (1 Cor 11:17–34).[26] Already in the early days, mutual support stretched beyond the respective individual communities. The Apostle Paul established regular collections in his communities for the poor in Jerusalem (Gal 2:10; Rom 15:26; 2 Cor 8:9). A fundamental truth was: "Bear one another's burdens, and in this way you will fulfill the law of Christ" (Gal 6:2). So the first Christians not only designated each other as brothers, they also acted like brothers.[27]

The pieces of evidence from the early church are numerous and staggering. Those early testimonies report that alms were given at the end of the Sunday worship services.[28] They served to support widows and orphans, the sick, the weak, the poor and those unable to work; the alms also provided for the remuneration of those who provided a service in the community and provided support for the care of prisoners, those languishing in the mines, and the slaves; they also provided support for hospitality to recently arrived brethren and assistance for poor and endangered communities. Tertullian reports that the way Christians cared for the needy very much amazed their pagan contemporaries. He reports that the pagans said: "See how they love one another!"[29] A beautiful testimony to the life of early Christians is found in the anonymous Letter to Diognetus, which stems from the second or third century. It describes how the Christians don't lead an outlandish life, but rather an outwardly and totally normal life, and yet they behave differently. "They love all, and by all they are persecuted…They are poor, and yet they make many rich; they are completely destitute, and yet they enjoy complete abundance."[30]

The bishop was in charge of this diaconal service and he made use of the deacons for this purpose. From the fourth century, there arose houses for the sick and for pilgrims and, alternatively, asylums for the poor, which became the model for the medieval hospitals that cared for the poor and the sick. Later, there arose numerous religious orders devoted to the care of the sick and others; they selflessly championed the cause of children, the poor, the old, the sick, and the handicapped and they continue to do so today. By doing this, Christianity exercised influence upon European culture and human civilization generally. That influence continues to be effective today, but mostly in a secularized form. Without this Christian impulse, neither the cultural and social history of Europe nor the history of humanity can be understood.

On the basis of the changed and changing social situation, new questions are being asked and new social challenges arise, which we will explore in detail.[31] In the present context, we shall only call attention to one problem: the danger of making the church bourgeois in the affluent West. In many communities, a milieu has developed in which people who do not fit within the parameters of a more or less middle-class lifestyle, people who have fallen on hard times, find a place only with difficulty. That is a situation that is scarcely compatible with Jesus' own praxis. For during his earthly life, nothing caused as much scandal as his care for sinners. "Why does he eat with tax collectors and sinners?" the reproachful question asks. Jesus' response was: "Those who are well have no need of a physician, but those who are sick; I have come to call not the righteous but sinners"

(Mark 2:16–17). Jesus also found more faith among the tax collectors and prostitutes than among those who belonged to the establishment of that time. Therefore, he said that the tax collectors and prostitutes are going into the kingdom of God before those who regard themselves as pious (Matt 21:31–32). To the accusers, who dragged a woman taken in adultery before him, he only said: "Let anyone among you who is without sin be the first to throw a stone at her." But when there was no one left who wanted to condemn her, he said to the woman: "Neither do I condemn you. Go your way, and from now on do not sin again" (John 8:7, 11).

The most serious criticism that can be leveled against the church, therefore, is the accusation that oftentimes only a few deeds follow, or appear to follow, its words. The church is reproached for speaking of God's mercy, while it is perceived by many people to be strict, harsh, and pitiless. Such accusations, among others, grow loud with regard to the issue of how the church deals with people whose lives are breaking down or have failed; with civilly divorced individuals who have remarried; with others who have left the church (as is their civil right), often only because they did not want to or could not pay the church tax, or who leave because of the criticism or even rejection of people who lead a way of life that doesn't conform to church order or, in some other way, does not fit into the ecclesial system of rules.

If the church wants not only to proclaim, but also to live Jesus' message of his forgiving Father and his way of dealing with those living on the margins back then, then it may not steer clear of those who, then as today, are not counted among the pious. Without denouncing the rich and the upper class in a sweeping fashion, the church must have a heart for the little people, for the poor, the sick, the disabled, the street people, the immigrants, those who are marginalized and discriminated against, the homeless, alcoholics and drug addicts, those infected with AIDS, criminals, and also for prostitutes, who, often because of great deprivation, see no other way to live than to sell their own bodies and, as a result, often have to accept terrible indignities. Of course, the church cannot justify the sin, but it should certainly attend to the sinners with mercy. In following

Jesus, the church must never be perceived to be the church primarily of the rich, the powerful, and the socially respectable. The preferential but not exclusive option for the poor, in the widest sense of the word, is in effect for the church.

The history of the saints is instructive also in this regard. The tax collector Levi became Matthew the evangelist and Saul became Paul. Some who later became saints, like Charles de Foucauld, were at first deadbeats. If one looked at his earlier life, an Augustine would not have made it even to the level of a head acolyte, according to today's criteria for episcopal appointments. These are all examples that show that God can make something useful out of crooked wood.

Fortunately, there are such spaces and places of mercy in the church. And to those who provide such merciful service, we cannot give them enough deep respect, gratitude, and recognition. The service that is meant is not only physical assistance in our hospitals and in the homes for senior citizens, the handicapped, the homeless and their dependents. A Christian culture of mercy should characterize these homes, hospices, and boards over and above the necessary external assistance. They should be equipped, as far as possible, with all of the modern medical apparatuses, but they must not let themselves be roped into becoming a technologically and increasingly economically and bureaucratically oriented system, in which there is no longer either time or place for humane care, for listening to others, and for comforting them. For this purpose, there is a need for caregivers, whether clergy or laity, who are merciful brothers and sisters. Jean Vanier's L'Arche communities for the developmentally disabled can serve in a special way as an exemplary model for such a Christian culture of mercy.

Whenever as bishop I visited prisoners on Christmas or, during the year, went to a pastoral ministry for the homeless and encountered people there whom our middle-class society most often steers clear of, then every time I experienced how very much these human beings perk up when they are perceived, taken seriously, and accepted in their human dignity by Christian or humanistic citizens' groups and when, at least for a few hours, they may experience brotherliness and security. In this way, hope's ray of light and warmth can light up for them too, in an otherwise gray and gloomy world.

A culture of mercy cannot confine itself to material assistance for others; compassionate interactions with one another are also necessary. Early on, Paul complained about the formation of parties in the community (1 Cor 1:10–17). He rigorously criticizes Christians for biting and devouring each other, rather than letting themselves be guided by the Spirit of God (Gal 5:15). Complaints about the lack of love among Christians do not go silent in the church fathers. One of the first postbiblical testimonies, the first letter of Clement, intervenes as an arbitrator in the community at Corinth. Gregory of Nazianzus complains bitterly with harsh words about the lack of love and the quarreling in the church, especially among the clergy. "Opprobrium is poured out over the leaders....We fall over each other and devour one another."[32] Similarly clear words are found also in Chrysostom. For him, the lack of love among Christians is simply disgraceful.[33] The contemporary reader thus finds in these texts from the church fathers some small comfort: what we often painfully experience nowadays in the church is anything but new; apparently it was not better in the past.

The culture of mercy among Christians should become concrete above all in the liturgy, in which we make God's mercy present in our celebration. In this regard, the Letter of James issues a clear lesson for us.

> If a person with gold rings and in fine clothes comes into your assembly, and if a poor person in dirty clothes also comes in, and if you take notice of the one wearing the fine clothes and say, "Have a seat here, please," while to the one who is poor you say, "Stand there," or, "Sit at my feet," have you not made distinctions among yourselves, and become judges with evil thoughts? Listen, my beloved brothers and sisters. Has not God chosen the poor in the world to be rich in faith and to be heirs of the kingdom that he has promised to those who love him? But you have dishonored the poor (Jas 2:2–6).

James emphasizes twice that Christ shows no partiality with respect to persons and, therefore, the same must hold true for Christians.

Again in this respect, Chrysostom is especially clear. It is worthwhile to cite in detail the words of this great bishop and church father.

> What excuse shall we have then, when eating a lamb, we become wolves? When feeding on the lamb, we begin to ravish like lions? This mystery demands that we be perfectly clear not only from violence, but even from mere enmity. In fact, this mystery is a mystery of peace; it does not permit us to chase after wealth by unjust means....Let us flee then from this abyss; neither let us think it sufficient for our salvation, if after we have robbed widows and orphans, we offer for the altar a gold and bejeweled chalice....For the church is not a gold or silver boutique, but rather an assembly of angels glorifying God....That table at the last supper was not of silver nor was the cup of gold, out of which Christ gave his disciples his own blood; but it was nonetheless precious and awesome because it was full of the holy spirit. Do you wish to honor Christ's body? Don't pass by him when you see him naked; do not honor him here in the church with silken garments, while you neglect him perishing outside from the cold and nakedness! For he that said, "This is my body," and by his word confirmed the fact, this same one said, "You saw me starving, and fed me not;" and, "Inasmuch as you did it not to one of the least of these, you did it not to me." For this purpose there is no need of silk coverings, but indeed a pure soul. But that requires much attention....God has no need of golden chalices, but of golden souls.[34]

What is true for liturgy must also be true for the life of the church as a whole, and especially for the style of life that its representatives lead. The church proclaims Jesus Christ, who for our sake emptied himself of his divine glory and lowered himself, becoming poor and like a slave (Phil 2:6–8; 2 Cor 8:9). Therefore, the church cannot give credible testimony to Christ, who became poor for us, if it, and in particular the clergy, give the impression of being rich lords. The Second Vatican Council, in the constitution on the church *Lumen Gentium*, put forth an important, but—unfortunately—infrequently cited paragraph about the ideal of a poor church.[35] While the paragraph about the institutional structures of the church is found in the same chapter and is cited repeatedly, this paragraph conspicuously receives little attention. In following Jesus, the church can be a church for the poor only if it, and particularly the clergy, seek—if not to live like the poor—at least to adopt a simple and unassuming lifestyle. The age of feudalism should nowadays also be over for the church. For this reason, the council fundamentally renounced worldly privileges.[36] Two weeks before the close of the council, forty bishops from around the world concluded a Catacombs' Pact, in which they renounced privileges and everything that had the appearance of wealth, committing themselves to being a poor church in the service of the poor.

Pope Benedict XVI, at the end of his pastoral visit to Germany on September 25, 2011, recalled these statements in his speech in Freiburg im Breisgau, a speech that received a lot of attention and elicited contentious discussion. He spoke of removing worldly elements from the church. Of course, by this utterance he did not mean a retreat from the world. Rather, he recalled the Gospel of John, according to which the church, to be sure, is in the world and has its mission in the world, but is not of the world and may not orient itself according to the world's standards (John 17:11, 14). Naturally, no insightful person will deny that the church in this world needs temporal means and institutional structures in order to fulfill its task. But means must then remain means and may not secretly become an end in itself. Therefore, institutional and bureaucratic points of view may not become so overly powerful and determinative of everything that, instead of serving the spiritual life, they crush and suffocate it. Release from temporal power and earthly wealth can, therefore, constitute new freedom for the church for accomplishing its true mission.

Thus, the secularization at the beginning of the nineteenth century that initially was experienced as an act of divestment and injustice—and actually was—has turned out to be a point of departure for spiritual renewal. Even if we cannot equate the situation then with the situation today, nonetheless nowadays—at least in Germany—a similar danger is posed by an overinstitutionalization and overbureaucratization of the church, which really is a form of secularization that makes the church hardly distinguishable from temporal organizations and leads to institutional conduct that obscures the church's spiritual profile. The removal and destruction of such structures, which are alien to the church in principle, in favor of more simplicity and poverty, can gain more credibility for the church today and become its path into the future.

If we don't voluntarily embark on this path ourselves, we could soon be forced to do so by outside forces. For the less the church (more specifically, the two big churches in Germany) represents mainstream society and the less it is, in this sense, the people's church—already today and even more so in the future—things will permanently be like what they have become at other times under different premises. Departure from the church's previous social structure, which is drawing to an end today, can thus become a new beginning for the church.[37]

5. Mercy in Canon Law?

One can misunderstand and misuse the word mercy not only in the personal realm, but also in the institutional realm of the church. That happens in both places when one confuses mercy with feeble indulgence and a laissez-faire point of view. Where that happens, the following is true: *corruptio optimi pessima* (the corruption of the best is the worst that can happen). The danger then exists of making cheap grace out of God's precious grace, which was "purchased" and "earned" with his own blood on the cross, and turning grace into a bargain-basement commodity. That is what Dietrich Bonhoeffer meant when he clearly stated, without mincing words: "Cheap grace means the justification of the sin and not the sinner....Cheap grace is the preaching of forgiveness without requiring repentance; baptism without church discipline; communion without acknowledging sin; absolution without personal confession."[38]

The extensive breakdown of church discipline is one of the weaknesses in the contemporary church. It represents a misunderstanding of what the New Testament means by mercy and what the pastoral dimension of the church means. The dismantling of a rigid, legalistic praxis, without simultaneously building up a new praxis of church discipline that conforms to the gospel, has led to a vacuum, which has permitted scandals that have led to a serious crisis in the church. Only recently, in the context of the horrifying cases of sexual abuse, does one appear to recollect that church discipline is necessary.

Therefore, it is necessary, in the context of the message about mercy, to ask anew about the sense and praxis of church discipline. For the breakdown of church discipline can in no way appeal to Jesus and the New Testament. The primary New Testament word for church, *ecclesia* (ἐκκλησία), contained legal elements from the very beginning. The idea of an original church of love that subsequently is supposed to have become a church of law cannot be substantiated.[39] According to Matthew's Gospel, Jesus gave Peter the power of the keys and gave to him, as well as to all of the apostles, the authority to bind and to loose, which means the authority to expel individuals from the community and to readmit them. Already Matthew established a clear rule for the exercise of this authority (Matt 16:19; 18:18).[40]

Expulsion from the community occurred even in the early days of the church (Acts 5:1–11; cf. 19:19). In many passages, the New Testament enumerates the sins that exclude one from the kingdom of God and that can have no place in the church. Paul names fornication, greed, thievery, and idolatry (1 Cor 6:9).[41] Therefore, he does not hesitate to exclude from the community a person who committed incest (1 Cor 5:4f.). In other passages, there are also warnings about dissension and divisions in the community: Avoid them! (Rom 16:17); Do not associate with them! (1 Cor 5:11).[42] Paul, therefore, implores his student Timothy and those in the church to take to heart his words: "Proclaim the message; be persistent whether the time is favorable or unfavorable; convince, rebuke, and encourage, with the utmost patience in teaching" (2 Tim 4:2).

Especially in light of participation in the Eucharist, examination and exclusion is necessary (1 Cor 11:26–34). The Eucharist is the church's supreme possession, which may not be turned into a bargain-basement commodity that is offered to everyone without distinction and to which everyone believes that he or she has a right. Paul passes a very harsh judgment here: whoever eats the bread or drinks the cup in an unworthy manner will be answerable for the body and blood of the Lord; they eat and drink judgment against themselves (1 Cor 11:27, 29). If one reads these words in context, then membership in the Catholic Church cannot be the only criterion for determining admission to the Eucharist, however much that is an important criterion according to ancient ecclesial tradition. But even Catholics must engage in serious self-examination whether their life fits in well with the Eucharist as the celebration of the death and resurrection of Christ. It was not for nothing that the ancient penitential praxis was directly connected with exclusion and readmission to the Eucharist. Such differentiation and separation involves nothing less than the holiness of the church.[43]

Because church discipline is in keeping with the sense of the gospel, it must also be applied according to the sense and spirit of the gospel. For this reason, Paul makes it clear that the punishment of expulsion is to be understood as a punishment that intends to force the sinner to reflect on his or her conduct and to repent. Paul intends to hand the sinner over to the devil "so that his spirit may be saved in the day of the Lord" (1 Cor 5:5). If the sinner regrets his or her actions and repents, the community should let gentleness again prevail (2 Cor 2:5–11). Punishment is the last resort and, as such, is temporally limited. It is the drastic and final means used by mercy. One can speak of the educational and curative meaning of penitential praxis. Ultimately, it has an eschatological meaning; it anticipates the eschatological judgment and it saves people from eternal punishment by applying temporal punishment now. When understood in this way, the church's penitential praxis is not pitiless harshness, but rather an act of mercy.

Such an understanding of church discipline as the bitter but necessary medicine of mercy is neither a form of legalism nor of laxity. It conforms to a tradition that understood Jesus Christ, in light of his miraculous healings, as doctor, healer, and savior, a tradition in which saintly physicians (Luke, Cosmos, Damian among others) are honored and the pastor, in particular the confessor, is understood not only as a judge, but is understood primarily as a doctor of the soul.[44]

This therapeutic understanding of church law and church discipline leads us to the fundamental issue of how to interpret and explain church law, that is, the hermeneutics of church law.[45] That is a broad field that, in this context, we of course cannot treat in a comprehensive way, but can treat only from the perspective of the relation of church law to mercy.

In his debate with the Pharisees, Jesus himself gave us a decisive criterion for thinking about an application of church law that conforms to the gospel. In response to an interpretation of the commandment concerning the Sabbath that contradicts its originally humane sense, he asserts: "The sabbath was made for humankind, and not humankind for the sabbath" (Mark 2:27). "Woe to you, scribes and Pharisees, hypocrites! For you tithe mint, dill, and cumin, and have neglected the weightier matters of the law: justice and mercy and faith" (Matt 23:23). By doing this, Jesus did not abolish the Torah. For, indeed, he came not to abolish the law and the prophets, but to fulfill them (Matt 5:17). But he admonishes people to interpret the Torah in the sense of a hierarchy of truths, that is, in light of the central message of justice and mercy.

In this sense, the orthodox tradition developed the principle of "economy." According to this principle, it is necessary to speak the truth clearly and unambiguously, without subtraction or addition. It is necessary to interpret the truth with meticulousness (ἀϰϱιβεία). But it is just as necessary to interpret it economically in particular cases, according to its authentic intention, that is, according to the οἰϰονομία, the entire divine order of salvation.[46] The Catholic tradition is not familiar with the principle of economy, but it does know *epikeia*, a similar principle. Even Aristotle knew that general rules can never adequately cover all of the very complex individual cases.

Therefore, *epikeia* must fill in the gaps and, as the higher righteousness, not abrogate the objective legal norm in the individual case, but, on the contrary, apply it in a prudent way so that the respective application is truly just and not factually unjust.[47] Thomas Aquinas picked up this insight from the spirit of the biblical term *misericordia* and deepened it. He knew that God accepts every human being in his or her unique situation so that he or she is never only one case among many. Therefore, human laws can be valid only *ut in pluribus*, that is, in the majority of cases. Because of their general character, they can never cover all of the often very complex individual cases. *Epikeia* does not, therefore, dismiss justice; rather, it is the higher righteousness.[48]

Mercy does not abolish justice, but fulfills it and exceeds it.[49] Thomas can even say: justice without mercy is cruelty; mercy without justice is the mother of disintegration; therefore, both must be bound together.[50] Mercy is concerned not only with the fair distribution of material goods. Mercy wants to do justice to the other in his or her unique personal dignity; it is a person-oriented, not a thing-oriented justice. Mercy brings it about that people "meet one another in that value which is man himself, with the dignity that is proper to him." Thus, according to a formulation of Pope John Paul II, it is capable "of restoring man to himself." It is "in a certain sense…the most perfect incarnation of justice."[51]

On the legal level, the *aequitas canonica*, canonical fairness, corresponds to *epikeia*. According to the classical definition, it is supposed to sweeten the harshness of the law's justice with mercy.[52] Thus, according to traditional canonical theory, justice and mercy together are authoritative for the concrete, practical application of church law so that fair and just solutions can be achieved. The code of canon law deliberately concludes with the declaration that the highest norm is the salvation of souls.[53]

Pope Benedict XVI, in an address to the Roman Rota on January 21, 2012, offered important and fundamental remarks concerning the issue of legal hermeneutics. He made a crucial statement in favor of a hermeneutics of mercy, equity, economy, and generally in support of the so-called pastoral interpretation of the law.[54] These remarks stand only in apparent contradiction to the position represented here. For the pope criticized positions that put human considerations in the place of the objective character of the law in determining what is just in particular cases. By doing this, he said, legal hermeneutics is emptied of its meaning and is exposed to the danger of arbitrariness because the situation, and not the objective law, becomes normative in those considerations and, therefore, the danger arises of opening wide the door to subjective caprice, which interprets the law contrary to its objective sense and literal meaning.

Of course, we agree with the criticism of the hermeneutics of mercy, understood in that way. Naturally, it cannot be the case of a subjective or, indeed, an arbitrary interpretation contrary to the sense of the objective law; nor can it be a matter of a purely situational ethics of justice. On the contrary, the point is to apply the objective sense of the legislation analogously in an often complex concrete situation so that the law's application truly is fair and just in the given situation. It is, therefore, not a matter of an arbitrary reinterpretation, but rather a matter of bringing to bear the sense of the objective law in a way that is appropriate to the matter at hand and to the situation. This is not a problem of theoretical, but rather a problem of practical reason; alternatively, it is a problem for the power of judgment, which has the responsibility of applying general principles to concrete situations.[55] Practical reason is concerned with the analogous and practical application of a predefined law in a specific situation. According to Aristotle, the application is not a purely logical deduction or a purely positivistic subsumption, in contrast to Socratic-Platonic intellectualism. Rather, the objective claim of the law only becomes effective in the concrete application.[56]

This kind of application of general principles to the concrete situation is, according to the opinion of Thomas Aquinas, the task of the virtue of prudence. Prudence may not be confused with arbitrariness, shrewdness, craftiness, slyness, cleverness, or the like. Rather, it must be understood as the *recta ratio agibilium* [right reason applied to practice].[57] Prudence is concerned with the application of the objective norm in a manner appropriate to the facts, the reality, and, therefore, also the situation; it presupposes human discernment and experience. The judge must be not only legally trained, but also experienced in human affairs.[58] Indeed, it is no accident that the judge's discipline is called jurisprudence and not juris-*science*.

Theologically, the point is to do the truth in love (Eph 4:15), that is, to do what is right, guided by love. The ecclesial judge, in addition to possessing the human power of judgment, is expected to be a just and merciful judge, following the example of Jesus. Naturally, he or she will not twist the objective sense of the law according to each situation out of an erroneously understood good-heartedness, but will apply it in a way that is just and fair in each situation. In addition, the judge will allow him- or herself, out of a sense of Christian mercy, to be touched by the other's situation and will attempt to understand the other from the perspective of that situation.[59] The judge will then render a fair judgment, but nevertheless not a judgment that functions like a guillotine, but rather a judgment that leaves open "a loophole of mercy," that is, that makes possible a new beginning for the other, if he or she is of good will. The judge should take Jesus Christ, the merciful judge, as his or her example.[60] His or her benchmark must be the gentleness and kindness (ἐπιείκεια) of Jesus Christ (2 Cor 10:1).

When Pope Benedict rightly insists that the interpretation of canon law has to take place in the church, that also means that it should take place in the spirit of Christ and in Christian fraternity, in the spirit of a justice that is not diluted by a properly understood mercy, but finds its fulfillment therein and thus can be transmitted into the realm of society.

VIII

FOR A CULTURE OF MERCY

1. The Size and Parameters of the Modern Social Welfare State

JESUS SENT HIS DISCIPLES and the church out into the world. Consequently, with its message of mercy, the church cannot restrict its activities to the individual, personal sphere or the intra-ecclesial sphere. The church, so to speak, cannot retire to the sacristy. It must be yeast, salt, and light for the world (see Matt 5:13f.; 13:33) and it must be engaged on behalf of the world. However, it has no specific competence for the technical questions of economic or social policies. For issues concerning the economic or social order possess a legitimate, factually based autonomy. Not theologians, but competent lay people are chiefly responsible for these issues.[1]

It would, of course, be totally wrong to think that the economic and social order deals only with technical factual issues. It deals with people as well as with the design and culture of human life, communal existence, and, in many cases, human survival. Bread is absolutely necessary for living, but human beings don't live by bread alone. The human person is more than what he or she eats. We need human care and we depend on others to deal with us with at least a modicum of mercy. The currently prevalent economization of the social sphere, therefore, constitutes a diminishment and even an "amputation" of the human person. When that happens, society loses its soul and becomes a soulless system.

The current economic and financial crisis is ultimately, there-fore, an anthropological and spiritual crisis. One worries about the cost of things and asks what is worth the money, but forgets to ask what is valuable or worthwhile for the human person and for human society. In order not to allow the question about what is valuable and life-giving for human beings to be forgotten, the church must have a say in the fundamental, ethical questions concerning the economy and society; it must get involved, not on its own account nor out of self-interest, but rather out of interest for people and the humaneness of society.[2]

Essential for proper social order is the issue of justice. According to Cicero's classical definition, justice consists in giving each his or her due (*suum cuique*).[3] Early on Augustine had empha-sized the fundamental meaning of justice for a political system:

> If justice is set aside, then, what are kingdoms but great bands of robbers? For what are bands of robbers but little kingdoms. The band itself is made up of men, which is ruled by the authority of a ringleader, is knit together by a pact of confederacy, and divides the booty according to a firm agreement among them.[4]

While the widest possible agreement exists, in principle, con-cerning the significance of justice for the proper ordering of society, many will raise objections about the significance of mercy. They will argue: mercy is without a doubt a fundamental Christian virtue, but it has no place in the design of secular society. It is alleged that mercy undermines engagement in the cause of justice and only serves, by means of almsgiving, to plug holes in the social network, without reshaping the system itself to be more just. Through spontaneous assistance here and there, mercy is accused of masking the injustices of the social system, instead of changing the system in a fundamen-tal way.[5] Even Mother Teresa of Calcutta, and her exemplary advo-cacy for the poorest of the poor, has not been spared this criticism.

From a completely different perspective, Adam Smith, the ancestor of liberal economic theory, came to a similar critique. In order to overcome the social problems of his age, he did not want to rely on love of neighbor and merciful beneficence, but wanted to take advantage of self-interest, or rather, the pursuit of profit. He built his theory not on altruism, but rather on egoism and he trusted that the "invisible hand" of the market would bring about social order.[6] As the social misery of early capitalism demonstrates, that was a rather naïve assumption.

Marx poured all of his ridicule upon this pre-established harmony. In fact, the cruel system of early capitalism of the nineteenth century did not lead to social order, but to the indescribable misery of industrial workers. While the optimistic assumptions of Adam Smith proceeded from a purely individualistic, in fact, purely egoistic image of humanity, Marx and Marxism proceeded from an equally one-sided, collectivist image of humanity that failed to recognize the inalienable dignity of every human being and, in practice, trampled it underfoot, violating it without mercy. Compassion and mercy fell by the wayside.

Both liberalism and Marxism proceed from different starting points; both proceed from a one-sided and false image of humanity. As a result of the impoverishment of the masses caused by industrial development in the nineteenth century, the idea of the modern social welfare state arose as a counterdevelopment of a completely different sort. In contrast to the care of the poor, as it had developed in the church in the first few centuries, the modern social welfare state is concerned not only about assistance or about the mitigation of poverty and deprivation in individual cases, but is concerned about the elimination of collective poverty, which is now understood as a socially bad state of affairs.[7] The task of ensuring what is right and just for everyone and constructing a just order for the entire body politic is not something that can be accomplished solely on an individual basis; it requires governmental regulatory policies. Therefore, the basic idea of the social market economy is that the state establishes the parameters in which a free market economy is then possible.[8] The parameters are supposed to give everyone the chance autonomously to shape his or her life in a way that respects human dignity and the opportunity to participate in the development of society. Moreover, these parameters are supposed to cushion the blow from threats to life (age, illness, joblessness, accident), thus representing a kind of institutionalized solidarity.

The idea of the social market economy has proven itself. In principle, it conforms to rules, already found in the Bible, for ordering the life of society, namely, the dignity of each individual, the mandate to work and shape the world, justice, and the protection of property, but also the social obligations that are thereby entailed.[9] Thus, this idea represents progress in humanitarianism that, also from a Christian perspective, is to be maintained and further developed in response to changing situations.

It is nevertheless apparent that the modern idea of the social welfare state in the meantime is hitting its limits for various reasons and in diverse ways; consequently, it must be further developed.[10] One can no longer, as in the past, take as a starting point for the financing of the welfare system regularly increasing economic growth rates. The numerical relation between the productive sector of the population and the sector supported by it has changed to a considerable degree because of demographic changes and longer average life expectancy. Technological developments, which can, in multiple ways, mechanically and electronically take care of what was previously done by hand, can cost work places and produce unemployment. Especially in the case of the youth and the long-term unemployed, this represents not only a material, but also a holistic human problem, affecting feelings of personal self-worth. It can become a social powder keg.

The real problem arises from the contemporary economic and financial processes of globalization. They lead to the fact that national economies can act less and less independently and end up in a system of global dependencies. In the face of economic globalization, the days of self-contained welfare states that are immune to outside influences are over.[11] Because there are hardly any global, state-like systems of control or only very weak ones, the weight of influence shifts to the benefit of the free and often unfettered play of the markets, concretely to the benefit of capital, for which purely economic data, not human values and what is humanly worthwhile, count. What matters most for capital markets, therefore, is profit and rate of return. As a result, the individual fate of many human beings, and even the fate of entire peoples, can be put at risk. The vast majority of people are more or less powerless as they are handed over to these convulsive forces and the concomitant threats to their existence.

In addition, the gap between rich countries in the North and poor countries in the South increases. The gap also increases between zones of prosperity (also in the South), where individuals live in excess, and zones of misery, where many people, above all children, starve. The extremely unjust distribution of goods in the world leads to massive migratory pressure that overtaxes the economic and social system of the economically and socially developed countries and, furthermore, can push them into a crisis. All attempts at overcoming this extremely unjust situation and arriving at a somewhat just world economic order have made little progress up to now. What we would need is a global market economy, but this presupposes a form of global governance,[12] which realistically, however, might best be attainable in the form of intergovernmental agreements. Unfortunately, even they are difficult enough to realize.

On the other hand, consumptive behavior and consumer demands have grown in recent decades. As a result, demands on the social system have grown in a way that, in many cases, cannot be covered any longer by economic strength and tax revenue. We have lost the right measure, we have been living beyond our means and thus have brought our own social system out of balance. Nations have had to incur debts, which have led to their excessive indebtedness and the current financial crisis. So there is a new poverty, not only of individuals, but also of nations and communities, which are no longer able to finance themselves and to provide necessary social services. The debt crisis can endanger the economic and social system as a whole. In many cases, the crisis made cutbacks in state social services necessary. The restructuring or dismantling of the social welfare state can then lead to new social problems. Excessive indebtedness, moreover, leads to an interest burden that the present generation cannot pay or is not willing to pay, a burden with which we saddle coming generations. For this reason, the issue of generational justice arises.

Understandably, all of that has caused many citizens to be anxious and fearful. They see that the idea of the social welfare state is being challenged anew in view of globalization and the neocapitalistic tendencies that have come to light that enable individuals to get rich as a result of an often shameless greed, at the expense of very many others. In this situation, the church's social teaching is also challenged in a new way. The question is: What can Christians in this situation do for a social-minded and merciful society? How can and how should the church's social teaching be further developed? In this situation, over and above the still fundamental issue of justice, can Christian mercy acquire new significance?

2. The Continuation of the Church's Social Teaching

Since the emergence of social problems and scandalous injustices, caused by the industrial revolution in the nineteenth century, the Catholic Church has been developing its social teaching. In this process, the church could draw upon the teaching concerning justice as it had developed in connection with Aristotle and, above all, with Thomas Aquinas. After precursors and pioneers like Bishop Wilhelm Emmanuel von Ketteler from Mainz, the popes—since Pope Leo XIII's encyclical *Rerum Novarum* (1891)—have put themselves at the head of this Catholic ecclesial social movement. They have denounced social injustice and promoted the development of the modern welfare state.[13]

The starting point and foundation of the church's social teaching is the Christian image of humanity, concretely, the unconditional dignity of each human being and of all people. This dignity is given to human beings not by society, but by the Creator and, therefore, it is sacrosanct and inalienable. Because it is given to all human beings in common, human dignity entails the solidarity of all people. The dignity of each human being entails a claim upon a humane life, in free self-determination and in solidarity with all other human beings. So we can say that the freedom of every individual and the common freedom of all is the principle by which Catholic social teaching is constructed. The most important resource is not the possession of land or capital, but the human person with his or her cognitive faculties, initiative, and creative work.

Proceeding from the twin perspectives of human freedom and social bonding and responsibility, the church has promoted the development of the modern social welfare state. The starting point and foundation of the church's social teaching is the Christian image of humanity, concretely, the inalienable dignity of each individual person and of all people in common, which is given to us not by society, but by the Creator. The church's social teaching is thereby distinguished both from liberal capitalism as well as from ideological socialism and communism, which socializes everything. According to the church's social teaching, everyone is, first of all, responsible for him- or herself, but each must also have the real chance of assuming this responsibility for self.

With these principles, the church neither can nor wants to deduce from the gospel, for instance from the Sermon on the Mount, a concrete social program or some kind of Christian political platform. The Second Vatican Council issued a rejection of such integralism, which is a kind of Christian totalitarianism,[14] and it also rejected the idea of a Catholic state. The council advocated the legitimate autonomy of politics as well as the autonomy of all other secular matters belonging to the sphere of culture.[15] The church's social teaching is no abstract, finished, deductive system. Rather, it seeks to reflect upon the changing human social situations in light of Christian anthropological principles. In this way, on the basis of its understanding of the human person, the church has attempted to respond to the challenges of the modern situation that have arisen from industrialization.

Because the economy ultimately has to do with people, legitimate autonomy does not mean that politics and the economy are ethically neutral. The state may not make decisions only from the points of view of power, the maintenance of power, success, or economic utility. It must be oriented toward human dignity, fundamental human rights, law and justice, the common good, and internal and external peace. The state must establish a corresponding just framework, within which free competition is possible and, for the sake of freedom and the common good, is also necessary.[16]

At the same time, the issue of generational justice acquires today an ever-greater significance. The present generation ought not impose on future generations the burden of public debts that this generation itself is neither ready nor able to pay back. Moreover, by preserving creation, we must ensure that we leave future generations a humanly livable natural environment by dealing responsibly with nature and its resources. Such environmental justice is rooted in reverence for creation, which is founded upon Christian beliefs about creation. The goods of creation are given to people, in fact to all people, for their use, but also for their conservation.

Proceeding from the dignity of each individual person and his or her social location, the popes' social teaching, since the time of Leo XIII, has rightly emphasized the demand for justice by means of the two principles of subsidiarity and solidarity, principles that complement each other.

Subsidiarity takes the dignity and autonomy of the person seriously. Social assistance, therefore, must be assistance directed toward self-help. It ought not undermine or discourage personal responsibility and achievement, but rather give it a chance. The ideal, therefore, is not a bureaucratic social system that regulates everything. The principle of subsidiarity means that the respectively smaller unit, above all the family, and then manageable units, like communities or associations—whether developed or free—should do everything and also should be able to do everything that they can accomplish by their own means. Larger entities like the state should only intervene in a supportive or regulatory way when the smaller unit can no longer help itself or is fundamentally overtaxed. Government intervention should not consist in taking over everything and wanting to regulate all things in a centralized way; rather, it should consist, not in bureaucratically bossing around individuals, the smaller entities, or the spontaneous civic engagement of individuals, but in supporting and promoting them in such a way that they can act responsibly and autonomously.

Solidarity takes seriously the fact that the human person is a social being. But solidarity consists, first of all, in the attitude and conduct of one human being toward another. It begins in one's respective vicinity, in the family, the neighborhood, or in the circle of one's friends and acquaintances. The principle of social proximity means simultaneously social friendliness and warmth. Beyond that, solidarity must stamp the body politic as a whole and lead to a just order of institutionalized solidarity for the entire community. This ensures that everyone has an appropriate share in the prosperity that has been generated.

Unfortunately, both the principle of subsidiarity and the principle of solidarity in one's vicinity have been largely undermined and replaced by a centralized, bureaucratic system that—instead of providing assistance to enable self-help—creates dependency and, therefore, neither serves freedom nor promotes established social units. When social systems bump up against the limits of their effectiveness, recollection of the bases of the church's social teaching could provide further assistance. In that process, the Christian idea of mercy could acquire significance anew, not as an alternative to the idea of the welfare state, but within its parameters and as its supplement.

In fact, the social encyclicals of the popes have not stood still with their ever-relevant demand for justice. They have repeatedly pointed out that the eyes of love and mercy are necessary in order first to recognize, in a timely fashion, new social challenges and sources of distress and that only love provides the necessary impetus for energetically addressing those perceived needs and overcoming them.[17] Moreover, Pope John Paul II, who campaigned for human rights and justice with all of his strength, has recognized:

> The experience of the past and of our own time demonstrates that justice alone is not enough, that it can even lead to the negation and destruction of itself, if that deeper power, which is love, is not allowed to shape

human life in its various dimensions. It has been precisely historical experience that, among other things, has led to the formulation of the saying: *summum ius, summa iniuria* [greatest justice, greatest injustice].[18]

He therefore seized upon the idea of a "culture of love," which was first formulated by Pope Paul VI. Pope Benedict XVI also made this idea his own.[19]

In his first encyclical, *Deus Caritas Est* (2005), Pope Benedict XVI already went a decisive step further, which, in its fundamental significance, has previously been little appreciated. He made love, not justice, the systematic point of departure for his social doctrine.[20] In his third encyclical *Caritas in Veritate* (2009), which was explicitly dedicated to social doctrine, he expressly characterized love as the chief path and principle of the church's social teaching.[21] For him, love is the normative principle, not only in microrelationships—in friendships, the family, and small groups—but also in macrorelationships, that is, in social, economic, and political contexts. In this way, Benedict XVI has introduced an important, additional idea into the church's social teaching.

Obviously, the word love may not be understood as mere sentimentality or as mere feeling. It is profoundly anchored in our God-given human essence. It, therefore, has an ontological dimension. For, according to Christian conviction, life is not the product of a pure accident, but rather is a gift. We have been created out of love and created for love. Because life has the character of a gift, we live by the gift of the unmerited, free care of other human beings. What is meant thereby is not only the great acts of caring, but also the many small signs of esteem for others, to which belong the gifts of time and understanding.

Love as the principle of social doctrine, of course, does not replace justice. On the contrary, justice is the minimal measure of love, while love is the abundant measure. Love does not lag behind justice, but goes beyond the justice that is owed to others. Consequently, it is not an addendum or appendix to justice. The other, as a person, relies not only on temporal goods, but also on the gift of love. Therefore, love, which gratuitously exceeds what is legally required, is the form of justice appropriate to the person of the other. In this context, Benedict XVI speaks of the "logic of the gift."[22]

In this way, the pope takes up the postmodern criticism of pure transactional justice and refers to the fundamental ideas of Paul Ricoeur and Jean-Luc Marion concerning this matter.[23] This shows that the encyclical *Caritas in Veritate*, with its further development of the church's social teaching, stands right at the apex of contemporary reflection. The question that the encyclical thus poses to us is: Where do such key reflections lead in practice? We must now turn to this question.

3. The Political Dimension of Love and Mercy

It would far exceed my competence if I wanted to attempt to draw comprehensive, concrete conclusions for the exceedingly complex spheres of social and economic life from what has been said. I will restrict myself to a few suggestions.

From love as the principle of social teaching, we can derive, first of all, negative norms that exclude ways of behaving that stand in contradictory opposition to love and, therefore, that are forbidden in every case. The killing of human life, first and foremost, belongs in this category. That applies to murder and genocide as well as to the killing of unborn human life and assisted suicide (which is often euphemistically called "active assistive dying"). The prohibition also extends to unlawful detention, slavery, mutilation, torture, robbery, severe injustice, oppression, rape and sexual abuse, and hatred of foreigners and discrimination of every kind. The prohibition also includes lying, defamation, and mendacious propaganda and advertising, which cause serious damage to the life and limb of others or to their honor, or which intentionally misleads. An especially sorry chapter in this story, besides drug trafficking, is the scandalous arms trade. It is good for nothing other than killing people and destroying cultural and material goods.

Most difficult of all is the issue of war. Every war involves killing, destruction, and suffering, even for noncombatants. War as such cannot be God's will; it stands in contradiction to the posture of love. In light of the love commandment and, in particular, the command to love one's enemies and to renounce violence, whether and, if so, how Christians can actively participate in hostilities is a serious question.[24] In the early church, Christians refused military service. Down to the present day, many free churches do the same, the so-called peace churches (Bohemian Brethren, Quakers, Mennonites). On the other hand, as paradoxical as it sounds, defense of one's own fundamental human rights or those of innocent individuals, especially women and children, against aggressive force and oppression, can be an act of neighborly love and, under certain conditions, an obligation of love of neighbor, provided that all other means have been exhausted and proportionality is maintained.

The theory of a just war (better: a justified war), which was founded by Augustine and further developed by Thomas Aquinas, represents an ethical compromise. In a violent and often evil world, it can be necessary, for the sake of peace, to constrain and suppress evil. In this sense, a war that aims to defend the peace can be justified as the *ultima ratio*, if, after other means are exhausted, it serves to defend fundamental human goods and restricts violence to the means appropriate for achieving this goal, that is, if it renounces cruelty, acts of revenge, and similar things, and if there is the sound prospect that things will be better, not worse, as a result of limited hostilities—in other words, that pacification can be achieved. This is true provided that war is a last resort and that proportionality in the use of military means is maintained, even in cases of humanitarian interventions.

Because of the development of modern weapon systems, especially atomic weapons with their tremendous destructive force, a new situation has arisen. The question is whether the conditions of a justified war can be met at all with these weapons. Without being able in this context to explore the difficult and complex individual questions that are relevant, one must say at any rate that a total war, involving the destruction of entire cities or wide regions and their population, must be unconditionally condemned and proscribed.[25]

Because the goal must be, not war, not even the so-called just war, but peace, people are talking today more appropriately about a just peace rather than about a just war. A just peace can be built neither with bayonets nor with panzers. Peace is the work of justice (*Opus iustitiae pax*, cf. Isa 32:17). In this sense, one seeks today to develop not an ethics of war, but an ethics of peace, whose goal is to do everything to make war impossible, not only in particular cases, but structurally impossible. Since Benedict XV the popes have repeatedly advocated such a politics of peace.[26] The Second Vatican Council picked up this idea again: "It is our clear duty, therefore, to strain every muscle in working for the time when all war can be completely outlawed by international consent."[27] That duty leads to a preventative politics of peace, which includes the removal of injustices, development aid (Paul VI: development as the new norm for peace), advocacy for the enforcement and protection of fundamental human rights, rights and protection for minorities, procedures for finding justice that balances legitimate interests, interreligious and intercultural dialogue, sanctions for potential assailants, and other things. The presupposition for this is a supranational authority, which currently only the United Nations can be.

Those are important steps that move in the direction of Jesus' commandment. In these processes, love and mercy can prove to be resourceful in finding, in the least-violent way, a just order that is accepted by all participants. That can be the task not only for politics. Individual Christians, Christian groups and movements (Pax Christi, Action Reconciliation Service for Peace, Swords to Ploughshares, Terre des hommes, the Sant' Egidio community, among others) can and should also effectively contribute a lot to peace in the world and prove themselves to be peacemakers (Matt 5:9) through dialogue, reconciliation work, services on behalf of peace and development— even without a political mandate.

4. Love and Mercy as the Source of Inspiration and Motivation

In negative terms, love fundamentally excludes reprehensible acts and attitudes; in positive terms, one cannot deduce from love generally binding, concrete, and detailed norms—or, as is often said, technical norms—for economic and political conduct. But it has already become clear that love, considered positively, can be a kind of regulative idea and a source of motivation and inspiration for finding and realizing concrete solutions. The Second Vatican Council speaks of "light and energy."[28] One could also say: love provides the conditions for seeing what must be done. It is the eye-opener and driving force for a praxis and culture of mercy and justice. It is the driving force of justice.[29] In this sense, love can make an important contribution, in the current critical situation, to developing further the modern social welfare state under changed conditions.

We begin with a first consideration. Even if the "social net" catches the most serious forms of deprivation, there are always people who fall through the cracks in the law. Only "officially documented cases" of deprivation are integrated into the social assistance offered by state and community. In addition, distress has many different and ever-changing new faces. Therefore, every social system, no mater how well thought out, will necessarily have holes in it and will continue to have holes. Whoever wants to resolve every hardship or emergency bureaucratically would have to build an unwieldy bureaucratic system, which, in the end, would be overtaxed by its own overregulation because it cannot cover every situation. It would suffocate life under a mass of regulations and hand the needy individual over to an anonymous bureaucratic system, in which the individual, in the end, is only a number and a case. Such a system may be technically appropriate to a certain degree, but it is not humane.

In the encyclical *Deus Caritas Est*, Pope Benedict writes:

> Love—*caritas*—will always prove necessary, even in the most just society. There is no ordering of the State so just

that it can eliminate the need for a service of love. Whoever wants to eliminate love is preparing to eliminate man as such. There will always be suffering which cries out for consolation and help. There will always be loneliness. There will always be situations of material need where help in the form of concrete love of neighbour is indispensable. The State which would provide everything, absorbing everything into itself, would ultimately become a mere bureaucracy incapable of guaranteeing the very thing which the suffering person—every person—needs: namely, loving personal concern. We do not need a State which regulates and controls everything, but a State which, in accordance with the principle of subsidiarity, generously acknowledges and supports initiatives arising from the different social forces and combines spontaneity with closeness to those in need. The Church is one of those living forces: she is alive with the love enkindled by the Spirit of Christ. This love does not simply offer people material help, but refreshment and care for their souls, something which often is even more necessary than material support. In the end, the claim that just social structures would make works of charity superfluous masks a materialist conception of man: the mistaken notion that man can live "by bread alone" (*Matt* 4:4; cf. *Deut* 8:3)—a conviction that demeans man and ultimately disregards all that is specifically human.[30]

There is a second consideration. The world is never finished; new situations of deprivation, poverty, or other crises always appear. Without mercy, the new emergencies are very often not discovered. We need people who first perceive the new crisis, which often arises unexpectedly, and who let themselves be touched by it, who have the heart and the courage, as far as that is possible for them, to ensure a remedial action in response to that concrete case. Without such mercy, the motivating basis for the further development of social legislation gets lost. For this reason, our society, even with a generally well-functioning social system, cannot manage without mercy. Jürgen Habermas has pointed out that, particularly in light of the enormous problems with which we are confronted today, without this religious foundation, the emotional impetus is lacking for engagement on behalf of a just world.[31] Accordingly, one can characterize mercy as the innovating and motivating wellspring of justice.

A concrete example is the issue of asylum and immigration. Both are "signs of the times." Asylum for people who are being persecuted is a human right. This is true: "I was a stranger and you welcomed me" or "did not welcome me" (Matt 25:35, 43). In light of these clearly unambiguous words, one must honestly ask whether the policies for asylum that are in effect in many states, which describe themselves as nations of law, are nothing other than problematic, in fact, often scandalous policies. The issue of immigration is more difficult. Unlimited immigration is certainly impossible. Even in our society, it would disrupt everything to the point that our society no longer could be a place of refuge. Politics must intervene here with regulations. The question is how to do that. The admission of aliens conforms to the virtue of hospitality (Matt 25:38, 41), which is highly regarded in the Old and New Testaments as well as in the entire ecclesial tradition. One must describe as a scandal the way in which we Europeans so often deal with human beings who come to us, driven by poverty and hunger as well as by persecution and discrimination. Thus, worldwide migration raises further questions for us and poses new challenges for the social teaching of the church.

Moreover, a third consideration is that there are forms of deprivation and poverty that cannot be expressed in terms of the per capita income that would be necessary for the satisfaction of the bare necessities for life. There is also psychological or emotional poverty and deprivation, a poverty of relationships, loneliness and isolation; there is cultural poverty as well as poor access to education and to active participation in social-cultural life; finally, there is also spiritual poverty, which is expressed in inner emptiness, in a loss of meaning and orientation, which can end in the deterioration of the human spirit.[32] Those are desperate situations that are widespread even in, and precisely in, developed and prosperous societies. Even the best social system can provide only limited relief in these situations. Only personal concern and relationship can provide assistance in most of these situations. Human life and a truly humane society are not possible without friendship, community, solidarity, and also mercy.

Fourth: the pure welfare state is, in the end, in danger of turning even mercy into an economic business. Public welfare is commercialized and itself is turned into a partially lucrative business. Today we see that happening when the hospital sector is increasingly structured according to purely economic measures and becomes an economic, profit-oriented, large-scale enterprise. It is no different with geriatric care. Care that is only interested in keeping senior citizens clean and fed does not do justice to their human needs. An economized and commercialized social welfare state produces coldness and insensitivity in society, which no longer has a place for hidden, lonely tears and deep-seated personal questions. The social welfare state can provide quite a few amenities, but it cannot give what people need the most, namely, human beings who listen to them, empathize, and show compassion. Without such empathy and sympathy, understood in the original sense of the word, that is, compassion and shared joy, the world grows cold and life can become unbearable. We cannot engineer and federally regulate concern and mercy; we can't turn them into a universal ideology. Mercy and concern are something personal. We can only motivate and inspire others to be merciful and caring.

Finally: love and mercy have their place, in the first instance, in our close relationships. But they are also the fundamental condition for communal life and for the coexistence of peoples. After the atrocities of the Second World War, not only were material reparation payments necessary; there was a need for a much deeper reconciliation of Germans with the French, the Poles, and especially the Jews. Such reconciliation presupposed rethinking, and, in fact, conversion and forgiveness. Pope John Paul II said:

> A world from which forgiveness was eliminated would be nothing but a world of cold and unfeeling justice, in the name of which each person would claim his or her own

rights vis-à-vis others; the various kinds of selfishness latent in man would transform life and human society into a system of oppression of the weak by the strong, or into an arena of permanent strife between one group and another.[33]

As first formulated by Pope Paul VI and then repeated by Pope John Paul II and Pope Benedict XVI, it is, therefore, necessary to build, over and above a culture of justice, a "culture of love."[34] If anywhere, then certainly here the church and ecclesial groups can contribute something to the humanizing of society and social services. They can assist our social welfare state in preserving its soul.

5. The Societal Significance of the Works of Mercy

To make what has been said more concrete, we can recall one more time the corporal and spiritual works of mercy.[35] From them an inspirational and motivating force can emanate even into the political and social spheres. It is not difficult to relate the works of mercy to important social tasks and challenges in our society in order to realize what the church's message of mercy can mean in the present situation. Today this message has become anything but superfluous.[36]

With regard to the corporal works of mercy, one can perhaps think of the already-mentioned fourfold dimension of poverty, or individual and structural poverty. We can think about the fact that everyday many thousands of people, especially children, die from undernourishment and malnutrition; we can also think of the lack of potable water for millions of human beings. We can also think of migration as a sign of the times and, therefore, also as a challenge of our time: the task of absorbing aliens, who have fallen on hard times at home and seek acceptance from us. In this context, we can think of the task of combatting growing xenophobia and hostility toward foreigners. We can think, furthermore, of the problem of the homeless and the street children in many of the large cities of the world. We can easily relate the injunction to visit the sick to the current economizing and concomitant depersonalizing trends in the health care system, or relate the injunction to visit prisoners to the task of humanizing the penal system.

The spiritual works of mercy are equally relevant. The requirement to teach others becomes relevant in light of deficiencies in educational systems or the unavailability of education and training, which is a reason that many fail to have access to social advancement. The injunction to comfort the sorrowful leads to the task of grief counseling; the injunction to counsel the doubtful leads to the task of providing counseling services. Such services are doubly relevant in a situation in which there are hardly any more universally valid standards and many people are overwhelmed by the complexity of modern life. The injunction to admonish the sinner leads, among other things, to raising awareness about unjust structures and disclosing structural injustice. The task patiently to bear what is irksome has a lot to do with tolerance in our pluralistic society. Finally, the exhortation to forgive calls to mind the political meaning of working for peace and reconciliation.

In order to be able to accomplish this service in society, the church needs humane means, but it does not need to be big and powerful nor does it have to have at its command a large bureaucratic apparatus. The church is not reliant on worldly privileges and, in fact, it should renounce them.[37] It is supposed to live and work and must live and work in this world, but the church is not of this world (John 17:11, 14) and, consequently, it should not act as the world does nor operate according to the criteria of this world. From the life of Saint Don Bosco, we know that he began many of his deeds with little or nothing and that, in the end, trust in providence never disappointed him. More than other institutions, the church can and should draw on the voluntary, but highly motivated engagement of volunteers. As a poor church for the poor, in an otherwise intellectually impoverished time, it can develop all the more its moral authority and new missionary persuasive power and charisma.[38] The kingdom of God comes in the form of a very small mustard seed that becomes a large shrub; it is like a little bit of yeast that leavens an entire trough of flour (see Matt 13:31–33). And precisely as a small, but creative minority, the church too can have a great moral, intellectual, and spiritual influence.[39]

6. Mercy and the Question of God

Concrete problems are important; for many people, in fact, they mean life or death. Nonetheless, theology ought not get lost in these complex and concrete issues. It must be theology, which means it must be and remain speech about God, and it must show how, in the concrete problems with which we are currently confronted, fundamental questions—and ultimately the God question—are raised. One could also say this the other way around: it is God, his justice, and his mercy that literally force us to come to grips with these issues. That is what we would like to pursue as we conclude this chapter.

We said that the principle by which the church's social teaching is constructed is the inalienable dignity and freedom of the human being. In so doing, the church's social teaching can proceed from a decidedly modern starting point and can complete the modern turn to the subject, which means anything but subjectivism. We, therefore, ask: What is freedom and what does it mean? Certainly not individualistic free license, because license makes itself dependent— more so than it realizes—on the predominant moods, interests, and emotional impulses of the moment. Individual license is also extremely dangerous politically. It can be seduced by propaganda and advertising and, as a result, very quickly and suddenly change into either an open or devious form of totalitarianism.

Freedom that is conscious of its own dignity will always respect the freedom of others. It will be in solidarity with their freedom, and will stand up for it. Freedom, therefore, is not "freedom from others," but "freedom with and for" others. Freedom is realized in justice, which gives everyone his or her due. Freedom concretely presupposes that everyone else will respect their own freedom. It presupposes thereby a system of justice that is, at the same time, a regulated system of freedom.[40]

But what is justice and what is a just society? Already Aristotle pointed out that justice and injustice are ambiguous concepts. He himself understood justice as a concept of proportion, that is, as the median between too much and too little. Moreover, he knew that the law cannot regulate all of the many diverse situations in life and that justice; therefore, is dependent upon goodness as the higher value.[41]

Since the natural law foundation of justice, as it existed in Aristotle and in the medieval tradition until late into the modern period, was, to a large extent, abandoned in the modern period, the most varied interpretations of the concept of justice have been proposed.[42] A consensus is not in sight. Some regard talk of justice and a just society, in fact, as empty formulas and clichés that are suited for populist political propaganda and can be misused for the purposes of power. Fyodor Dostoevsky powerfully described this danger in his novel, *The Brothers Karamazov*, in the figure of the grand inquisitor. He showed how people, for the sake of getting some bread, are prepared to surrender their freedom at the feet of power and say: "Better that you enslave us, but feed us."[43] Democracy without values can very quickly be transformed into an overt or covert totalitarianism.[44]

Famous is the much-cited dictum from Ernst-Wolfgang Böckenförde, that democracy lives by presuppositions that it itself cannot guarantee.[45] If these presuppositions are no longer operative or if they are forgotten or displaced because they are regarded as self-evident, then we arrive at relativism, which currently is much criticized by the church and which no longer recognizes any absolute values, but makes decisions about everything according to a utilitarian or power calculus.[46] What is so dangerous about such relativism is the threat of its changing into a far more dangerous totalitarianism. If, after the end of metaphysics, which has been proclaimed by many, there is no final truth and no absolute values orienting and directing political action, then even the noblest democratic, political ideas are finally not only without a foundation; they are then without orientation and can be misused in a populist fashion. Tolerance can then very easily be converted into intolerance against anyone who dares to hold a conviction that departs from the mainstream. Indications of going in this dangerous direction are multiplying.

It is, therefore, good one more time to proceed from the general concept of justice, according to which justice is acting in such a way that allows each to get his or her due (*suum cuique*). The question, then, is: What is due to each person? Opinions differ on this question. The issue elicits recurring political debates. For the median between extremes envisioned by Aristotle cannot be determined once and for all. Time and again it must be determined anew in the concrete situation, and, because it is conditioned by different interests, it will then most often be debated and argued. In this process, Christians too can come to different opinions and alignments.

As soon as one addresses this issue in a fundamental way, the question arises: What does the human being need as a human being? What is due to him or her in order to be able to live in a way worthy of human beings, that is, to be able to live a self-determined life in moderation? Of course, for that purpose he or she needs bread to eat and an appropriate measure of material goods. How much or how little is enough is always debated and varies according to circumstances. In such arguments, however, what is very often forgotten is that what is due to a person as a human being is not only material goods and cannot be only material goods. Nothing would be so disastrous as if, after the failure and the end of ideological Marxism, its place would be taken by an individualism and consumerist social order of wealth that seek the happiness of human existence solely in material consumption. In that case, Marxist and communist materialism would be replaced by consumerist materialism. Both forms of materialism misjudge and disregard the true dignity of the human person. Both lead, albeit in different ways, to the objectification of the human person.

What is due to the human being as a human being, and that means as a free entity, is first and foremost the acknowledgment of his or her human dignity. What is owed to every human being on the basis of his or her dignity is personal respect, personal acceptance, and personal care. In this sense, one can understand justice as the minimal measure of love and love as the full measure of justice.[47]

The unconditional element, which we have largely lost with the often-proclaimed end of metaphysics, can arise anew for us in the encounter with the otherness of the other and with the unconditional acknowledgment that is owed to the other.[48] In the interpersonal encounter, something absolute is revealed that excludes every strict form of relativism. Concretely, this means that the demand for justice, which in concrete situations cannot be made in a totally unambiguous way, is to be interpreted in light of love and its unconditional claim. Practically, the demand for justice must be surpassed in loving and merciful care for the other.

Admittedly, we human beings come from a damaged mold; we have an inextinguishable tendency towards evil (Kant).[49] All of our interpersonal relationships are also influenced by it. Therefore, we cannot and are not permitted to proceed from an ideal situation of encounter. All of our relationships are burdened and impaired by injustice, which preceded us and, as it were, was inherited by us. Our relationships are also burdened and impaired by injustice that we ourselves experienced and that we ourselves have done. For the sake of the survival of a relationship, as well as for the sake of the survival of an entire society, it can be necessary to pardon severe violations of justice in the past and to be reconciled again. For only by means of such reconciliation can the vicious circle of guilt and retribution be broken—and with it a new cycle of guilt. Only in this way can a new beginning be made and a common future become possible. So, justice too lives because of forgiveness, reconciliation, and mercy, which—as has been shown—is defined by disclosing a way out of a desperate situation and offering a new future.

But what happens when there is such forgiveness and reconciliation? It does something that fundamentally is impossible per se; it pardons what, from the view of justice, is not at all pardonable. A murder, a gory war, and especially genocide are unpardonable. Forgiving such an unpardonable act that basically cannot be forgiven violates a sense of justice that is eager for retribution. But precisely by acting against the demand for retributive justice, forgiveness becomes the foundation and starting point of a new, just, and reconciled coexistence.[50]

Already Jesus was accusingly asked by what authority he could forgive sins. As a matter of fact, his opponents were right when they objected that only God could forgive (Mark 2:5–7). As human beings, we can help another to live with his or her guilt. But we cannot forgive it. Forgiveness is a creative new beginning that cannot be derived from the world. By forgiving and reconciling ourselves, we do "something" that we cannot make happen, something that is rather inaccessible to us and must be bestowed upon us. In the gift of reconciliation, in which communal life in justice is granted to us anew, we are pointing to "something" that is transcendent to us. In reconciliation, we bestow on the other "something" that we don't "have"; consciously or unconsciously, we are grasping after that which theologically is called grace and which scripture testifies is God's infinite mercy.

Ultimately, neither the demand for justice nor mercy, which is ready to pardon, can work out in this world. Perfect justice could be established only by means of a violent system, which itself then could only be an evil system. Whoever wants to create heaven on earth, as we know in the meantime from the bitter experience of totalitarian systems, installs not heaven, but hell on earth. That is also generally true for ecclesial perfectionists, who want to establish a church of the pure (καθαρός: Cathars) by force. The excesses of the Cathar movement, on the one hand, and of the Inquisition, on the other, should continue to make us recoil.

That is anything but an argument for doing nothing in society and in the church. On the contrary, we should and we must curb injustice and evil, as far as humanly possible. As far as possible, we must help justice and mercy achieve a breakthrough in society and in the church. Everywhere we can, in situations of physical or spiritual need, we should let the warm rays of mercy shine and thereby ignite a hope-bestowing light of love.

But in our world there are not only pitiless injustices and unrelenting perfectionism, there is also an unrelenting this-worldliness. Nowadays, it generally consists in the consolation of a purely this-worldly happiness and no longer in the consolation of the afterlife. This attitude wants perfect justice and full mercy, that is, perfect happiness right now—everything now and everything immediately. In this way, life moves ever faster; it becomes strenuous, demanding, indeed overwhelming. We not only work ourselves to death; we also enjoy ourselves to death. We demand that another's love should give us heaven on earth and, in the process, we overwhelm him or her without mercy.[51]

In light of injustice, which can never be completely abolished, and in light of mercy and love in this world, which can never be completely fulfilled, all that remains in the end, in many cases, is only an appeal to God's mercy. It alone can guarantee that, in the end, the murderer does not triumph over the innocent victim and that, in the end, what is right and just is meted out to all. Hope for eschatological justice and eschatological reconciliation at the resurrection of the dead makes life in this world truly livable and worthy of living. It bestows serenity as patient impatience and impatient patience.[52]

In the face of imminent despair or consumerist stupefaction, nothing else finally remains but to see the world and life in the light of hope for perfect justice and definitive reconciliation and to insist on it. Therefore, the cry of "Kyrie eleison" in this world will never be silenced, but will continually grow louder. That this cry can and may be voiced publicly belongs to the cultural legacy of the human race; it belongs to a culture of justice and mercy and to the humanitarianism of a truly free society.

MARY, MOTHER OF MERCY

1. Mary in the Gospels

HOLY SCRIPTURE AND THE CHURCH do not speak only abstractly and theoretically about God's mercy; the theology of scripture, like that of the church fathers, is a theology in images. In the person of Mary, they present us with a concrete image, indeed, a mirror image of divine mercy and an archetype of human and Christian mercy. Mary is a type of the church, and, therefore, she is also a type of Christian mercy.[1] This conviction has been deeply rooted in the religious consciousness of the church since the first centuries down to the present day in Catholic and Orthodox Christianity. Increasingly, this conviction is also gaining a greater place in the consciousness and hearts of many evangelical Christians.[2]

One may and, indeed, must certainly criticize many of the attempts to exaggerate Mary's status, which are to be assessed by the criterion of the Bible's testimony to Jesus Christ, who is the foundation—laid once and for all—and the permanent center of Christian faith. However, one must equally question a Marian minimalism that would frivolously, arrogantly, and somewhat smugly brush aside the evidence of countless Christians from every century, who, in their diverse internal and external difficulties, have appealed to the mother of God as the mother of mercy and have experienced her assistance and consolation—acting as if all of that was only exuberant pious emotions and Marian devotion going over-the-top. One must after all acknowledge: Mary appears in the gospel and, in fact, in a prominent position.

There are two texts above all in the New Testament that form a solid basis for Marian spirituality: the annunciation scene at the beginning of the gospel (Luke 1:26–38) and the scene at the end, in which Mary stands beneath the cross (John 19:26f.). The latter scene in John's Gospel refers back to the report about the wedding at Cana, which stands at the beginning of Jesus' public ministry (John 2:1–12). Thus, the scenes relevant for Mariology frame, so to speak, the entire gospel and, even when superficially considered, they accord Mary a prominent place in the history of salvation. By doing that, the few lines about Mary that are found in holy scripture make clear that Mary has an important role and unique significance in the story of God's dealings with us mortals.

The annunciation scene at the beginning of the gospel, like the entire prehistory to Jesus' public appearance, presents historical and literary-critical problems. What needs to be said in this context has already been said.[3] There it was already clear that an important theological significance accrues to this prehistory in Luke's conception of the gospel. In the prehistory, all of the important motifs of the gospel are already sounded, just like in a musical prelude. Thus, in the Magnificat, Mary summarizes the entire history of salvation and describes it as the story of God's mercy. "His mercy is…from generation to generation" (Luke 1:50). With her election and calling to become the mother of the redeemer, this history has entered upon its all-decisive and final phase. In his infinite mercy, God now makes his last, decisive, and conclusive attempt to save his people and to save humanity.

Mary is chosen to cooperate in this great work of redemption. She has "found favor with God" (Luke 1:30). That means: she is absolutely nothing on her own, but she is everything on account of pure grace. She is only the "servant of the Lord" (Luke 1:38). All of the glory belongs not to her, but to God alone, for whom nothing is impossible (Luke 1:37f.). Therefore she sings:

My soul magnifies the Lord,
  and my spirit rejoices in God my Savior....
For the Mighty One has done great things for me,
  and holy is his name.

(Luke 1:46–47, 49)

She is entirely a vessel and simply a humble instrument of God's mercy. Martin Luther brilliantly brought out this point in his exegesis of the Magnificat.[4] For him Mary is nothing less than an archetype of *sola gratia*, "by grace alone."

Because Mary exists only by grace, she also lives "by faith alone." She is an instrument of God's mercy by means of the faithful "yes" that she gives in reply to the angel's incomprehensible message, which initially surprises and overwhelms her. With her "yes," Mary defines herself as the handmaiden, essentially as the slave (δοῦλος) of the Lord. With this word, she expresses both her entire, purely passive availability as well as her active readiness to cooperate in the work of salvation. She gives God space for performing his miracle.[5] Even this "yes" to what exceeds the human capacity to imagine, she can only say as someone who has been blessed by God.

By this obedient "yes," Mary enabled the coming of God into this world. In this way, she has become the new Eve. Whereas the first Eve brought pain and suffering to humanity because of her disobedience, Mary, by her faithful obedience in the place of all humankind,[6] has loosed the knot of disobedience that Eve had tied. Thus she has become the mother of all the living.[7] By her obedient "yes," Mary became the handmaiden chosen and blessed by God to be his servant of mercy. Indeed, the fact that, for the work of mercy that only he could make possible, he chose and graciously enabled her—a human being and a simple young woman—to be the instrument of his mercy, this itself is an expression of divine mercy that exceeds every expectation and every human claim.

In the grace-filled election of Mary and in her faithful "yes," which clears a space for God to come into the world and which makes her the Christ-bearer, the ark of the new covenant, as well as the temple of the Holy Spirit, the church has become reality in Mary. She sums up in herself the history of the Old Testament people of God and, at the same time, she is the primordial cell of the New Testament people of God. She is this before the apostles were called and embarked on the plan. She, the representative of the little people and the voiceless of the land, the "woman of the people" as she is called in the church's hymn,[8] she is church because of God's pure mercy, even before the foundation was laid for what later became the hierarchically structured church. Even before that, she represents the church in her innermost being, as the one who lives entirely out of God's merciful grace and who has been chosen as his ready-for-service instrument. In light of Mary's preferential status, it is surely ideological delusion to say that the male-dominated church created an oppressive image of woman.[9] The opposite is the case. Mariology is the most radical critique of a pure male church that is theologically possible.

Mary too had to walk the pilgrim's path of faith. In her life, as reported in the Gospels, there are none of those wondrous things with which the apocryphal gospels and pious legends wish to embellish it. Quite to the contrary, Mary, the woman of the people, had to bear and survive many difficulties and hardships: childbirth in an emergency shelter; the flight to Egypt; the search for her child; her disconcertment over the public life of her son, whom she wanted to keep at home with his family; and finally her brave endurance under her son's cross. She was spared nothing.

Mary endured even the darkest night of the cross with her son. She did not evade it nor did she flee. It is expressly said: "She stood there," "*stabat mater iuxta crucem* [his mother stood near the cross]" (John 19:25). In the end, according to countless artistic representations of the Pietà, she held the battered body of her dead son on her lap—the most grievous experience of anguish that can befall a mother. Thus in the Magnificat, Mary not only anticipates the beatitudes of the poor, the sorrowful, and the persecuted in the Sermon on the Mount (Matt 5:2–12; Luke 6:20–26); she herself has had all of these experiences.

At the end of the fourth Gospel, the circle is closed. Mary, who stands at the beginning of the New Testament story of salvation, assumes an important position at its climax. For from the cross, Jesus entrusts Mary to John as his mother, and conversely he entrusts his disciple John to Mary as her son (John 19:26f.). This scene, again, is full of meaning. John is the disciple whom Jesus loved (John 19:26); in the fourth Gospel, he serves as the archetype of a disciple of Jesus. That means that, in John, Jesus entrusts all of his disciples to Mary as sons and, conversely, he entrusts Mary to all of his disciples.[10] One can understand these words of Jesus as his last will and testament. By doing this, Jesus says something that is decisive and binding for the future of the church.[11]

One does well to read the words of the fourth Gospel precisely. It says that from then on John took Mary to himself. More accurately, one has to translate the sentence: he took her "into his own" (εἰς τὰ ἴδια). Augustine has reflected extensively on what this "his own" means. According to him, it does not mean that John took Mary "into his possession;" rather, it means that he took her "into his sphere of activity."[12] Because John is said to be the disciple who remains until Christ comes again (John 21:22), then Mary is thereby assumed into John's "remaining" and into what endures of his testimony. Therefore, Mary permanently belongs in the gospel of God's mercy; she is permanently a witness and an instrument of divine mercy.

2. Mary in the Faith of the Church

The few spare but nevertheless central statements in holy scripture about Mary have burrowed deeply into the hearts of the faithful of every century and have found a resounding echo in Christian spirituality of every age. Mary herself prophetically predicted: "From now on all generations will call me blessed" (Luke 1:48). A living and rich tradition that continues to this day has developed out of the testimonies of the New Testament.

The most important dogmatic anchor of this living tradition was the Council of Ephesus (431 CE), which confessed Mary as the God-bearer (θεοτόκος).[13] In doing so, it is important to note that the fight over this honorific title, which was carried out primarily between Nestorius and Cyril of Alexandria, was not a mariological, but rather a christological debate. It dealt with the question whether Jesus is the son of God in reality and in terms of his hypostasis. Thus, from the very beginning, the mariological tradition was no alien, adventitious growth on Christology; rather, from the very beginning, it stands in relation to Christology and rests upon that foundation. Only in this way can the mariological tradition be—and continue to be—salutary and spiritually fruitful.

On this basis, many prayers, hymns, and songs in the history of Christianity have repeatedly taken up the statements of the New Testament, interpreted them spiritually, and made them fruitful. The most important are the testimonies of the liturgy. Besides them, there are countless sermons and treatises, already in the patristic period. This spiritual exegesis of scripture is found in all of the ecclesial traditions of the first millennium; it is found among the Greeks as well as among the Latins, among the Copts as well as among the Syrians and Armenians, in Russia as well as in the Latin West.[14] It has left noticeable traces even in the sixteenth-century Reformers' praise of Mary.[15]

That is expressed already in the oldest Marian prayer, which originated around 300 CE and is widely disseminated: "We fly to thy patronage, O holy Mother of God." Originally it read: "We fly to thy mercy, O Mother of God."[16] We find the same confident attitude in many later prayers. One can think of the *Ave Maris Stella* (Hail Star of the Sea), alternatively Star of the Sea, We Greet Thee (nineteenth century), where it says: "Show thyself a mother, that thy Infant may graciously hear the prayers of your children through thee."[17] In one of the best-known prayers to Mary, the *Salve Regina* (eleventh century), we appeal to Mary as "the mother of mercy" and ask her: "Turn thine eyes of mercy toward us." The Marian antiphon from the Advent and Christmas season, *Alma Redemptoris Mater* (twelfth century), likewise concludes with the cry *peccatorum miserere* (have mercy on sinners). In the litany of Loreto (the original version, going back to the Eastern Church, stems from the twelfth century), we call on Mary as "mother of divine mercy," "health of the sick," "refuge of sinners," "comforter of the afflicted," and "help of Christians." She was called upon as a helper in every affliction, not only in response to capricious acts of nature, in famines, pestilence, and hail, but also in the hardships of war and in response to violent rulers.

Already in the second century, the great church father Irenaeus of Lyons put it in a nutshell when he described Mary as the Undoer of Knots, the one who loosed again the knot that Eve had tied. Thus Mary has become the undoer of knots for many Christians.[18] She has helped them to undo the knots of the most varied sort in their personal lives, knots in human relationships, knots in their own soul, and not least knots caused by entanglement in sin and guilt.

Sometimes this piety has also sprouted strange blossoms, like in the description and portrayal of Mary as the "Madonna of the scoundrels," as the one who sided with failures and sinners, thieves and adulterers, and who was virtually regarded as their accomplice. This portrayal was not so much an expression of frivolity as it was a humorous expression of a solid understanding of faith, even if, on occasion, the mantel of mercy was spread somewhat too broadly.[19]

What was uttered with words in prayers throughout all of the centuries was also expressed in diverse ways in the visual and performing arts, above all in the pilgrimage paintings and devotional images [Gnadenbilder]* of Mary.[20] From the seventh to the ninth century, we find in Syria representations of Eleusa, the Tender One: Mary, who holds and caresses the divine child at her breast. The most famous icon of this type is the Virgin of Vladimir, which originated in the twelfth century in Constantinople and which today is located in the Tretyakov Gallery in Moscow. Reproductions are found in the West in the Notre Dame de Grace in Cambrai, in the Carmelite Madonna (Rome, St. Maria in Traspontina), and in Lucas Cranach's painting of Mary of Succor. Another famous icon that, according to tradition, stems from Luke the evangelist, but actually is to be dated from the thirteenth century, is venerated in St. Maria Maggiore in Rome as Salus Populi Romani. A replica is found in the

---

*Translator's note: A Gnadenbild was an image or statue of Mary before which a believer would pray, asking for her intercession in obtaining grace or a particular favor from her Son. Miraculous cures or healing were sometimes reported in the Middle Ages as a result of this devotional practice.

cocathedral* of St. Eberhard in Stuttgart, where it is called the Mother of Consolation. Finally, mention must be made of the gracious image of the Mother of Perpetual Help, which was painted according to a Byzantine prototype. In the fifteenth century, it was moved for security from Crete to Rome ahead of the advancing Turks. It is highly venerated in Rome, beyond whose borders it is well known as a devotional image.

Above all, mention must be made of the representations of the Pietà, the image of God's mother holding her dead son in her lap. We know of such representations since the fourteenth century. The most famous is the sculpture by Michelangelo in St. Peter's Basilica in Rome, a sculpture that is known throughout the world and is rightly much admired. In these representations, Mary is presented as the mother of all who are suffering, who are sorrowful, who are beleaguered, and who are in need of consolation. These depictions enable the pious viewer, especially countless mothers in a similar situation, to identify with Mary. Less well known are the representations of Mary's fainting, which belong in the same context.[21] They show how Mary shares in her son's falling into unconsciousness and how she is caught by God's merciful omnipotence. This too is an image of solace for many who have been overwhelmed by anguish or have begun to unravel, yet who receive power and strength in faith.

Finally, mention must be made of the representations of the *Mater Dolorosa* (the Sorrowful Mother), which derive from the early baroque period and show Mary's heart being pierced by a sword (Luke 2:35). Closely connected to this image is the representation of Mary's seven wounds by means of seven swords in her breast. These representations, which, at first glance, we nowadays find strange because of their realism, show how Mary shares in the cruel death of her son.

---

*Translator's note: A cocathedral is a cathedral church that shares the function of being a bishop's seat with another cathedral. Saint Eberhard in Stuttgart and Saint Martin in Rottenbrug are the two cocathedrals of the diocese of Rottenburg-Stuttgart in the state of Baden-Württemberg, Germany. Cardinal Kasper was bishop of this diocese from 1989 to 1999.

That every one of these portrayals is concerned not only with Mary as an individual figure, but is concerned with Mary as a type—as an archetype and model—providing reassurance for Christians, becomes clear in the representations of the Madonna with the Sheltering Cloak. The Sheltering Cloak Madonna in Ravensburg acquired special fame. It shows that in every adversity, especially in the dangers of war, we may know that we are safe under her maternal, protective cloak. According to ancient German law, by sheltering them under the mother's cloak, children born out of wedlock were declared to be children born of a marital union (*filii mantellati*). Thus, this representation also says: all of us, who are born in sin (cf. Ps 51:7), have been made children of God, according to the archetype and model of Mary, by divine mercy. The cloak motif is again found in the Marian hymn from the seventeenth century, *Maria breitet den Mantel aus*, in which the last strophe says: "O Mother of Mercy, spread your cloak over us."[22] I still remember very vividly the nights of bombing during the Second World War, when this song had a very realistic meaning for us.

3. Mary as Archetype of Mercy

What becomes impressively visible in many prayers and pictorial representations has found theological expression in Ambrose. In his commentary on Luke's Gospel, he describes Mary as the archetype (type) of the church.[23] The Second Vatican Council explicitly adopted this assertion.[24] As the first of those who are redeemed, Mary is the type, that is, the archetype of all the redeemed. As the mother of the redeemer, she is at the same time the mother of all the redeemed. In the order of grace, Mary is our mother.[25] The Second Vatican Council expressed this conviction, held by countless Christians, in the following way: "By her maternal charity, she takes care of the brethren of her Son, who still journey on earth surrounded by dangers and difficulties, until they are led into their blessed home."[26]

In the course of its history, the church has learned to understand Mary not only as a witness and archetype, but also as a special creature of divine mercy. Mary is redeemed just like all others who are redeemed, but, different from them, she was free of every stain of sin from the first moment of her existence.[27] The Eastern Church, for this reason, calls Mary the All Holy (Παναγία). In her and in her entire life, divine mercy, which opposes sin, represses it, and gives room to life, victoriously prevailed. Thus, she is a sign that the power of sin could not fundamentally foil God's original salvific plan for humanity. At the same time, she is the safe ark in the flood, the sacred remnant of humanity, and also the dawn of the new creation. The original beauty and the ultimate, perfect beauty of creatures shines in her beauty, which has been praised in the religious poetry and art of every century. She is the perfect creature. "In Mary we see, so to speak, the Creator's original plan and, at the same time, the goal: the redeemed man."[28]

Such statements may appear fanciful to a secularized way of thinking, with its stunted and poor understanding of reality, for which, paradoxically, nothing is as sacred as the profane. Nevertheless, a look at the literature in which Mary has been a constant theme down to this very day can disabuse us of this impression. One can think of Gretchen in Goethe's *Faust*: "O lean down, you who are full of sorrow, incline your countenance graciously to my distress!" The theme appears again in Romanticism, in the works of Brentano and Eichendorff. Hölderlin and Rilke also make use of the traditional material, even if not in an ecclesial and spiritual way, but they show, all the same, how Mary continues to have an effect as a transfigured exemplar and ideal image of humanity. The traditional elements are not only picked up in Gertrud von Le Fort's *Hymnen an die Kirche*, but are made present in powerful, poetic language.[29]

Speaking of Mary as a concrete mirror and special realization of divine mercy has not finished serving its usefulness, even in our modern world. This talk also shows us today that the Christian message of mercy has assumed concrete temporal and human form, so that we can grasp the transformative power of God's mercy not only with our heads, but also with our hearts.

Among all creatures, Mary embodies the gospel of divine mercy most purely and most beautifully. She is the purest creaturely representation of God's mercy and the mirror of what is the heart and sum of the Gospel. She radiates the total congeniality of divine mercy and displays the splendor and the all-transforming beauty that descends upon the world from God's gracious mercy. Precisely in the face of today's often austere living conditions and the often very flat or trite understanding of life, Mary can, therefore, be an archetype and shining model for a new culture of mercy. She can be that for the life of every Christian, for the church and its renewal on the basis of the idea of mercy, and, ultimately, for the construction of a culture of mercy in our society. Thus we can quite rightly describe Mary as the archetype and exemplar of a renewed Christian culture and spirituality of mercy.

The Catholic Church goes a step further. Mary is not only archetype and exemplar, she is also the merciful advocate of the church and of Christians. Thus, ever since the fifteenth century, the following request was added to the Hail Mary, the most famous and most widely disseminated Marian prayer, which traces its origin to the angel's and Elizabeth's greeting (Luke 1:28, 42): "Pray for us sinners, now and at the hour of our death."[30] Praying in this way is also not foreign to the young Martin Luther. In his exegesis of the Magnificat, he sees therein the hope for God's action through the mediation of a creature.[31] Thus he concludes his exegesis: "May Christ grant us this through the intercession and for the sake of His dear Mother Mary."[32]

Evangelical Christians today are usually worried that, by relying on such an intercessory prayer, the uniqueness of Jesus Christ's role as mediator runs into danger. That is a gross misunderstanding. Of course, we do not set Mary on a level with Christ or put her into competition with him. Indeed, Mary herself lives entirely and undividedly out of divine mercy. She points to the divine mercy revealed in Jesus Christ and bears witness to it. Then how should the church give Mary an independent role alongside Christ or a role supplemental to his? Mary takes nothing away from Christ and adds nothing to him, who is the only mediator of salvation.[33] In her intercession, rather, she actualizes, in a special and unique way, the representative advocacy for others that is supposed to be a distinguishing mark of every Christian. If one wanted to express what is meant in Scholastic terminology, then one could say: Mary lives and works entirely in the power of the first cause of salvation; enabled by and completely dependent on the first cause, she shares in it as a secondary cause.

Therefore, we do not worship Mary. Worship is due only and exclusively to God. But we venerate her above all other creatures as God's most perfect creature and as an instrument in God's hands.[34] For God is a God of human beings and he wants to effect his salvation for them through human beings. That too is a sign of his benevolence and his mercy, which shines in Mary in an exemplary and unique way.

Thus, Mary sums up in herself the greatest mysteries of faith and radiates them outward.[35] In her shines an image of the new, redeemed, and reconciled person and the new, transformed world that can fascinate us in its inimitable beauty and should pull us out of much torpor and indigence. Mary says to us and shows us: the good news of God's mercy in Jesus Christ is the best thing that can ever be said to us and the best thing that we can ever hear. At the same time, it is the most beautiful thing there can be because it can transform us and our world by means of God's glory, expressed in his gracious mercy. This mercy is God's gift and, simultaneously, our task as Christians. We are supposed to enact mercy. We should live it in word and deed and give witness to it. In this way, our often dark and cold world can become somewhat warmer, lighter, more endearing, and more worth living because of a ray of mercy. Mercy is the reflection of God's glory in this world and the epitome of the message of Jesus Christ, which was given to us as a gift and which we are to further bestow on others.

NOTES

Translator's Preface

1. See Friedrich Kluge, *An Etymological Dictionary of the German Language*, trans. from 4th German edition by John Francis Davis (New York: Macmillan & Co., 1891), 20.

2. Friedrich Kluge, *Etymologisches Wörterbuch der deutschen Sprache*, 17. Auflage, unter Mithilfe von Alfred Schirmer, bearbeitet von Walther Mitzka (Berlin: Walter de Gruyter & Co., 1957), 52–53.

3. *Oxford English Dictionary*, 2nd ed., 20 vols., ed. J. A. Simpson and E. S. C. Weiner (Oxford: Clarendon Press, 1989), 9:625–26.

I

1. For an extensive analysis of the theodicy question, see chap. V, 7.

2. Odo Marquard, "Der angeklagte und der entlastete Mensch in der Philosophie des 18. Jahrhunderts," in *Abschied vom Prinzipiellen* (Stuttgart: Reclam, 1981), 39–66.

3. Fyodor M. Dostoevsky, *The Brothers Karamazov*, trans. Richard Pevear and Larissa Volokhonsky (New York: Vintage Classics, 1991), 242–43.

4. Cited by Eugen Biser, *Interpretation und Veränderung: Werk und Wirkung Romano Guardinis* (Paderborn: Schöningh, 1979), 132f.

5. Concerning the older atheism problematic, see Walter Kasper, *The God of Jesus Christ*, trans. Matthew J. O'Connell (New York: Crossroad, 1986), 16–46. Concerning the so-called "new atheism," see Magnus Striet, ed., *Wiederkehr des Atheismus: Fluch oder Segen für die Theologie?* (Freiburg i. Br.: Herder, 2008); Gregor M. Hoff, *Die neuen Atheismen: Eine notwendige Provokation* (Kevelaer: Topos, 2009).

6. See Jürgen Habermas, *Glauben und Wissen* (Frankfurt a. M.: Suhrkamp, 2001), 27f.

7. Jürgen Habermas et al., *An Awareness of What is Missing: Faith and Reason in a Post-Secular Age*, trans. Ciaran Cronin (Malden, MA: Polity Press, 2010), 15–23.

8. Jürgen Habermas, *Zeitdiagnosen: Zwölf Essays 1980-2001* (Frankfurt a. M.: Suhrkamp, 2003), 47.

9. Albert Camus, *The Myth of Sisyphus and Other Essays*, trans. Justin O'Brien (New York: Vintage Books, 1955), 3.

10. Rüdiger Safranski, *Romantik: Eine deutsche Affäre* (München: C. Hanser, 2007).

11. Friedrich Nietzsche, *The Gay Science*, trans. Walter Kaufmann (New York: Vintage Books, 1974), 167, 181–82, 279–80.

12. Nietzsche, *The Gay Science*, 181.

13. Martin Heidegger, *Elucidations of Hölderlin's Poetry*, trans. Keith Hoeller (New York: Humanity Books, 2000), 46.

14. Martin Buber, *Eclipse of God: Studies in the Relation between Religion and Philosophy* (New York: Harper, 1952), 13–24.

15. Second Vatican Council, *Gaudium et Spes*, sec. 19. Official translation from: http://www.vatican.va/archive/hist_councils/ii_vatican _council/documents/vat-ii_const_19651207_gaudium-et-spes_en.html.

16. Max Horkheimer, *Die Sehnsucht nach dem ganz Anderen: Ein Interview mit Kommentar von H. Gumnior* (Hamburg: Furche, 1970), 69.

17. Theodor W. Adorno, *Negative Dialektik* (Frankfurt a. M.: Suhrkamp, 1966), 376.

18. Theodor Adorno, *Minima Moralia: Reflections from Damaged Life*, trans. E. F. N. Jephcott (New York: Verso, 1978), 247.

19. See chap. II, 1.

20. Robert Spaemann, *Das unsterbliche Gottesgerücht: Die Frage nach Gott und die Täuschung der Moderne* (Stuttgart: Klett-Cotta, 2007).

21. For the complex topic of secularization, see this standard work: Charles Taylor, *A Secular Age* (Cambridge, MA: Harvard University Press, 2007).

22. See Kasper, *The God of Jesus Christ*, 7–12.

23. Augustine, *Confessions*, VI, 16. This translation from *The Confessions of St. Augustine*, trans. F. J. Sheed (New York: Sheed & Ward, 1943), 126.

24. Augustine, *Confessions*, VI, 7. F. J. Sheed translation, 116.

25. Pope John XXIII, *Il giornale dell'anima e altri scritti di pietà*, a cura di L. F. Capovilla (Milan: Edizioni paoline, 1989), 452.

26. Pope John XXIII, *Il giornale dell'anima*, 149.

27. Pope John XXIII, "Opening Speech to the Council," in *The Documents of Vatican II*, ed. Walter M. Abbott (New York: Guild Press, 1966), 716.

28. Pope John XXIII, *Il giornale dell'anima*, 465.

29. See Walter Kasper, *Katholische Kirche: Wesen–Wirklichkeit–Sendung* (Freiburg i. Br.: Herder, 2011), 32, 39–41, 453f. Translator's note: An English translation, entitled *The Catholic Church: Nature, Reality and Mission*, is expected to be published in 2014.

30. For a good compilation of texts, see Pope John Paul II, *Barmherzigkeit Gottes: Quelle der Hoffnung* (Einsiedeln: Johannes, 2011). There are a number of publications about Pope John Paul II's contribution to the topic of mercy. Only two are mentioned here: Christoph von Schönborn, *We Have Found Mercy: The Mystery of Divine Mercy* (San Francisco: Ignatius Press, 2012). Edith Olk, *Die Barmherzigkeit Gottes als zentrale Quelle des christlichen Lebens* (St. Ottilien: EOS, 2011). This latter book offers a detailed overview of other contributions.

31. Pope John Paul II, *Dives in Misericordia* (1980): Mit einem Kommentar von K. Lehmann (Freiburg i. Br.: Herder, 1981).

32. *Tagebuch der Schwester Maria Faustina Kowalska* (Hauteville: Parvis-Verlag, 1996). Cf. Hans Buob, *Die Barmherzigkeit Gottes und der Menschen: Heilmittel für Seele und Leib nach dem Tagebuch der Schwester Faustina* (Fremdingen: UNIO-Verlag, 2007).

33. Pope John Paul II, *Memory and Identity: Conversations at the Dawn of a Millennium* (New York: Rizzoli, 2005), 55.

34. See chap. III and IV.

35. Franz Diekamp devotes just eleven lines to mercy and treats it alongside other divine attributes. For a dogmatic theology that is supposedly structured according to the principles of Saint Thomas, in whose theology are found many magnificent statements about mercy, this is strange. See his *Katholische Dogmatik nach den Grundsätzen des heiligen Thomas*, Bd. 1, (Münster: Aschendorff, 1957), 225. Joseph Pohle and Joseph Gummersbach treat mercy almost like an appendix, discussing it as the last of the divine attributes. See their *Lehrbuch der Dogmatik*, Bd. 1, (Paderborn: Schöningh, 1952), 338–40. In Ludwig Ott's dogmatics, mercy takes up about a page in his treatment of God's moral attributes: *Grundriss*

katholischer Dogmatik (Freiburg i. Br.: Herder, 1970), 57f. In Michael Schmaus's dogmatics, mercy takes up two and a half pages, but again towards the end of the 678 pages that deal with the doctrine of God and, consequently, in a place where it can exercise no determinative influence on the dogmatic system. See Schmaus's *Katholische Dogmatik*, Bd. 1 (München: Hueber, 1960). There is a brief reference to mercy in the doctrine of creation in Wolfgang Beinert's book: *Glaubenszugänge: Lehrbuch der katholischen Dogmatik*, Bd. 1 (Paderborn: Schöningh, 1995), 392. These are merely samples, which can be easily multiplied.

36. In *Mysterium salutis: Grundriss heilsgeschichtlicher Dogmatik*, Bd. 2 (Einsiedeln: Benziger Verlag, 1967), God's mercy is mentioned only in passages dealing with biblical theology, but it is not discussed systematically (264, 268, 279, 1113). This is also true of *Initiation à la pratique de la théologie* by Bernard Lauret und François Refoulé, (Paris: Editions du Cerf, 1983), vol. 3 (German edition: *Neue Summe Theologie*, hrsg. von Peter Eicher, Bd. 1 [Freiburg i. Br.: Herder, 1988]). There is nothing to report concerning the *Handbuch der Dogmatik* by Theodor Schneider, Bd. 1 (Düsseldorf: Patmos Verlag, 1992); Gerhard Ludwig Müller's overall presentation, *Katholische Dogmatik*, (Freiburg i. Br.: Herder, 1995), 238 and 241; and Harald Wagner's *Dogmatik* (Stuttgart: Kohlhammer, 2003), 361ff. It is surprising that Otto Hermann Pesch, in his dogmatics, which is formulated with an eye to ecumenical experience, does not devote a single word to God's mercy, even though it certainly must have arisen from the perspective of Luther's experience: *Katholische Dogmatik*, Bd. I/2 (Ostfildern: Matthias-Grünewald Verlag, 2008). Unfortunately, I cannot exclude myself from this criticism. Even I overlooked and passed over the idea of mercy in my exposition of the doctrine of God in *The God of Jesus Christ*.

37. A laudable exception, first and foremost, is Matthias Joseph Scheeben, *Handbuch der katholischen Dogmatik*, Bd. 2 (Freiburg i. Br.: Herder, 1948), § 101, 265–67. A positive example from more recent theology is Bertrand de Margerie, *Les perfections du Dieu de Jésus Christ* (Paris: Cerf, 1981), 255–68.

38. See chap. V, 1.

39. See chap. V, 6.

40. Thomas Aquinas, *Summa theologiae*, pt. I, q. 21 a. 3.

41. See chap. III.

42. As Otto Pesch rightly observes. See his article, "Gerechtigkeit

Gottes II," *Lexikon für Theologie und Kirche*, 3rd ed., ed. Walter Kasper et al. (Freiburg: Herder, 1993–2001), 6:506.

43. *Official Common Statement of the Lutheran World Federation and the Catholic Church* and the *Joint Declaration on the Doctrine of Justification* (October 31, 1999). Both documents are available at the official Vatican website: http://www.vatican.va/roman_curia/pontifical _councils/chrstuni/sub-index/index_lutheran-fed.htm. Cf. chap. V, 3.

44. Karl Marx, "A Contribution to the Critique of Hegel's 'Philosophy of Right,'" in *Critique of Hegel's "Philosophy of Right,"* trans. Annette Jolin and Joseph O'Malley (Cambridge: Cambridge University Press, 1970), 131.

45. See chap. VIII, 1.

46. Daniil Granin, *Die verlorene Barmherzigkeit: Eine russische Erfahrung* (Freiburg i. Br.: Herder, 1993).

47. Friedrich Nietzsche, *Human, All Too Human*, trans. R. J. Hollingdale (New York: Cambridge University Press, 1996), 55–56.

48. Friedrich Nietzsche, *Thus Spake Zarathustra*, trans. Thomas Common (New York: Carlton House, no date), 93–96.

49. Friedrich Nietzsche, *Ecce Homo*, trans. Duncan Large (New York: Oxford University Press, 2007), 95.

50. Nietzsche, *Thus Spake Zarathustra*, 168; *Ecce Homo*, 76.

51. Friedrich Nietzsche, *Beyond Good and Evil: Prelude to a Philosophy of the Future*, trans. Helen Zimmern (London: George Allen & Unwin Ltd., 1967), 227–30.

52. Friedrich Nietzsche, *Aus dem Nachlass der Achtzigerjahre*, in *Friedrich Nietzsche: Werke in Drei Bänden*, ed. Karl Schlechta (Munich: Carl Hanser Verlag, 1956), 521.

53. See chap. VIII.

54. Additional examples in Käte Hamburger, *Das Mitleid* (Stuttgart: Klett-Cotta, 2001). Hamburger holds the view that compassion is a distancing and ethically neutral phenomenon. Nina Gülcher and Imelda von der Lühe respond critically in *Ethik und Ästhetik des Mitleids* (Freiburg i. Br.: Rombach, 2007).

55. Carl Rogers, "Empathie–eine unterschätzte Seinsweise," in Carl Rogers and Rachel L. Rosenberg, *Die Person als Mittelpunkt der Wirklichkeit* (Stuttgart: Klett-Cotta, 1980). Cf. K. Hilpert, "Mitleid," *Lexikon für Theologie und Kirche*, 3rd ed., 7:334–37.

56. Johann Baptist Metz, Lothar Kuld, Adolf Weisbrod, eds.,

Compassion: Weltprogramm des Christentums: Soziale Verantwortung lernen (Freiburg i. Br.: Herder, 2000). Cf. D. Mieth, "Mitleid," in the same volume, 21–25.

57. Originally as an essay in the *Süddeutsche Zeitung*, Dec. 24, 2007. It was then published as "Compassion: Zu einem Weltprogramm des Christentums im Zeitalter des Pluralismus der Religionen und Kulturen," in Metz, Kuld, and Weisbrod, *Compassion*, 9–18.

58. Above all, see Johann Baptist Metz, "Plädoyer für mehr Theodizee-Empfindlichkeit in der Theologie," in *Worüber man nicht schweigen kann*, ed. Willi Oelmüller et al. (Munich: W. Fink Verlag, 1992), 125–37; "Theodizee-empfindliche Gottesrede," in Johann Baptist Metz, *Landschaft aus Schreien: Zur Dramatik der Theodizeefrage* (Mainz: Matthias Grünewald,1995), 81–102; Metz, *Memoria Passionis: Ein provozierendes Gedächtnis in pluraler Gesellschaft* (Freiburg i. Br.: Herder, 2006).

59. See Peter Hünermann and Adel Theodor Khoury, eds., *Warum leiden? Die Antwort der Weltreligionen* (Freiburg i. Br.: Herder, 1987).

II

1. In what follows, only a few references are possible. A comprehensive, historical, and philosophical presentation can be found in: L. Samson, "Mitleid," *Historisches Wörterbuch der Philosophie*, ed. Joachim Ritter, Karlfried Gründer, and Gottfried Gabriel (Basel: Schwabe Verlag, 1971–2007), 5:1410–16; R. Hauser and J. Stöhr, "Barmherzigkeit," *Historisches Wörterbuch der Philosophie* 1:754f. Dirk Ansorge provides a comprehensive presentation: *Gerechtigkeit und Barmherzigkeit Gottes: Die Dramatik von Vergebung und Versöhnung in bibeltheologischer, theologiegeschichtlicher und philosophiegeschichtlicher Perspektive* (Freiburg i. Br.: Herder, 2009).

2. See chap. III, 1.

3. Friedrich Kluge and Elmar Seebold, *Etymologisches Wörterbuch der deutschen Sprache*, 23rd ed. (Berlin: De Gruyter, 1999), 82.

4. Plato, *Apology*, 34 c ff.; Republic, 415 c.

5. Aristotle, *Rhetoric*, 1385 b.

6. Aristotle, *Poetics*, 1449 b.

7. Seneca, *On Clemency*, II, 6.

8. Augustine, *City of God*, IX, 5.

9. Thomas Aquinas, *Summa theologiae*, pt. I, q. 21 a. 3; pt. II/II, q. 30 a. 1 ad 2, a. 2 and 3; *Super Ioannem* 2, lect. 1, n. 3.

10. Thomas Aquinas, *Summa theologiae*, pt. II/II, q. 30 a. 1 c. a.

11. Thomas Aquinas, *Summa theologiae*, pt. I, q. 21 a. 3. Cf. Bertrand de Margerie, *Les perfections du Dieu de Jésus Christ* (Paris: Cerf, 1981), 255–57.

12. Yves Congar, "La miséricorde: Attribut souverain de Dieu," *Vie spirituelle* 106 (1962): 380–95; Cf. Ansorge, *Gerechtigkeit und Barmherzigkeit Gottes*, 301–26; Edith Olk, *Die Barmherzigkeit Gottes als zentrale Quelle des christlichen Lebens* (St. Ottilien: EOS, 2011), 97–102.

13. Thomas Aquinas, *Summa theologiae*, pt. I, q. 21, a. 1 ad 2 and 3.

14. Thomas Aquinas, *Summa theologiae*, pt. I, q. 21, a. 3 ad 2. For more details, see chap. V, 1.

15. Cf. chap. VII, 4.

16. See bk. IV of *Émile*: Jean-Jacques Rousseau, *Émile or On Education*, trans. Allan Bloom (New York: Basic Books, 1979), 221–24.

17. Henning Ritter, *Nahes und fernes Unglück: Versuch über das Mitleid* (Munich: C.H. Beck, 2004). Cf. also Norbert Bolz, *Diskurs über die Ungleichheit: Ein Anti-Rousseau* (Munich: Wilhelm Fink, 2009).

18. Gotthold Ephraim Lessing, *Hamburg Dramaturgy*, trans. Helen Zimmern with a new introduction by Victor Lange (New York: Dover, 1962). See esp. essay #74, 175–78.

19. Lessing's letter to Friedrich Nicolai, November 1756, in *Lessings Briefwechsel mit Mendelssohn und Nicolai über das Trauerspiel*, ed. Robert Petsch (Leipzig: Dürrsche Buchhandlung, 1910), 50–57.

20. Friedrich Schiller, "Was kann eine gute, stehende Schaubühne eigentlich wirken?" (1784), in *Schillers Werke* (Frankfurt a. M.: Insel, 1966), IV:7–19; "Über den Grund des Vergnügens an tragischen Gegenständen," IV:60–73. Cf. Schiller, "The Stage Considered as a Moral Institution" in *Friedrich Schiller: An Anthology for Our Time*, trans. Frederick Ungar (New York: Frederick Ungar, 1959), 263–83.

21. G. W. F. Hegel, *Aesthetics: Lectures on Fine Art*, trans. T. M. Knox, 2 vols. (New York: Oxford University, 1975), 2:1198.

22. Arthur Schopenhauer, *The Basis of Morality*, trans. Arthur Brodrick Bullock (London: Swan Sonnenschein, 1903), 170.

23. Immanuel Kant, *Groundwork of the Metaphysic of Ethics, in The Metaphysic of Ethics*, trans. J.W. Semple (Edinburgh: T &T Clark, 1871), 51.

24. Immanuel Kant, *The Metaphysic of Morals*, Part II in *Immanuel Kant: The Doctrine of Virtue*, trans. Mary J. Gregor (Philadelphia: University of Pennsylvania, 1964), 126.

25. Kant, *Metaphysic of Morals*, 126.

26. Immanuel Kant, *Critique of Practical Reason and Other Writings in Moral Philosophy*, trans. Lewis White Beck (Chicago: University of Chicago, 1949), 236, 244ff.

27. Kant, *Critique of Practical Reason*, 245–46.

28. Immanuel Kant, *Religion within the Boundaries of Mere Reason and Other Writings*, trans. Allen Wood and George DiGiovanni (New York: Cambridge University, 1998), 58–59.

29. Kant, *Religion within the Boundaries of Mere Reason*, 65–73.

30. Kant, *Religion within the Boundaries of Mere Reason*, 71. Cf. Ansorge, *Gerechtigkeit und Barmherzigkeit Gottes*, 435f. Helmut Hoping, *Freiheit im Widerspruch: Eine Unter-suchung zur Erbsündenlehre im Ausgang von Immanuel Kant* (Wien: Tyrolia Verlag, 1990).

31. In this context, we don't need to go again into Nietzsche's criticism of pity and mercy. See chap. I, 4.

32. Edith Stein, *Zum Problem der Einfühlung* (Freiburg i. B.: Herder, 2010).

33. Max Scheler, *Wesen und Formen der Sympathie* (Bonn: Cohen, 1926).

34. Max Horkheimer and Theodor W. Adorno, *Dialectic of Enlightenment*, trans. John Cumming (New York: Herder and Herder, 1972), 101–3, 119. Theodor W. Adorno, *Negative Dialektik* (Frankfurt a. M.: Suhrkamp, 1966), 279f. and 356.

35. Walter Schulz, *Philosophie in der veränderten Welt* (Pfullingen: Neske, 1972), 749–51, here 751.

36. Emmanuel Levinas, *Die Spur des Anderen: Untersuchungen zur Phänomenologie und Sozialphilosophie*, trans.W. N. Krewani (Freiburg i. Br.: Karl Alber, 1999); Bernhard Casper, *Angesichts des Anderen: Emmanuel Levinas–Elemente seines Denkens* (Paderborn: Schöningh, 2009).

37. Ansorge, *Gerechtigkeit und Barmherzigkeit Gottes*, 469–86.

38. See Martin Heidegger, *Being and Time*, trans. Joan Stambaugh (Albany, NY: State University of New York, 1996), 17–23.

39. Jacques Derrida and M. Wieviorka, "Jahrhundert der Vergebung" in *Lettre internationale* 48 (2000): 10–18, quoted in Jan-Heiner

Tück, "Versuch über die Auferstehung," *Internationale Katholische Zeitschrift* 31 (2002): 279 n. 25.

40. Plato, *Republic,* 509 b 9f.

41. Ansorge, *Gerechtigkeit und Barmherzigkeit Gottes*, 486–504. Jacques Derrida's position was often critically analyzed. Criticism came from analytic philosophy. Noam Chomsky criticized Derrida for a lack of clarity and indeed for a pretentious and abstruse rhetoric. Criticism has also come from critical theory, esp. from Jürgen Habermas. See his "Die Moderne–ein unvollendetes Projekt" in *Habermas, Kleine Politische Schriften* (I-IV) (Frankfurt a. M.: Suhrkamp, 1981), 444–64.

42. Paul Ricœur, *Liebe und Gerechtigkeit, Amour et Justice* (Tübingen: J.C.B. Mohr, 1990). Cf. Ansorge, *Gerechtigkeit und Barmherzigkeit Gottes*, 504–24.

43. Jean-Luc Marion, *Being Given: Toward a Phenomenology of Givenness*, trans. Jeffrey L. Kosky (Stanford: Stanford University, 2002).

44. Jean-Luc Marion, *The Crossing of the Visible*, trans. James K. A. Smith (Stanford: Stanford University, 2004).

45. Cf. Walter Kasper, *Katholische Kirche: Wesen–Wirklichkeit–Sendung* (Freiburg i. Br.: Herder, 2011), 91–93, 99–101, 156–59. Also see what is said in n. 68 concerning the problem of determination in connection with Thomas Aquinas.

46. Karl Rahner, *Hearers of the Word*, rev. ed. Johannes B. Metz (Montréal: Palm Publishers, 1969). Concerning the context and background, as well as discussion about Rahner's position, see vol. 4 of the *Gesamtausgabe der Werke von Karl Rahner* (Freiburg i. Br.: Herder, 1997).

47. Above all, mention should be made of Thomas Pröpper, whose views are summarized in *Theologische Anthropologie*, 2 Bde. (Freiburg i. Br.: Herder, 2011); and Hans-Jürgen Verweyen, *Gottes letztes Wort: Grundriss der Fundamentaltheologie*, (Düsseldorf: Patmos Verlag, 1991). I cannot explore here the discussion that has developed between these two proposals.

48. *Nostra Aetate*, "Declaration on the Relation of the Church to Non-Christian Religions," sec. 1. Official translation from the Vatican website: http://www.vatican.va/archive/hist_councils/ii_vatican_council/documents/vat-ii_decl_19651028_nostra-aetate_en.html.

49. Helmut von Glasenapp, *Die fünf Weltreligionen* (Düsseldorf: Eugen Diederichs Verlag, 1963); Emma Brunner-Traut, ed., *Die fünf grossen Weltreligionen* (Freiburg i. Br.: Herder, 1974).

50. Concerning Hinduism, see P. Hacker, G. Oberhammer, H. Bürkle, A. Michaels. For a summary, see Heinrich von Stietencron, *Der Hinduismus* (München: Beck, 2006).

51. See H. Bürkle, "Hinduismus," VII und X, *Lexikon für Theologie und Kirche*, 3rd ed., ed. Walter Kasper et al. (Freiburg: Herder, 1993–2001), 5:139–42.

52. Concerning Buddhism, see H. M. Enomya-Lasalle, H. Dumoulin, H. Waldenfels. For a summary, see Michael von Brück, *Einführung in den Buddhismus* (Frankfurt a. M.: Verlag der Weltreligionen, 2007).

53. Concerning Islam, see Annemarie Schimmel, *Im Namen Allahs des Allbarmherzigen: Der Islam* (Düsseldorf: Patmos Verlag, 2002); Schimmel, *Die Religion des Islam: Eine Einführung* (Stuttgart: Reclam, 2010); Tilman Nagel, *The History of Islamic Theology from Muhammad to the Present*, trans. Thomas Thornton (Princeton: Markus Weiner, 2000); Bassam Tibi, *Die islamische Herausforderung: Religion und Politik im Europa des 21. Jahrhunderts* (Darmstadt: Wissenschaftliche Buchgesellschaft, 2008). Concerning the relation of the Bible to the Quran, see: Joachim Gnilka, *Bibel und Koran: Was sie verbindet, was sie trennt* (Freiburg i. Br.: Herder, 2004); Gnilka, *Der Nazarener und der Koran: Eine Spurensuche* (Freiburg i. Br.: Herder, 2007).

54. *Nostra Aetate*, sec. 3.

55. This is the oft-quoted thesis from Hans Küng. See his *Global Responsibility: In Search of a New World Ethic*, trans. John Bowden (New York: Crossroad, 1991), 75–76.

56. *Nostra Aetate*, sec. 2.

57. Concerning the foundation of interreligious dialogue, see Kasper, *Katholische Kirche*, 439–52.

58. See H. P. Mathys, R. Heiligenthal, and H. H. Schrey, "Goldene Regel," *Theologische Realenzyklopädie*, ed. Gerhard Müller, Horst Balz, and Gerhard Krause (Berlin: Walter de Gruyter, 1977–2007), 13:570–83; H. H. Schrey, "Goldene Regel," *Historisches Wörterbuch der Philosophie*, 8:450–64; A. Sand and G. Hunold, "Goldene Regel," *Lexikon für Theologie und Kirche*, 3rd ed., 4:821–23.

59. See Paul Billerbeck and Hermann Leberecht Struck, eds., *Kommentar zum Neuen Testament aus Talmud und Midrasch* (Munich: C.H. Beck, 1985–89), 1:459f.

60. See Heinz Schürmann, *Das Lukasevangelium* (Freiburg i. Br.: Herder, 1969), 349–52; Ulrich Luz, *Matthew 1-7: A Commentary*, trans. James E. Crouch, Hermeneia (Minneapolis: Fortress, 2007), 362–68; Joachim Gnilka, *Das Matthäusevangelium* (Freiburg i. Br.: Herder, 1986), 264–68. In light of these interpretations, Rudolf Bultmann's opinion, that the Golden Rule is a morality of naïve egoism, may be regarded as outdated. See Rudolf Bultmann, *The History of the Synoptic Tradition*, trans. John Marsh (New York: Harper & Row, 1963), 103.

61. Augustine, *On Order*, II, 25; *Confessions*, I, 18, 29; *Expositions on the Psalms*, 57, 1f.; Sermon, IX, 14. Cf. Eberhard Schockenhoff, *Das umstrittene Gewissen: Eine theologische Grundlegung* (Mainz: Matthias-Grünewald Verlag, 1990), 70–77.

62. The Golden Rule was fundamental especially for the World Ethic Project, which Hans Küng developed and which has attracted a lot of attention since then. See Küng, *Global Responsibility*, 58–59.

63. We cannot engage in further consideration here of the problem of religious violence, a problem that has been raised particularly by J. Assmann and René Girard and currently is much discussed. Reference to the Golden Rule, nonetheless, demonstrates that we have to be careful with generalizing judgments. This is particularly true with regard to the Old Testament. Concerning this issue, see: J. Niewiadomski, "Unbekömmlicher Monotheismus? Der christliche Gott unter Generalverdacht," in *Streitfall Gott: Zugänge und Perspektiven*, Herder Korrespondenz Spezial, ed. Ulrich Ruh et al. (Freiburg i. B.: Herder, 2011), 6–11; J.-H. Tück, "Arbeit am Gottesbegriff: Ein Erkundungsgang anhand jüngerer Veröffentlichungen," in the same volume, 24f.

64. Augustine, *City of God*, bk. XIV, 8.

65. Immanuel Kant, *Groundwork of the Metaphysic of Morals*, trans. by H. J. Paton (New York: Harper Torchbooks, 1964), 97.

66. *Didache*, 1:2f.; Justin Martyr, *Dialogue with Trypho*, 93:2; Clement of Alexandria, *The Instructor*, II, 2.

67. Thomas Aquinas, *Summa theologiae*, pt. I/II, q. 100 a. 11; cf. pt. III q. 84 a. 7 ad 1; q. 60 a. 5; q. 61 a. 3 ad 2. The problem has already been encountered in the relation of philosophy and theology (see sec. 1 of chap. II and n. 46 previously). We will again encounter this problem when determining the relation of the philosophical and the theological understandings of God (chap. V, 1) as well as the relation of a monotheistic and a trinitarian understanding of God (chap. V, 2).

68. In similar fashion, Martin Luther subjected the Golden Rule to a critical interpretation. See Schrey, "Goldene Regel," *Historisches Wörterbuch der Philosophie*, 576f.

III

1. Friedrich Nietzsche, *Beyond Good and Evil*, trans. Helen Zimmern (London: Allen & Unwit), 3.

2. For understanding the imprecatory psalms, see E. Zenger, "Fluchpsalmen," *Lexikon für Theologie und Kirche*, 3rd ed., ed. Walter Kasper et al. (Freiburg: Herder, 1993–2001), 3:1335f. Also see chap. II previously, n. 62.

3. Helmut Köster, "σπλάγχνον," *Theologisches Wörterbuch zum Neuen Testament*, ed. Gerhard Kittell et al. (Stuttgart: Kohlhammer, 1949–79), 7:553–57.

4. Rudolf Bultmann, "οἰκτίρω," *Theologisches Wörterbuch zum Neuen Testament*, 5:162f.

5. F. Baumgärtel and J. Behm, "καρδία," *Theologisches Wörterbuch zum Neuen Testament*, 3:609–16; Hans Walter Wolff, *Anthropologie des Alten Testaments* (Munich: Kaiser, 1973), 68–95.

6. Abraham Joshua Heschel, *The Prophets* (New York: Harper & Row, 1975); Peter Kuhn, *Gottes Selbsterniedrigung in der Theologie der Rabbinen* (Munich: Kösel Verlag, 1968); Peter Kuhn, *Gottes Trauer und Klage in der rabbinischen Überlieferung* (Leiden: E.J. Brill, 1978).

7. Rudolf Bultmann, "ἔλεος," *Theologisches Wörterbuch zum Neuen Testament*, 2:474–82.

8. Walther Zimmerli, "χάρις," *Theologisches Wörterbuch zum Neuen Testament*, 9:366–77.

9. Gen 18:18; 22:18; 26:4; 18:14; Sir 44:21; Gal 3:6–18.

10. See W. Beyer, "εὐλογέω, εὐλογία," *Theologisches Wörterbuch zum Neuen Testament* 2:751–63.

11. For this formulation and point of view, I am indebted to the beautiful book by Gerhard Lohfink and Ludwig Weimer: *Maria–nicht ohne Israel: Eine neue Sicht der Lehre von der Unbefleckten Empfängnis* (Freiburg i. Br.: Herder, 2008).

12. For the interpretation of the name Yahweh, see Walther Zimmerli, "Ich bin Jahwe," in *Gottes Offenbarung: Gesammelte Aufsätze zum Alten Testament* (Munich: Kaiser, 1963); Gerhard von Rad, *Old Testament Theology*, trans. D. M. G. Stalker (New York: Harper, 1962).

For more recent research, see M. Rose, "Jahwe," *Theologische Realenzyklopädie*, ed. Gerhard Müller, Horst Balz, and Gerhard Krause (Berlin: Walter de Gruyter, 1977–2007), 16:438–41; R. Brandscheidt, "Jahwe," *Lexikon für Theologie und Kirche*, 3rd ed., 5:712–13.

13. *Die fünf Bücher der Weisung*: Verdeutscht von M. Buber gem. m. F. Rosenzweig (Heidelberg: Schneider, 1981). See also Martin Buber, *Moses: The Revelation and the Covenant* (New York: Harper & Row, 1958), 52–55.

14. Tertullian, *The Prescription of Heretics*, bk. VII, 9.

15. Blaise Pascal, *Pensées*, trans. A.J. Krailsheimer (Baltimore: Penguin Books, 1966), 309. Concerning the systematic theological problem, see chap. V, 1.

16. Ulrich Wilckens, *Theologie des Neuen Testaments*, 2/1 (Neukirchen-Vluyn: Neukirchener Verlag, 2007), 93. The concept *Proexistenz*, as far as I know, stems from the Protestant exegete W. Schmauch and was then taken up by Catholic New Testament exegetes, such as H. Schürmann and W. Thüsing. It fits well with this idea that some authors regard not *hajah* (to be), but rather *hasah* as the root of Yahweh's name. *Hasah* means to love passionately. According to this interpretation, Yahweh would be the passionate lover of his chosen people. Cf. Edith Olk, *Die Barmherzigkeit Gottes–zentrale Quelle des christlichen Lebens* (St. Ottilien: EOS, 2011), 46.

17. Wilckens, *Theologie des Neuen Testaments*, 2/1:96.

18. Ibid.

19. See Deut 4:31; Ps 86:15; 103:8; 116:5; 145:8; Jonah 4:2; Joel 2:13; etc.

20. Hans Walter Wolff, *Dodekapropheten*, XIV/1 (Neukirchen-Vluyn: Neukirchener Verlag, 1976), 261.

21. O. Proksch and G. Kuhn, "ἅγιος," *Theologisches Wörterbuch zum Neuen Testament* 1:87–112.

22. Friedrich Nietzsche, *Thus Spake Zarathustra*, trans. Thomas Common (NY: Carlton House), 96.

23. J. Fichtner and G. Stählin, "ὀργή," *Theologisches Wörterbuch zum Neuen Testament*, 5:395–410, 442–48. Günther Bornkamm, "Die Offenbarung des Zornes," in *Studien zum Neuen Testament* (Munich: Kaiser, 1985), 136, 189; Walter Groß, "Zorn–ein biblisches Theologumenon," in *Gott–ratlos vor dem Bösen?*, ed. Wolfgang Beinert (Freiburg i. Br. : Herder, 1999), 47–85.

24. G. Quell, "δικαιοκρισία," *Theologisches Wörterbuch zum Neuen Testament*, 2:176–80.

25. See Isa 44:26, 28; 49:10–13; Jer 3:12; 12:15; 26:13; etc.

26. G. Quell, G. Kittel and R. Bultmann, "ἀλήθεια," *Theologisches Wörterbuch zum Neuen Testament*, 1:233–51.

27. Friedrich Nietzsche, *The Twilight of the Idols*, trans. Anthony M. Ludovici (New York: Macmillan, 1924), 42–43.

28. F. Hauck, "πένης," *Theologisches Wörterbuch zum Neuen Testament* 6:37–40; F. Hauck and E. Bammel, πτωχός, *Theologisches Wörterbuch zum Neuen Testament*, 6:885–902; Norbert Lohfink, *Lobgesänge der Armen* (Stuttgart: Verlag Katholisches Bibelwerk, 1990); H.-J. Fabry, "Armut," *Lexikon für Theologie und Kirche*, 3rd ed., 1:1005–8.

29. Concerning Deuteronomy, see Norbert Lohfink, "Das deuteronomistische Gesetz in der Endgestalt: Entwurf einer Gesellschaft ohne marginale Gruppen," *Biblische Notizen* 51 (1990): 25–40.

30. Hauck and Bammel, πτωχός, 894–902.

IV

1. As Joachim Gnilka rightly observes in *Das Matthäusevangelium* (Freiburg i. Br.: Herder, 1986,) 1f.

2. This is not the place to discuss in detail the literary genre of the childhood stories and the question of their historicity. I am drawing upon the work of Heinz Schürmann, who rules out their interpretation as legendary and purely edifying stories. He speaks, instead, of their homologous narrative style, such as is found in late Jewish (better: early Jewish) haggadah. With this characterization, nothing is predetermined concerning the historical character of the reports. See Schürmann, *Das Lukasevangelium* (Freiburg i. Br.: Herder, 1969), 18–25.

3. We neither can nor need to go into this matter in detail here. I have already expressed my thoughts on this issue in *Jesus the Christ*, trans. V. Green (New York: Paulist Press, 1977), 251 and in *Katholische Kirche: Wesen–Wirklichkeit–Sendung* (Freiburg i. Br.: Herder, 2011), 219. Concerning the exegetical discussion, see Gnilka, *Das Matthäusevangelium*, 22–33; G. L. Müller, "Jungfrauengeburt," *Lexikon für Theologie und Kirche*, 3rd ed., ed. Walter Kasper et al. (Freiburg: Herder, 1993–2001), 5:1090–95.

4. Ulrich Luz, *Matthew 1—7: A Commentary*, trans. James E. Crouch (Minneapolis, MN: Fortress, 2007), 72–73; Gnilka, *Das Matthäusevangelium*, 1.

5. See Gnilka, *Das Matthäusevangelium*, 33–37. Concerning the ecclesiological meaning of this passage, see Kasper, *Katholische Kirche*, 131–33.

6. Ernst Bloch, *The Principle of Hope*, trans. Neville Plaice, Stephen Plaice, and Paul Knight, 3 vols. (Cambridge, MA: MIT, 1986), 3:1256.

7. Ignatius of Antioch, "Epistle to the Magnesians," 8, 23.

8. A. M. Haas, "Im Schweigen Gott zur Sprache bringen," in *Gott denken und bezeugen*, ed. George Augustin and Klaus Krämer (Freiburg i. B.: Herder, 2008), 344–55.

9. Rudolf Pesch, *Das Markusevangelium* (Freiburg i. Br.: Herder, 1976), 100–4; Joachim Gnilka, *Das Evangelium nach Markus* (Zürich: Benziger Verlag, 1978), 64–69.

10. Gnilka, *Das Matthäusevangelium*, 409f.; Ulrich Luz, *Matthew 8—20: A Commentary*, trans. James E. Crouch (Minneapolis: Fortress, 2001), 52–58.

11. Schürmann, *Das Lukasevangelium*, 231; Luz, *Matthew 1—7*, 190–93.

12. Jewish parallels in Paul Billerbeck and Hermann Leberecht Struck, eds., *Kommentar zum Neuen Testament aus Talmud und Midrasch* (Munich: C.H. Beck, 1985–89), IV/1:559–610.

13. Ulrich Wilckens, *Theologie des Neuen Testaments*, Bd. II/1 (Neukirchen: Neukirchener Verlag, 2007), 190–95.

14. G. Schrenk, "πατήρ," *Theologisches Wörterbuch zum Neuen Testament*, ed. Gerhard Kittell et al. (Stuttgart: Kohlhammer, 1949–79), 5:984–86; Joachim Jeremias, *Abba: Studien zur neutestamentlichen Theologie und Zeitgeschichte* (Göttingen: Vandenhoeck & Ruprecht, 1966). Pope Benedict XVI greatly emphasized the centrality of Jesus' message about God as Father, and particularly about God as "his Father." See *Jesus of Nazareth: From the Baptism to the Transfiguration*, trans. Adrian J. Walker (New York: Doubleday, 2007), 135–42.

15. Schürmann, *Das Lukasevangelium*, 358–65.

16. Fundamental for this interpretation: C. H. Dodd, *The Parables of the Kingdom* (New York: Scribner, 1961); Joachim Jeremias, *The Parables of Jesus*, trans. S. H. Hooke (New York: Scribner, 1972).

More recent interpretations: Eta Linnemann, *Die Gleichnisse Jesu: Einführung und Auslegung* (Göttingen: Vandenhoeck & Ruprecht, 1975); Hans-Josef Klauck, *Allegorie und Allegorese in synoptischen Gleichnistexten* (Münster: Aschendorff, 1986). For an introduction to the problem of interpreting the parables: Benedict XVI, *Jesus of Nazareth: From the Baptism to the Transfiguration*, 183–94.

17. For both of these parables, see Benedict XVI, *Jesus of Nazareth: From the Baptism to the Transfiguration*, 194–211.

18. Pope John Paul II, *Dives in Misericordia* (1980), sec. 6. This is the official Vatican translation, available at: http://www.vatican. va/holy_father/john_paul_ii/encyclicals/documents/hf_jp-ii_enc_ 30111980_dives-in-misericordia_en.html.

19. Wilckens, *Theologie des Neuen Testaments*, Bd. I/1, 316–19; Bd. II/1, 201–4. Cf. chap. V, 3.

20. Concerning Jesus' foreknowledge of his death and the issue of his own understanding of death, see Kasper, *Jesus the Christ*, trans. V. Green (New York: Paulist Press, 1977), 113–21.

21. For the discussion of this word by specialists, see Wilckens, *Theologie des Neuen Testaments*, Bd. I/2, 15–18.

22. W. Grundmann, "de...," *Theologisches Wörterbuch zum Neuen Testament*, 2:21–25.

23. H. Riesenfeld, "ὑπέρ," *Theologisches Wörterbuch zum Neuen Testament*, 8:510–18; Heinz Schürmann, *Gottes Reich, Jesu Geschick: Jesu ureigener Tod im Licht seiner Basileia-Verkündigung* (Freiburg i. Br.: Herder, 1983).

24. See Hans Urs von Balthasar, *Theo-Drama: Theological Dramatic Theory*, vol. 3, *The Dramatic Personae: The Person in Christ*, trans. Graham Harrison (San Francisco: Ignatius, 1992), 244–45.

25. Balthasar finds and criticizes this reduction also in the work of Karl Rahner, Edward Schillebeeckx, and Hans Küng, among others. See his *Theo-Drama: Theological Dramatic Theory*, vol. 4: *The Action*, trans. Graham Harrison (San Francisco: Ignatius Press, 1994), 273–84. For a constructive and penetrating treatment of the subject, see Karl-Heinz Menke, *Stellvertretung: Schlüsselbegriff christlichen Lebens und theologische Grundkategorie* (Einsiedeln: Johannes Verlag, 1991); Menke, *Jesus ist Gott der Sohn: Denkformen und Brennpunkte der Christologie* (Regensburg: Friedrich Pustet, 2011), 377–408. From a Protestant per-

spective, see Christof Gestrich, *Christentum und Stellvertretung* (Tübingen: Mohr Siebeck, 2001).

26. Hartmut Gese, "The Atonement," in *Essays on Biblical Theology* (Minneapolis: Augsburg, 1981), 93–116.

27. Pope Benedict XVI, *Jesus of Nazareth: Holy Week: From the Entrance into Jerusalem to the Resurrection*, trans. Philip J. Whitmore (San Francisco: Ignatius, 2011), 132–33.

28. Augustine, Sermon 169 c. 11 n. 13.

29. Menke clearly worked out this difference in his discussion with Karl Barth and Hans Urs von Balthasar. According to him, therefore, the satisfaction model is also excluded. See his *Jesus ist Gott der Sohn*, 133.

30. Joachim Jeremias, *The Eucharistic Words of Jesus*, trans. Norman Perrin (New York: Charles Scribner's Sons, 1966), 226–31. Jeremias, "πολλοί," *Theologisches Wörterbuch zum neuen Testament*, 6:544f.

31. This is the interpretation of: Jeremias, *The Eucharistic Words of Jesus*, 227–31; Rudolf Pesch, *Wie Jesus das Abendmahl hielt* (Freiburg i. Br.: Herder, 1977), 76f.; Wilckens, *Theologie des Neuen Testaments* I/2, 84; T. Söding, "Für euch–für viele–für alle: Für wen feiert die Kirche Eucharistie?" in *Gestorben für wen? Zur Diskussion um das "pro multis,"* ed. Magnus Striet (Freiburg i. Br.: Herder, 2007), 22–26; M. Theobald, "'Pro multis'–ist Jesus nicht für alle gestorben," in Striet, *Gestorben für wen?*, 30–34; Benedict XVI, *Jesus of Nazareth: Holy Week: From the Entrance into Jerusalem to the Resurrection*, 134–35.

32. This issue has become topical as a result of the planned translation of *pro multis* as "for many" in the Eucharistic words of institution, according to a text from the prefect of the Congregation for Divine Worship and the Discipline of the Sacraments on October 17, 2006. The more formal perspectives of a literal translation, in the spirit of the liturgical and patristic tradition, are determinative for this translation. This translation is, however, in need of a catechetical explanatory note that makes clear that, with this translation, the universal salvific will of God remains beyond question, but that the response of faith is necessary for the appropriation of salvation by individual human beings. Only after the printing of the prefect's text did a corresponding letter from Pope Benedict XVI to the German bishops on April 14, 2012, become known.

33. Concerning this topic in detail, see chap. V, 3.

34. The statement in *Gaudium et Spes* (sec. 22), according to which the Son of God is said to have united himself with every human being, must also be interpreted in this sense.

35. Bernard of Clairvaux, *Canticle of Canticles*, Sermon 62, 5. Cf. Bernard's *On Loving God*, chap. X.

36. *Evangelical Lutheran Worship* (Minneapolis: Augsburg Fortress Press, 2006), #351.

37. Concerning the theology of resurrection, see Kasper, *Jesus the Christ*, 124–59.

38. See Franz Mussner, *Der Jakobusbrief: Auslegung* (Freiburg i. Br.: Herder, 1964), 126f.

39. Concerning the Pauline understanding of God's justice: G. Schrenk, "δικαιοσύνη," *Theologisches Wörterbuch zum neuen Testament*, 2:204–14; Peter Stuhlmacher, *Gerechtigkeit Gottes bei Paulus* (Göttingen: Vandenhoeck & Ruprecht, 1965); Karl Kertelge, *Rechtfertigung bei Paulus* (Münster: Aschendorff, 1971); Kertelge, "Gerechtigkeit Gottes I", *Lexikon für Theologie und Kirche*, 3rd ed., 4:504–6 (Lit.); Ulrich Wilckens, *Der Brief an die Römer*, Bd. 1 (Neukirchen: Neukirchener Verlag, 1978), 202–33; Walter Klaiber, *Gerecht vor Gott* (Göttingen: Vandenhoeck & Ruprecht, 2000).

40. Kasper, *Jesus the Christ*, 156–58.

41. Augustine, *On the Spirit and the Letter*, 9:15.

42. Franz Posset, *The Real Luther: A Friar at Erfurt and Wittenberg* (Saint Louis: Concordia Publishing House, 2011).

43. See the Common Declaration on the Doctrine of Justification Issued by the Catholic Church and the Lutheran World Federation, accessible at http://www.vatican.va/roman_curia/pontifical_councils/chrstuni/documents/rc_pc_chrstuni_doc_31101999_cath-luth-joint-declaration_en.html.

44. See Irenaeus of Lyons, *Against Heresies*, III, 19, 1; V, 1, 1. Definitive for Christology was Athanasius's *Against the Arians*, III, 34. Also see Athanasius's *On the Incarnation*, 54. Cf. Balthasar, *Theo-Drama: Theological Dramatic Theory*, vol. 3: *The Dramatic Personae: The Person in Christ*, 237–45; vol. 4: *The Action*, 244–49; M. Herz, "Commercium," *Lexikon für Theologie und Kirche*, 2nd ed., ed. Josef Höfer and Karl Rahner (Freiburg: Herder, 1957–68), 3:20–22; E. M. Faber, "Commercium," *Lexikon für Theologie und Kirche*, 3rd ed., 2:1274f.

45. For example: Martin Luther, "The Freedom of a Christian," in *Luther's Works*, general eds. Jaroslav Pelikan and Helmut T. Lehmann, 55 vols. (Philadelphia: Muhlenberg Press, 1955–86), 31:351–52. For the interpretation of Luther on this point, Walter von Loewenich's book has become important: *Luthers Theologia crucis* (Munich: Kaiser, 1954). Luther's position has been misinterpreted by Theobald Beer. His misinterpretation has often been uncritically adopted by Catholic authors, even Hans Urs von Balthasar, and it has been turned into a position fundamentally opposed to the Catholic understanding. See Beer's *Der fröhliche Wechsel und Streit: Grundzüge der Theologie Martin Luthers* (Einsiedeln: Johannes Verlag, 1980). For a critique of Beer's position, see E. Iserloh, *Catholica (M)* 36 (1982): 101–14; Jared Wicks, *Theologische Revue* 78 (1982): 1–12.

46. Concerning the interpretation of this letter, see Ernst Käsemann, "Kritische Analyse von Phil 2, 5–11," in his *Exegetische Versuche und Besinnungen*, Bd. 1 (Göttingen: Vandenhoeck & Ruprecht, 1960), 51–95; Joachim Gnilka, *Der Philipperbrief* (Freiburg i. Br.: Herder, 1968), 111–47; Ulrich Wilckens, *Theologie des Neuen Testaments*, Bd. I/3, 247–49; II/1, 250–53.

47. Concerning this statement by Hegel, see Eberhard Jüngel, *God as the Mystery of the World: On the Foundation of the Theology of the Crucified One in the Dispute between Theism and Atheism*, trans. Darrell L. Guder (Grand Rapids: William B. Eerdmans, 1983), 63–100.

48. Pope John Paul II, *Dives in Misericordia* (1980), 7.

V

1. Clement of Rome, "First Epistle to the Corinthians," 23:1.

2. Irenaeus of Lyons, "Demonstration of the Apostolic Preaching," 60.

3. Tertullian, "On Repentance," 7; Cyprian, Epistle 55, 22, etc. For the continuation of the lines of research on this topic by B. Poschmann, K. Rahner, and others, see: Herbert Vorgrimler, *Buße und Krankensalbung* (Freiburg i. Br.: Herder, 1978).

4. This debate was taken up primarily by Irenaeus of Lyons, Tertullian, and Origen. See Dirk Ansorge, *Gerechtigkeit und Barmherzigkeit Gottes* (Freiburg i. Br.: Herder, 2009), 203–32.

5. See chap. III, 3.

6. This is the case with Thomas Aquinas, *Summa theologiae*, pt. I, q. 13 a. 11. It is also the case with Augustine and Bonaventure. See nn. 14 and 17 below.

7. Joseph Ratzinger emphasized this point in his inaugural lecture at Bonn in 1959: *Der Gott des Glaubens und der Gott der Philosophen: Ein Beitrag zum Problem der Theologie naturalis* (Trier: Paulinus, 2006.) Pope Benedict XVI returned to this point in his lecture at Regensburg in 2006: see James V. Schall, *The Regensburg Lecture* (South Bend, IN: St. Augustine's, 2007). Also cf. my farewell lecture at Tübingen, "Zustimmung zum Denken: Von der Unerlässlichkeit der Metaphysik für die Sache der Theologie," *Theologische Quartalschrift* 169 (1989): 257–71, and my essay "Glaube und Vernunft: Zur protestantischen Diskussion um die Regensburger Vorlesung von Papst Benedikt XVI," *Stimmen der Zeit* 132 (2007): 219–28.

8. Tertullian, "On the Prescription of Heretics," VII, 9.

9. Blaise Pascal, *Pensées*, trans. A.J. Krailsheimer (Baltimore: Penguin Books, 1966), 309.

10. For an overview of the problem of the Hellenization or de-Hellenization of Christianity, see: J. Drumm, "Hellenisierung," *Lexikon für Theologie und Kirche*, 3rd ed., ed. Walter Kasper et al. (Freiburg: Herder, 1993–2001), 4:1407–9.

11. In different ways: Wolfhart Pannenberg, "Die Aufnahme des philosophischen Gottesbegriffs als dogmatisches Problem der frühchristlichen Theologie," in *Grundfragen systematischer Theologie: Gesammelte Aufsätze* (Göttingen: Vandenhoeck & Ruprecht, 1967), 296–346; Eberhard Jüngel, *God as the Mystery of the World: On the Foundation of the Theology of the Crucified One in the Dispute between Theism and Atheism*, trans. Darrell L. Guder (Grand Rapids: William B. Eerdmans, 1983).

12. I made a first attempt in this direction in *Das Absolute in der Geschichte: Philosophie und Theologie der Geschichte in der Spätphilosophie Schellings* (Mainz: Matthias Grünewald, 1965). Drawing upon Johannes Evangelist Kuhn (*Katholische Dogmatik*, Bd. 1/2 [Tübingen, 1862], 758ff.), I further developed the idea in: *The God of Jesus Christ*, trans. Matthew J. O'Connell (New York: Crossroad, 1986), 151–52, 293–94. Most notably, Thomas Pröpper and his students have taken up this concern and have developed it further. See chap. II, n. 48.

13. See chap. II, nn. 46 and 68.

14. Augustine, *Confessions*, VII, 10, 16.

15. Augustine, *On the Trinity*, V, 3; VII, 5, 10.

16. Augustine, *On the Trinity*, XV, 19, 37.

17. Bonaventure, *The Mind's Journey to God*, prologue, 3.

18. Bonaventure, *The Mind's Journey to God*, V, 1.

19. In any case, this is clear in Augustine's *On the Trinity*. It is likewise clear in Bonaventure: I Sent. d. 2 q. 2 and q. 4; *The Mind's Journey to God*, V, 1 and *Breviloquium*, I c. 2–3.

20. Karl Rahner, "Theos in the New Testament," in *Theological Investigations*, trans. Cornelius Ernst, vol.1 (Baltimore: Helicon, 1965), 79–148.

21. See chap. I, 3.

22. Thomas Aquinas, *Summa theologiae*, pt. I, q. 21 a. 3: "misericordia est Deo maxime attribuendo: tamen secundum effectum, non secundum passionis affectum." Cf. Bertrand de Margerie, *Les perfections du Dieu de Jésus Christ* (Paris: Cerf, 1981), 263.

23. See chap. III, 5.

24. Matthias Joseph Scheeben, *Handbuch der katholischen Dogmatik*, Bd. 2, 3rd ed. (Freiburg i. Br.: Herder, 1948), 265.

25. Detailed analysis in Franz Diekamp, *Katholische Dogmatik*, Bd. 1, 13th ed. (Münster: Aschendorff, 1958), 144–48. Concerning the further development of the teaching about God's attributes, Margerie's work is helpful: Margerie, *Les perfections du Dieu de Jésus Christ*, and, from a Protestant perspective: Wolf Krötke, *Gottes Klarheiten: Eine Neuinterpretation der Lehre von den "Eigenschaften Gottes"* (Tübingen: Mohr Siebeck, 2001).

26. See chap. IV, 5.

27. See chap. V, 3.

28. Gershom Scholem, *Die jüdische Mystik in ihren Hauptströmungen* (Frankfurt a. M.: A. Metzner, 1957).

29. Hans Jonas, *Der Gottesbegriff nach Auschwitz: Eine jüdische Stimme* (Frankfurt a. M.: Suhrkamp, 1987).

30. See chap. III, 3.

31. Thus Søren Kierkegaard, *Die Tagebücher, 1834–1855* (Munich: Kösel Verlag, 1953), 239f. Also Karl Barth, *Church Dogmatics*, ed. G. W. Bromiley and Thomas F. Torrance, 5 vols. (Edinburgh: T&T Clark, 1956–77), II/1:599. Thomas Pröpper, "Allmacht III," *Lexikon für Theologie und Kirche*, 3rd ed., 1:416.

32. Thomas Aquinas, *Summa theologiae*, pt. I, q.25, a. 3 ad 3; pt.

II/II, q.30, a. 4, and, in each case, with reference to the oration of the tenth Sunday after Pentecost, which today is the 26th Sunday in the liturgical year.

33. *Story of a Soul: The Autobiography of St. Therese of Lisieux*, trans. John Clarke (Washington: ICS, 1975), 180.

34. See chap. I, 2.

35. Yves Congar, "La miséricorde: Attribut souverain de Dieu," *La Vie Spirituelle* 106 (1962): 380–95, with an appeal to Laberthonnière, as quoted by Margerie, *Les perfections du Dieu de Jésus Christ*, 264. Heinrich M. Christmann has also pointed in this direction in his book: *Thomas von Aquin als Theologe der Liebe* (Heidelberg: Kerle, 1958). We find approaches to a theology or ontology of love in Augustine and Bonaventure as well as in some representatives of contemporary philosophy. See chap. II, 1.

36. See Walter Kasper, *Katholische Kirche: Wesen–Wirklichkeit– Sendung* (Freiburg i. Br.: Herder, 2011), 47 n. 70 and the literature identified there.

37. In this context, we cannot treat all of the biblical, historical, and systematic problems involved in the establishment of the doctrine of the Trinity. On this issue, see Kasper, *Der Gott Jesu Christi*, new ed. (2008), 31–38 and the literature cited there. Also see Kasper, *The God of Jesus Christ*, 277–316.

38. On this issue, see Kasper, *Katholische Kirche*, 78–80, 91–93.

39. The analyses of this phenomenon are found primarily in the work of Jean Luc Marion. See chap. II, 1.

40. Thus, the famous axiom of the Fourth Lateran Council (1215): "For between creator and creature there can be noted no similarity so great that a greater dissimilarity cannot be seen between them." See *Decrees of the Ecumenical Councils*, 2 vols., ed. Norman P. Tanner (Washington: Georgetown University Press, 1990), 1:232.

41. Drawing upon Johannes Evangelist Kuhn concerning this point, see Kasper, *The God of Jesus Christ*, 294.

42. See Bonaventure, *The Mind's Journey to God*, VI, 1. Similar statements are found in *Breviloquium*, I c. 2–3 and I Sent d. 2 q. 2 and q. 4.

43. Concerning the relation of the economic and the immanent Trinity, see Kasper, *The God of Jesus Christ*, 273–77.

44. The idea of the self-withdrawal of God was represented in the Protestant *kenosis* theology of the nineteenth century in such a way that

God surrenders his Being as God. Pope Pius XII, in his encyclical *Sempiternus Rex* (1951), rightly condemned this teaching. On this matter, see Kasper, *Das Absolute in der Geschichte*, 521–30. Here it is not a matter of God giving up his Being as God in the act of self-kenosis, but rather that he reveals his Being as God in this very act. It is in this sense that *kenosis* is presented in the Orthodox theology of Sergei Bulgakov and in the contemporary Protestant theology of Jürgen Moltmann.

45. Thus, Preface I for Easter.

46. Drawing upon Schelling: Kasper, *Katholische Kirche*, 120f.

47. *Gaudium et Spes* ("Pastoral Constitution on the Church in the Modern World"), sec. 22.

48. Jüngel, *God as the Mystery of the World*, 261–98; in particular, 283f. Jüngel has done a good job exploring and working out this formula. However, he sets the two formulas in opposition to each other, when, in reality, both are correct: the one formula considered within the dimension of nature, and the other considered within the dimension of grace.

49. Concerning such interpretations (even if they are rejected there), see Rudolf Schnackenburg, *Das Johannesevangelium* (Freiburg i. Br.: Herder, 1975), 333.

50. Concerning the Johannine formulas of immanence, see the excursus by Rudolf Schnackenburg, *Die Johannesbriefe* (Freiburg i. Br.: Herder, 1953), 91–102.

51. See J. Eckert and J. Weismayer, "Christusmystik," *Lexikon für Theologie und Kirche*, 3rd ed., 2:1179–82.

52. Kasper, *Katholische Kirche*, 122–29, 161–65, 201–11, 241–42.

53. Thomas Aquinas, *In Psalmos* 24, n.7; 50, n.1, 4–6, 9. Cf. *Summa theologiae*, pt. III, q.1, a. 2. Thomas refers directly to Augustine (*Sermon* 138).

54. Bonaventure, *The Mind's Journey to God*, prologue, 2; VII, 3.

55. Bonaventure, *The Mind's Journey to God*, VII, 2–4.

56. Hugo Rahner's work is foundational on this issue. See his *Symbole der Kirche: Die Ekklesiologie der Väter* (Salzburg: Müller, 1964), 11–87.

57. Elisabeth de la Trinité, *Der Himmel im Glauben: Eine Auswahl aus ihren Schriften*, trans. Hans Urs von Balthasar (Einsiedeln: Johannes Verlag, 2000); Hans Urs von Balthasar, *Schwestern im Geist: Therese von Lisieux und Elisabeth von Dijon* (Einsiedeln: Johannes Verlag, 1990).

58. Trinitarian mysticism represents an important bridge between Western and Eastern ecclesial spirituality in the form of hesychasm. Particularly important is Russian Orthodox spirituality (Solovyov, Berdyaev, Lossky, Bulgakov). Cf. Mikhail G. Meerson-Aksenov, *The Trinity of Love in Modern Russian Theology* (Quincy, IL: Franciscan, 1998). Mention must also be made of the Pietist tradition (Johannes Arndt, Michael Hahn, et al.).

59. See Kasper, *Jesus the Christ*, trans. V. Green (New York: Paulist Press, 1977), 252–68.

60. Kasper, *Katholische Kirche*, 173–77.

61. Thomas Aquinas, *Summa theologiae*, pt. III, q. 8, a.3.

62. Ibid., pt. I, q. 21, a.3.

63. Ibid., pt. I, q. 21, a.4.

64. Thomas is thinking of Albert the Great and Alexander of Hales. See ibid., pt. III, q. 1, a. 3. From the time period after Aquinas, particular mention should be made of John Duns Scotus.

65. Thomas Aquinas, *Summa theologiae*, pt. III, q. 1 a. 1–6.

66. Concerning the doctrine of predestination, see Georg Kraus, *Vorherbestimmung: Traditionelle Prädestinationslehre im Licht gegenwärtiger Theologie* (Freiburg i. Br.: Herder, 1977); "Prädestination," Lexikon für Theologie und Kirche, 3rd ed., 8:467–73.

67. Augustine, *Confessions* IV, 4, 7; V, 2, 2; VI, 7, 12; 16, 26.

68. Gisbert Greshake, *Gnade als konkrete Freiheit: Eine Untersuchung zur Gnadenlehre des Pelagius* (Mainz: Matthias-Grünewald, 1972), 47–157; Ansorge, *Gerechtigkeit und Barmherzigkeit Gottes*, 232–56; Hans Urs von Balthasar, *Dare We Hope "That All Men Be Saved"? with a Short Discourse on Hell*, trans. David Kipp and Lothar Krauth (San Francisco: Ignatius, 1988), 65–69.

69. Augustine, *Handbook on Faith, Hope, and Love*, 8, 27; "On the Gift of Perseverance," 35; *City of God*, XXI, 12. For a critical discussion of Augustine's doctrine of original sin, see Thomas Pröpper, *Theologische Anthropologie*, Bd. 2 (Freiburg i. Br.: Herder, 2011), 981–1025. Concerning the relation of divine and human freedom, see 1351–401.

70. Already the second provincial council of Orange (529 CE) rejected the predestination of individuals to evil. See Heinrich Denzinger, *Enchiridion Symbolorum: Definitionum et declarationum de rebus fidei et morum* (Freiburg i. B.: Herder, 1963), 397. The Synod of

Quierzy (853 CE) condemned the monk Gottschalk's teaching concerning predestination (see Denzinger, 621–24), but the Synod of Valence (855 CE) did otherwise (see Denzinger, 625–33). In 1547 the Council of Trent condemned the double predestination teaching of the Reformers. See Denzinger, 1567.

71. Ambrose, *Expositio evangelii secundum Lucam*, 2, 90.

72. Ambrose, *On Christian Faith*, II, 2, 28.

73. Hans Urs von Balthasar, *A Short Discourse on Hell*, in *Dare We Hope*, 193–95.

74. Anselm of Canterbury, *Proslogion*, 8–12. Cf. H.-J. Verweyen, "Die Einheit von Gerechtigkeit und Barmherzigkeit bei Anselm von Canterbury," *Internationale katholische Zeitschrift Communio* 14 (1985): 52–55; Ansorge, *Gerechtigkeit und Barmherzigkeit Gottes*, 256–80, who gives the title "God's Mercy as Respect for Created Freedom" to his chapter on Anselm.

75. Thomas Aquinas, *Summa theologiae*, pt. I, q. 21, a. 1 ad 2 and 3. Cf. IV Sent d. 46, q. 2, a 2 qla. 2.

76. Thomas Aquinas, *Summa theologiae*, pt. I, q. 21, a. 4.

77. Karl Barth, *Church Dogmatics*, II/2, § 33.

78. B. Dahlke, *Die katholische Rezeption Karl Barths: Theologische Erneuerung im Vorfeld des Zweiten Vatikanischen Konzils* (Tübingen: Mohr Siebeck, 2010). Two works that have become especially important are: Hans Küng, *Justification: The Doctrine of Karl Barth and a Catholic Reflection*, trans. Thomas Collins, Edmund E. Tolk, and David Granskou (Philadelphia: Westminster, 1964) and Hans Urs von Balthasar, *The Theology of Karl Barth: Exposition and Interpretation*, trans. Edward T. Oakes (San Francisco: Ignatius, 1992).

79. Balthasar, *The Theology of Karl Barth*, 228–48; in particular, 247–48.

80. Karl-Heinz Menke, *Jesus ist Gott der Sohn: Denkformen und Brennpunkte der Christologie* (Regensburg: Friedrich Pustet, 2008), 378–85.

81. Thus, the famous Chalcedonian formula (451): Denzinger, *Enchiridion*, 302.

82. Thus, many formulas in the church's liturgical tradition of prayer. See Kasper, *Katholische Kirche*, 123f.

83. *Gaudium et Spes*, sec. 10.

84. *Gaudium et Spes*, sec. 45. Cf. *Ad Gentes* ("On the Mission Activity of the Church"), 3:8.

85. Immanuel Kant, *Critique of Pure Reason*, B 833.

86. Irenaeus of Lyons, *Against Heresies*, III, 18, 1:7.

87. Marius Reiser, *Die Gerichtspredigt Jesu: Eine Untersuchung zur eschatologischen Verkündigung Jesu und ihrem frühjüdischen Hintergrund* (Münster: Aschendorff, 1990); Hans-Josef Klauck, *Weltgericht und Weltvollendung: Zukunftsbilder im Neuen Testament* (Freiburg i. Br.: Herder, 1994).

88. Presented in detail in the five fascicles of the *Handbuch der Dogmengeschichte*, ed. Michael Schmaus et al., (Freiburg i. Br.: Herder, 1980–90), Bd. IV. Johann Auer offers a short summary: Johann Auer, *Siehe ich mache alles neu: Der Glaube an die Vollendung der Welt* (Regensburg: Friedrich Pustet, 1984), 121–28. M. Kehl, "Gericht Gottes III und IV," *Lexikon für Theologie und Kirche*, 3rd ed., 4:517–19.

89. Apostles' Creed (Denzinger, *Enchiridion*, 30); Niceno-Constantinopolitan Creed (Denzinger, *Enchiridion*, 125, 150). Other, older formulas: Denzinger, *Enchiridion*,10f.; 46; 48; 50; 61–64; 76.

90. Concerning linguistic use: A. Oepke, "ἀποκατάστασις," *Theologisches Wörterbuch zum neuen Testament*, ed. Gerhard Kittell et al. (Stuttgart: Kohlhammer, 1949–79), 1:388–90; C. Lenz, "Apokatastasis," *Reallexicon für Antike und Christentum*, ed. Theodor Klauser, Ernst Dassmann, and Georg Schöllgen, et al. (Stuttgart: Anton Hiersemann Verlag, 1950), 1:510–6; Balthasar, *A Short Discourse on Hell*, in *Dare We Hope*, 225–54. Concerning the concept: W. Breuning, "Zur Lehre von der Apokatastasis," *Internationale katholische Zeitschrift Communio* 10 (1981): 19–31; Leo Scheffczyk, "Apokatastasis: Faszination und Aporie," *Internationale katholische Zeitschrift Communio* 14 (1985): 35–46; Gisbert Greshake, *Gottes Heil–Glück des Menschen* (Freiburg i. Br.: Herder, 1984), 245–76. W. Breuning provides a good overview: "Apokatastasis," *Lexikon für Theologie und Kirche*, 3rd ed., 1:821–24. Recent discussion in Magnus Striet, "Streitfall Apokatastasis: Dogmatische Anmerkungen mit einem ökumenischen Seitenblick," *Theologische Quartalschrift* 184 (2004): 185–201.

91. See Max Seckler, *Das Heil in der Geschichte: Geschichtstheologisches Denken bei Thomas von Aquin* (Munich: Kösel Verlag, 1964), 26–57.

92. Origen, *On First Principles*, I, 6, 1 and 3.

93. Denzinger, *Enchiridion*, 411; cf. 433 and 801.

94. See Henri Crouzel, *Origen*, trans. A. S. Worrall (San Francisco: Harper & Row, 1989), 257–66; Henri de Lubac, *Geist aus der Geschichte: Das Schriftverständnis des Origenes* (Einsiedeln: Johannes Verlag, 1968), 23–61; De Lubac, *Du hast mich betrogen, Herr* (Einsiedeln: Johannes Verlag, 1984); Balthasar, *Dare We Hope*, 47–64.

95. See the historical overview and interpretation by Joseph Ratzinger, "Hölle II," *Lexikon für Theologie und Kirche*, 2nd ed., ed. Josef Höfer and Karl Rahner (Freiburg: Herder, 1957–68), 5:446–49.

96. Johann Baptist Metz, "Kampf um jüdische Traditionen in der christlichen Gottesrede," *Kirche und Israel* 2 (1987): 16f. Similarly: Scheffczyk, "Apokatastasis," 4.

97. Balthasar's position can appeal to significant French theologians such as H.de Lubac, H. Rondet, among others. It was taken up positively by J. Ratzinger, G. Greshake, H.-J. Verweyen, among others. The debate with his critics is found in Balthasar, *Dare We Hope?* and *A Short Discourse on Hell*. As much as I would like to share Balthasar's point of view, which excludes every claim to be truly in the know, many of his remarks nevertheless appear to want to know too much and are in danger of becoming Gnostic speculation about the inner nature of God. See his *Theo-Drama: Theological Dramatic Theory*, vol. 5: *The Last Act*, trans. Graham Harrison (San Francisco: Ignatius, 1998) 269–90; *Theologik*, Bd. 2, (Einsiedeln: Johannes Verlag, 1985), 269–321.

98. The New Testament expresses Judas's betrayal of Jesus with the word "handed over" (παραδίδωμι), a term that, in the Bible, expresses the mysterious interweaving of divine and human decision. Concerning the biblical transmission history and the increasingly negative characterization of Judas, see P. Dückers, "Judas Iskariot," *Lexikon für Theologie und Kirche*, 3rd ed., 5:1024–25.

99. Irenaeus of Lyons, *Against Heresies*, IV, 20, 7.

100. See Karl Rahner, *Foundations of Christian Faith: An Introduction to the Idea of Christianity*, trans. William V. Dych (New York: Crossroad Book, 1978), 102.

101. Irenaeus of Lyons, *Against Heresies*, V, 1, 1.

102. Augustine, *Sermon* 169, c. 11 n. 13.

103. Cf. the analyses of Meister Eckhart, E. Levinas, and E. Stein by H.-B. Gerl-Falkowitz, "Von der Gabe zum Geber," in *Gott denken*

und bezeugen, ed. G. Augustin and K. Krämer (Freiburg i. Br.: Herder, 2008), 356–73.

104. Edith Stein, *Welt und Person: Beitrag zum christlichen Wahrheitsstreben* (Freiburg i. Br.: Herder, 1962), 158ff.

105. Karl Rahner provides a summary: "Fegfeuer, III–V," *Lexikon für Theologie und Kirche*, 2nd ed., 4:51–55; G. L. Müller, "Fegfeuer III," *Lexikon für Theologie und Kirche*, 3rd ed., 3:1205–8; Joseph Ratzinger, *Eschatology, Death, and Eternal Life*, trans. Michael Waldstein (Washington: Catholic University of America, 1988), 218–33.

106. This is the position of H. U. v. Balthasar, J. Ratzinger, G. Greshake, M. Kehl, among others. Cf. Pope Benedict XVI, *Spe Salvi* (2007), 45–48.

107. Balthasar, *A Short Discourse on Hell*, in *Dare We Hope?*, 211–21. This is also the view of Karl Rahner, "Hölle," *Sacramentum mundi* II (Freiburg i. Br.: Herder, 1968), 737f.

108. Concerning the history of interpretation of this kind of intercession, see Balthasar, *A Short Discourse on Hell*, in *Dare We Hope*, 204–10.

109. Thomas Aquinas, *Summa theologiae*, pt. II/II, q. 17, a. 3.

110. Balthasar, *Dare We Hope*, 97–113 and *A Short Discourse on Hell*, in *Dare We Hope*, 211–21.

111. Quoted by Balthasar, *A Short Discourse on Hell*, in *Dare We Hope*, 214–15.

112. Catherine of Siena, *Engagiert aus Glauben: Briefe* (Zürich: Benziger, 1990), 30–33, 35f., 51f., 79, et al.

113. *Story of a Soul: The Autobiography of St. Therese of Lisieux*, 188–89.

114. Hans Urs von Balthasar, *Die Gottesfrage des heutigen Menschen*, expanded new ed. (Einsiedeln: Johannes Verlag, 2009), 175–88, 207–25. Also: *Dare We Hope*, 67–69.

115. Gisbert Greshake, *Leben–stärker als der Tod: Von der christlichen Hoffnung* (Freiburg i. Br.: Herder, 2008), 232–36.

116. Scheeben, *Handbuch der katholischen Dogmatik*, 2:266.

117. See Karl Rahner, "Some Theses for a Theology of Devotion to the Sacred Heart," in *Theological Investigations*, vol. 3, trans. Karl-H. and Boniface Kruger (Baltimore: Helicon, 1967), 331–52; Joseph Ratzinger, *Behold the Pierced One: An Approach to a Spiritual Christology* (San Francisco: Ignatius Press, 1986), 51–56.

118. Bonaventure, *The Mind's Journey to God*, III, 5. Joseph Ratzinger referred to it in *Behold the Pierced One*, 53

119. Denzinger, *Enchiridion*, 259, 431.

120. Pope Pius XII lays out this argument in detail in the 1956 encyclical *Haurietis Aquas* ("On Devotion to the Sacred Heart"). More recently, J. Ratzinger as well as L. Scheffczyk have pointed to the background to this devotion in the history of doctrine: Joseph Ratzinger, *Behold the Pierced One*, 51–69 and Leo Scheffczyk, "Herz Jesu II," *Lexikon für Theologie und Kirche*, 3rd ed., 5:53f.

121. Pope Pius XI, *Miserentissmus Redemptor* (1928).

122. Hugo Rahner, *Symbole der Kirche*, 177–235.

123. Augustine, *In evangelium Ioannis*, 120, 2.

124. Bernard of Clairvaux, *Commentary on the Song of Songs*, 61, 4.

125. Ibid.

126. Bonavenure, *Vitis mystica*, III, 4.

127. Karl Richtstätter, *Die Herz-Jesu-Verehrung des deutschen Mittelalters: Nach gedruckten und ungedruckten Quellen dargestellt* (Paderborn: Bonifacius, 1919).

128. *Tagebuch der Schwester Maria Faustina Kowalska* (Hauteville: Parvis Verlag, 1993).

129. See chap. I.

130. Especially Karl Rahner has pointed to this phenomenon: "Some Theses for a Theology of Devotion to the Sacred Heart," 339–40.

131. Pascal, *Pensées*, 323.

132. Ibid., 313.

133. Hans Urs von Balthasar, *Heart of the World*, trans. Erasmo S. Leiva (San Francisco: Ignatius, 1979).

134. Wilhelm Maas, *Unveränderlichkeit Gottes: Zum Verhältnis von griechisch-philosophischer und christlicher Gotteslehre* (Munich: Schöningh, 1974); Kasper, *The God of Jesus Christ*, 189–97; Peter Koslowski, *Der leidende Gott: Eine philosophische und theologische Kritik* (Munich: W. Fink Verlag, 2001).

135. Such ideas are found in the Jewish Kabbalah and, in a different form, in Hegel, the later Scheler, process theology (A. N. Whitehead, C. Hartshorne, J. Cobb, among others), as well as in the context of post-Auschwitz theology, such as Hans Jonas, *Der Gottesbegriff nach Auschwitz*.

136. Karl Rahner, *Schriften zur Theologie*, Bd. 15 (Einsiedeln: Benziger, 1983), 211f; Paul Imhof and Hubert Biallowons eds., *Karl Rahner im Gespräch*, Bd. 1 (Munich: Kösel Verlag, 1982), 245f.

137. Abraham J. Heschel, *The Prophets* (New York: Harper & Row, 1962); Peter Kuhn, *Gottes Selbsterniedrigung in der Theologie der Rabbinen* (Munich: Kösel Verlag, 1968); and his *Gottes Trauer und Klage in der rabbinischen Überlieferung* (Leiden: Brill, 1978).

138. Scheeben, *Handbuch der katholischen Dogmatik*, 2:266.

139. Preface I for Easter.

140. Søren Kierkegaard, *Die Tagebücher 1834–1855* (Munich: Kösel Verlag, 1949), 239f.; Karl Barth, *Church Dogmatics*, II/1:605–7; Eberhard Jüngel, "Gottes ursprüngliches Anfangen als schöpferische Selbstbegrenzung," in *Wertlose Wahrheit: Zur Identität und Relevanz des christlichen Glaubens* (Munich: Kösel Verlag, 1990), 151–62; Thomas Pröpper, "Allmacht III," *Lexikon für Theologie und Kirche*, 3rd ed., 1:416.

141. *Roman Missal*, Oration from the 26th Sunday in the liturgical calendar.

142. Only a few are mentioned here: Hans Urs von Balthasar, Joseph Ratzinger, Hans Küng, Jean Galot, H. Mühlen. On the Protestant side: Jürgen Moltmann, Eberhard Jüngel, among others. Cf. Walter Kasper, "Das Kreuz als Offenbarung der Liebe Gottes," *Catholica (M)* 61 (2007): 1–14.

143. Origen, *Homelia in Ezechielem*, VI, 8.

144. Bernard of Clairvaux, *Commentary on the Song of Songs*, 26, 5.

145. Augustine, *Expositions on the Psalms*, 87, 3. This translation from: *Readings from St. Augustine on the Psalms*, ed. Joseph Rickaby (New York: Benziger Brothers, 1925), 143.

146. Benedict XVI, *Spe Salvi* (2007), 39. The translation is from the Vatican website: http://www.vatican.va/holy_father/benedict_xvi/encyclicals/documents/hf_ben-xvi_enc_20071130_spe-salvi_en.html.

147. An overview of the theodicy issue in: Thomas Pröpper and Magnus Striet, "Theodizee," *Lexikon für Theologie und Kirche*, 3rd ed., 9:1396–98; P. Gerlitz and M. Köhlmoos, "Theodizee I-IV," *Theologische Realenzyklopädie*, ed. Gerhard Müller, Horst Balz, and Gerhard Krause (Berlin: Walter de Gruyter, 1977–2007), 33:210–37. From the rich literature on this topic: Karl Rahner, "Warum lässt Gott uns leiden?" in *Schriften zur Theologie*, Bd. XIV (Einsiedeln: Benziger, 1980), 450–66;

Peter Hünermann and Adel Theodor Khoury, eds., *Warum leiden? Die Antwort der Weltreligionen* (Freiburg i. B.: Herder, 1987); Thomas Pröpper, *Erlösungsglaube und Freiheitsgeschichte: Eine Skizze zur Soteriologie* (Munich: Kösel Verlag, 1988); Willi Oelmüller et al., *Worüber man nicht schweigen kann: Neue Diskussionen zur Theodizee Frage* (Munich: W. Fink Verlag, 1992); Gisbert Greshake, *Preis der Liebe: Besinnung über das Leid* (Freiburg i.b.: Herder, 1992); Walter Groß and Karl-Josef Kuschel, *Ich schaffe Finsternis und Unheil! Ist Gott verantwortlich für das Übel?* (Mainz, M. Grünewald, 1992); Johann Baptist Metz, ed., *Landschaft aus Schreien: Zur Dramatik der Theodizeefrage* (Mainz: Matthias Grünewald, 1995); Johann Baptist Metz, *Memoria passionis: Ein provozierendes Gedächtnis in pluralistischer Gesellschaft* (Freiburg i.br.: Herder, 2009); Harald Wagner et al., eds., *Mit Gott streiten: Neue Zugänge zum Theodizee-Problem* (Freiburg i. Br.: Herder, 1998); Armin Kreiner, *Gott im Leid: Zur Stichhaltigkeit der Theodizee-Argumente* (Freiburg i. Br.: Herder, 2005); Magnus Striet, "Das Versprechen der Gnade: Rechenschaft über die eschatologische Hoffnung," in *Theologische Anthropologie*, Bd. 2, ed. Thomas Pröpper (Freiburg i. Br.: Herder, 2011), 1490–1520.

148. This argument was handed on by the Christian apologist Lactantius and was ascribed to Epicurus.

149. Post-Auschwitz theology is found, in different forms, among some Jewish theologians as well as among Catholic and Protestant theologians such as J. B. Metz, J. Moltmann, D. Sölle, among others. Cf. J. B. Metz, "Auschwitz II," *Lexikon für Theologie und Kirche*, 3rd ed., 1:1260f.; M. Sarot, "Holocaust," *Die Religion in Geschichte und Gegenwart*, 4th ed., ed. Hans Dieter Betz, Don S. Browning, Bernd Janowski, and Eberhrad Jüngel (Tübingen: Mohr Siebeck, 1998–2007), 3:1866–68; Franz Mussner, "Theologie nach Auschwitz: Eine Programmskizze," *Kirche und Israel: Neukirchner theologische Zeitschrift* 10 (1995): 8–23. An important work is: Hans Jonas, *Der Gottesbegriff nach Auschwitz*.

150. Immanuel Kant, "On the Failure of All Attempted Philosophical Theodicies" (1791), *Kant on History and Religion*, trans. Michel Despland, (Montréal: McGill-Queen's University Press, 1973), 283–97.

151. See chap. II, 1.

152. Habermas, *Glauben und Wissen* (Frankfurt a. M.: Suhrkamp, 2001), 28.

153. Ibid., 24f.

154. So says Jürgen Habermas. See Michael Reder and Josef Schmidt, eds., *An Awareness of What is Missing: Faith and Reason in a Post-secular Age* (Malden, MA: Polity, 2010).

155. Gisbert Greshake and Jakob Kremer, *Resurectio mortuorum: Zum theologischen Verständnis der leiblichen Auferstehung* (Darmstadt: Wissenschaftliche Buchgesellschaft, 1986).

156. Fridolin Stier, *Das Buch Ijjob* (Munich: Kösel Verlag), 1954, 252–55; H. Spieckermann, "Hiob/ Hiobbuch," *Die Religion in Geschichte und Gegenwart*, 4th ed., 3: 1777–81.

157. Similarly: Hartmut Gese, "Die Krisis der Weisheit bei Koheleth," in *Vom Sinai zum Zion* (Munich: Kaiser, 1974), 168–79.

158. B. Janowski, "Klage II," *Die Religion in Geschichte und Gegenwart*, 4th ed., 4:1389–91.

159. To understand Jesus' cry of abandonment: Hartmut Gese, "Psalm 22 und das Neue Testament: Der älteste Bericht vom Tode Jesu und die Entstehung des Herrenmahls," in *Vom Sinai zum Zion*, 180–201.

160. See also *Didache*, 10, 6.

161. Kuhn, "μαρανα θά," *Theologisches Wörterbuch zum Neuen Testament*, 4:470–75.

162. Benedict XVI, *Spe Salvi*, 35.

163. U. Diese, "Gelassenheit," *Historisches Wörterbuch der Philosophie*, ed. Joachim Ritter, Karlfried Gründer, and Gottfried Gabriel (Basel: Schwabe Verlag, 1971–2007), 3:219–24; R. Körner, "Gelassenheit," *Lexikon für Theologie und Kirche*, 3rd ed., 4:403f.

164. Ignatius of Loyola, *Spiritual Exercises*, "The Principle and Foundation."

165. Thomas Pröpper, *Evangelium und freie Vernunft: Konturen einer theologischen Hermeneutik* (Freiburg i. Br.: Herder, 2001), 275.

166. Thomas Pröpper, *Erlösungsglaube und Freiheitsgeschichte*, 179.

VI

1. Martin Buber, "Nachahmung Gottes," in *Gesammelte Werke* (Frankfurt-a-Main: S. Fischer, 1964), 2:1953–65; Ulrich Luz, *Matthew*

1—7: A Commentary, trans. James E. Crouch (Minneapolis: Fortress, 2007), 289.

2. See chap. III.

3. Paul Billerbeck and Hermann Leberecht Struck, eds., *Kommentar zum Neuen Testament aus Talmud und Midrasch* (Munich: Beck, 1922–61), I:203–5; IV:559–610.

4. See chap. IV.

5. For the exegesis and the history of interpretation of this commandment, see Joachim Gnilka, *Das Evangelium nach Markus* (Neukirchen-Vluyn: Neukirchener Verlag, 1979), 162–68; Luz, *Matthew 21—28: A Commentary*, trans. James E. Crouch (Minneapolis: Fortress, 2005), 75–87.

6. For the Jewish interpretation, see Billerbeck and Struck, *Kommentar zum Neuen Testament aus Talmud und Midrasch*, I:900–8.

7. Augustine, *On the Trinity*, VIII, 8. Translation from *Augustine: Later Works*, trans. John Burnaby (Philadelphia: Westminster, 1955), 52–53. Many other passages in: T. J. van Bavel, "Love," in *Augustine through the Ages: An Encyclopedia*, ed. Allan Fitzgerald et al. (Grand Rapids, MI: W.B. Eerdmans, 1999), 510f.

8. See Luz, *Matthew 21—28*, 81–85. We are indebted to Karl Rahner for his powerful (if somewhat one-sided) reflections on the unity of love of God and love of neighbor and their contemporary meaning: Karl Rahner, "Reflections on the Unity of the Love of Neighbour and the Love of God," in *Theological Investigations*, vol. 6, trans. Karl-H. and Bonfiace Kruger (Baltimore: Helicon, 1969), 231–49; cf. also "The 'Commandment' of Love in Relation to the Other Commandments" in *Theological Investigations*, vol.5, trans. Karl-H. Kruger (Baltimore: Helicon, 1966), 439–59.

9. See Wolfgang Schrage, *Der erste Brief an die Korinther* (Zürich: Benziger, 1999), 273–373, especially the summary on 319f.

10. Augustine, *In evangelium Ioannis*, 76, 2.

11. Leo the Great, *Tractatus*, 74.

12. Basil, Homily 6.

13. John Chrysostom, *Commentary on Matthew*, Homily 18, n. 8.

14. Basil, "Sermon to the Rich," 3.

15. Chrysostom, *Commentary on Matthew*, Homily 77, n. 5f.

16. Chrysostom, Homily 47, n. 4.

17. Thomas Aquinas, *Summa theologiae*, pt. II/II, q. 30, a. 4, ad 2.

18. Dietrich Bonhoeffer, *The Cost of Discipleship*, trans. R. H. Fuller (New York: Macmillan, 1972), 100–1.

19. Luz, *Matthew 1—7*, 285–87.

20. Athenagoras, *A Plea for the Christians*, 11; Tertullian, *To Scapula*, 1; Origen, *Against Celsus*, 59–61.

21. 2 Clement, 13f.

22. Tertullian, *Of Patience*, 6.

23. Chrystostom, *Commentary on Matthew*, Homily 18, n. 3.

24. Ambrose, *On the Duties of the Clergy*, 48, nn. 242–48.

25. Augustine, *Handbook on Faith, Hope, and Love*, 73–74.

26. Thomas Aquinas, *Summa theologiae*, pt. II/II, q. 25, a. 8; cf. a. 9.

27. Luz, *Matthew 1—7*, 290–91.

28. Ibid., 291. On the issue of war, see chap. VII.

29. Ibid., 292.

30. On this issue, see the document from the International Theological Commission, *Memory and Reconciliation: The Church and the Faults of the Past* (1999). Text available at: http://www.vatican.va/roman_curia/congregations/cfaith/cti_documents/rc_con_cfaith_doc_2 0000307_memory-reconc-itc_en.html.

31. See Paul M. Zulehner, *Gott is größer als unser Herz* (Ostfildern: Schwabenverlag, 2006), 146–52.

32. See *Catechism of the Catholic Church* (Washington: United States Catholic Conference, 1994), n. 2447.

33. *Rule of St. Benedict*, IV, 74.

34. Christoph Schönborn, *We Have Found Mercy: The Mystery of Divine Mercy*, trans. Michael J. Miller (San Francisco: Ignatius, 2012), 102–5.

35. *Tagebuch der Schwester Maria Faustyna Kowalska* (Hauteville: Parvis Verlag, 1990), 80f.

36. Heinrich Schlier, "Vom Wesen der apostolischen Ermahnung," in *Die Zeit der Kirche*, (Freiburg i. Br.: Herder, 1958), 74–89.

37. Irenaeus, *Against Heresies*, III, 25, 7.

38. Ephraim the Syrian, *Hymns Against Heresies*, 1.

39. A. Fitzgerald, "Mercy, Works of Mercy," in Fitzgerald, *Augustine through the Ages*, 558.

40. Augustine, Sermon 38, 8; 53A, 6; 206, 2; 236, 3.

41. See, for example: Navin Chawla, *Mother Teresa: the Authorized Biography* (Rockport, MA: Element, 1997).

42. Mother Teresa, *Worte der Liebe*, trans. Franz Johna (Freiburg i. Br.: Herder, 1977), 117f.

43. See chap. VIII.

44. Karl Hermann Schelkle, *Jüngerschaft und Apostelamt* (Freiburg i. Br.: Herder, 1957); Hans Dieter Betz, *Nachfolge und Nachahmung Jesu Christi im Neuen Testament*, (Tübingen: Mohr Siebeck, 1967); Martin Hengel, *Nachfolge und Charisma: Eine exegetisch-religionsgeschichtliche Studie zu Mt 8, 21 f. und Jesu Ruf in die Nachfolge* (Berlin: A. Töpelmann, 1968); Bonhoeffer, *The Cost of Discipleship*.

45. Karl-Heinz Menke, *Stellvertretung: Schlüsselbegriff christlichen Lebens und theo-logische Grundkategorie* (Einsiedeln: Johannes, 1997).

46. Ulrich Luz et al., "Nachfolge Jesu," *Theologische Realenzyklopädie*, ed. Gerhard Müller, Horst Balz, and Gerhard Krause (Berlin: Walter de Gruyter, 1977–2007), 23:678-713.

47. Tertullian, *Apology*, 50, 14.

48. Bernard of Clairvaux, *Song of Songs*, 62,5. Cf. Bernard of Clairvaux, *Rückkehr zu Gott: Die mystischen Schriften*, trans. Bernardin Schellenberger (Düsseldorf: Patmos, 2001), 27–33.

49. Karl-Heinz Menke, *Jesus ist Gott der Sohn: Denkformen und Brennpunkte der Christologie* (Regensburg: Friedrich Pustet, 2008), 291–99.

50. Concerning the *kenosis* and night motifs, see: Paul Rheinbay, "Voller Pracht wird die Nacht, weil dein Glanz sie angelacht," in *Gott denken und bezeugen: Festschrift für Kardinal Walter Kasper zum 75. Geburtstag*, ed. G. Augustin and K. Krämer (Freiburg i. Br.: Herder, 2008), 384–86.

51. *Story of a Soul: The Autobiography of St. Therese of Lisieux*, trans. John Clarke (Washington, DC: Institute of Carmelite Studies, 1975), 193–96. Cf. Hans Urs von Balthasar, *Schwestern im Geist: Therese von Lisieux und Elisabeth von Dijon* (Einsiedeln: Johannes Verlag, 1970), 316–20; Balthasar, *Dare We Hope "That All Men Be Saved?" with a Short Discourse on Hell*, trans. David Kipp and Lothar Krauth (San Francisco: Ignatius, 1988), 101–6.

52. *Story of a Soul: The Autobiography of St. Therese of Lisieux*, 211–12.

53. Ibid., 216–17, 252.

54. Ibid., 253.

55. Romaeus Leuven, *Heil im Unheil: Das Leben Edith Steins: Briefe und Vollendung*, Edith Steins Werke, Bd. 10 (Freiburg i. Br.: Herder, 1983), 166: "Komm, wir gehen für unser Volk." Concerning this, see: A. Ziegenaus, "Benedicta a Cruce – Jüdin und Christin," in *Edith Stein: Leben, Philosophie, Vollendung*, ed. Leo Elders (Würzburg: Verlag J.W. Naumann, 1991), 129–43, esp. 137ff.

56. *Mother Teresa: Come Be My Light: The Private Writings of the "Saint of Calcutta,"* ed. Brian Kolodiejchuk (New York: Doubleday, 2007).

57. Bonhoeffer, *The Cost of Discipleship*, 81–82.

VII

1. See Walter Kasper, *Katholische Kirche: Wesen-Wirklichkeit-Sendung* (Freiburg i.Br.: Herder, 2011), 126–29, 190–96, 247–54.

2. Augustine, *In evangelium Ioannis*, 13, 15–17; cf. 6, 23.

3. Augustine, "On Baptism," I, 8, 10 etc.

4. Augustine, "On Baptism," VI, 28, 39. Cf. *Lumen Gentium*, sect. 14.

5. *Lumen Gentium*, sect. 15; *Unitatis Redintegratio*, sect. 3.

6. Karl Bopp, *Barmherzigkeit im pastoralen Handeln der Kirche: Eine symbolisch-kritische Handlungstheorie zur Neuorientierung kirchlicher Praxis* (Munich: Don Bosco Verlag, 1998); Paul M. Zulehner, *Gott ist größer als unser Herz (1 John 3, 20): Eine Pastoral des Erbarmens* (Ostfildern: Schwabenverlag, 2006).

7. Pope John XXIII, "Opening Speech to the Second Vatican Council," in *The Documents of Vatican II*, ed. Walter M. Abbott, (New York: Guild Press, 1966), 716.

8. Pope John Paul II, *Dives in Misericordia* (1980), 7.

9. According to its substance, the program promoting a new evangelization is not new. Repeatedly in the history of the church, there have been stirring preachers and movements that have called for penance, conversion, and renewal. In the period after the Council of Trent, popular missions, and later regional and city missions, have proven to be valuable instruments for this purpose. In more recent times, one can think of the Mission de France and the Mission de Paris. Since the Second Vatican Council, Pope Paul VI's apostolic letter, *Evangelii Nuntiandi* (1975), and Pope John Paul II's encyclical, *Redemptoris Missio*, sec. 32–38 (1990), have become decisive. By means of his *Motu Proprio, Ubicumque et Semper*

(2010), Pope Benedict XVI established a distinct Pontifical Council for Promoting New Evangelization and he announced a bishops' synod on this theme for the fall of 2012. Concerning this topic, see: Walter Kasper, "Neue Evangelisierung als theologische, pastorale und geistliche Herausforderung," in *Das Evangelium Jesu Christi* (Freiburg i. Br.: Herder, 2009), esp. 284–91.

10. Prayer of the third Christmas Mass during the day.

11. Augustine, *Confessions*, I, 1.

12. John Chrysostom, *Commentary on the Letter to the Romans*, 2.

13. This is true concerning the way in which the New Testament presents the Pharisees. This is altogether true of the way in which the Second Letter of Peter deals with its opponents.

14. See Kasper, *Katholische Kirche*, 47f., 417f.

15. Ibid., 170–72.

16. Augustine, *In evangelium Ioannis*, 26, 6, 13; Thomas Aquinas, *Summa theologiae*, pt. III, q. 73, a. 6. Cf. *Sacrosanctum Concilium*, sec. 47; *Lumen Gentium*, sec. 3, 7, 11, and 26.

17. Walter Kasper, *Die Liturgie der Kirche* (Freiburg i. Br.: Herder, 2010), 70–74.

18. Hugo Rahner, "Der Schiffbruch und die Planke des Heils," in *Symbole der Kirche: Die Ekklesiologie der Väter* (Salzburg: Müller, 1964), 432–72.

19. Gregory of Nazianzus, Oratio 39, 17. Cf. Heinrich Denzinger, *Enchiridion Symbolorum: Definitionum et declarationum de rebus fidei et morum* (Freiburg i. B.: Herder, 1963), 1672.

20. See the essays on penance in: Kasper, *Die Liturgie der Kirche*, 337–422.

21. Concerning this topic, see the research of Bernhard Poschmann, Karl Rahner, and Herbert Vorgrimler, among others.

22. Council of Trent, in Denzinger, *Enchiridion*, 1680 and 1707; in opposition to the Synod of Pistoia, 2639. Pope John Paul II, "Apostolic Exhortation," *Reconciliation and Penance* (1984).

23. Karl Rahner, "The Meaning of Frequent Confession of Devotion," in *Theological Investigations*, vol. 3, trans. Karl-H. and Boniface Kruger (Baltimore: Helicon, 1967), 177–89.

24. Johann Baptist Metz, in the draft of the resolution of the general synod of German bishops, which he essentially wrote: *Unsere Hoffnung: Ein Bekenntnis zum Glauben in dieser Zeit: Ein Beschluss der*

Gemeinsamen Synode der Bistümer in der Bundesrepublik Deutschland (Bonn: Sekretär der Gemeinsamen Synode der Bistümer in der Bundesrepublik Deutschland, 1976), 93–95.

25. Of course, it is not possible nor is it my intention in what follows to describe the entire history of the church's care of the poor and its social services. On this topic, see W. Schwer, "Armenpflege B. Christlich," *Reallexicon für Antike und Christentum*, ed. Theodor Klauser, Ernst Dassmann, and Georg Schöllgen, et al. (Stuttgart: Anton Hiersemann Verlag, 1950), 1:693–98; F. Hauck, "πτωχός," *Theologisches Wörterbuch zum Neuen Testament*, ed. Gerhard Kittell et al. (Stuttgart: Kohlhammer, 1949–79), 6:887f.; W.-D. Hauschild, "Armenfürsorge II," *Theologische Realenzyklopädie*, ed. Gerhard Müller, Horst Balz, and Gerhard Krause (Berlin: Walter de Gruyter, 1977–2007), 4:14–23; T. Becker, "Armenhilfe III," *Lexikon für Theologie und Kirche*, 3rd ed., ed. Walter Kasper et al. (Freiburg: Herder, 1993–2001), 1:999. Still informative is: Adolf von Harnack, *Die Mission und Ausbreitung des Christentums in den ersten Jahrhunderten* (Leipzig: Hinrichs, 1924), 170–220.

26. Concerning the history of interpretation of this passage, see Wolfgang Schrage, *Der erste Brief an die Korinther* (Neukirchen-Vluyn: Neukirchener Verlag, 1999), 58–107.

27. Concerning this topic, see the early publication by Joseph Ratzinger, *Christian Brotherhood*, trans. W. A. Glen-Doepel (London: Sheed & Ward, 1966). Walter Kasper, "Christliche Brüderlichkeit," in *Kirche–Sakrament–Gemeinschaft: Zur Ekklesiologie bei Joseph Ratzinger*, ed. Christian Schaller (Regensburg: Verlag Friedrich Pustet, 2011), 55–66.

28. Justin Martyr, 1 *Apology*, 67; Tertullian, *Apology*, 39.

29. Tertullian, *Apology*, 39.

30. Letter to Diognetus, 5.

31. See chap. VIII.

32. Gregory of Nazianzus, *Second Oration*, 78–90; here 78, 81.

33. Chrysostom, *Commentary on the Letter to the Romans*, Homily 9, n. 7f.

34. Chrysostom, *Homilies on the Gospel of Matthew*, Homily 50, n. 3 and 4.

35. *Lumen Gentium*, sec. 8, par. 3.

36. *Gaudium et Spes*, 76.

37. Kasper, *Katholische Kirche*, 463–68.

38. Dietrich Bonhoeffer, "Costly Grace," in *The Cost of Discipleship*, trans. R. H. Fuller, rev. ed. (New York: Macmillan, 1972), 36–37.

39. Kasper, *Katholische Kirche*, 141–48, 274–76. Cf. also Dietrich Bonhoeffer, "The Church of Jesus Christ and the Life of Discipleship," in *The Cost of Discipleship*, 201–68.

40. See E. Ernst, "Binden und Lösen," *Lexikon für Theologie und Kirche*, 2nd ed., ed. Josef Höfer and Karl Rahner (Freiburg: Herder, 1957–68), 2:463f.

41. Cf. Gal 5:19–21; Eph 5:5; Col 3:5; 1 Thess 4:4–8; Rev 21:8; 22:15.

42. Cf. 2 Thess 3:6, 14; 1 Tim 6:4; 2 Tim 3:5.

43. See Kasper, *Katholische Kirche*, 238–54.

44. R. Herzog, "Arzt," *Reallexicon für Antike und Christentum*, 1:723f.; V. Eid, "Arzt III," *Lexikon für Theologie und Kirche*, 2nd ed., 1:1049f.

45. In *Truth and Method*, Hans-Georg Gadamer has done a good job explicating the legal hermeneutical problem in the context of the fundamental hermeneutical problem and the parallels to theological hermeneutics. In the process, he has also emphasized the relevance of Aristotle. His remarks are important in this context because they also draw on Aristotle and his reception by Thomas Aquinas. See *Truth and Method*, rev. trans. Joel Weinsheimer and Donald G. Marshall, 2nd rev. ed. (New York: Continuum, 1993), 307–41. From a theological perspective: H. Müller, "Barmherzigkeit in der Rechtsordnung der Kirche?," *Archiv für katholisches Kirchenrecht*, 159 (1990): 353–67; Thomas Schüller, *Die Barmherzigkeit als Prinzip der Rechtsapplikation in der Kirche im Dienst der salus animarum: Ein kanonistischer Beitrag zu Methodenproblemen der Kirchenrechtstheorie* (Würzburg: Echter, 1993); Walter Kasper, "Gerechtigkeit und Barmherzigkeit: Überlegung zu einer Applikationstheorie kirchenrechtlicher Normen," in *Theologie und Kirche*, (Mainz: Matthias Grünewald Verlag, 1999), 183–91; Kasper, "Canon Law and Ecumenism," *The Jurist* 69 (2009): 171–89.

46. See Yves Congar, *Diversity and Communion* (Mystic, CT: Twenty-Third, 1985), 54–69.

47. Aristotle, *Nicomachean Ethics*, V, 14; 1127b–1138a. Cf. Günter

Virt, *Epikie: verantwortlicher Umgang mit Normen: Eine historisch-systematische Untersuchung* (Mainz: Matthias Grünewald Verlag, 1983).

48. See Thomas Aquinas, *Summa theologiae*, pt. II/II, q. 120, a. 2.

49. Thomas Aquinas, *Summa theologiae*, pt. I, q. 21, a. 3, ad 2.

50. Thomas Aquinas, *Super Ev. Matthaei*, cap. 5, lc. 2.

51. Pope John Paul II, *Dives in Misericordia* (1980), 14. This is the official Vatican translation, available at: http://www.vatican.va/holy_father/john_paul_ii/encyclicals/documents/hf_jp-ii_enc_30111980_dives-in-misericordia_en.html.

52. See Kasper, "Gerechtigkeit und Barmherzigkeit," 188.

53. *Code of Canon Law: Latin-English Edition* (Washington: Canon Law Society of America, 1983), c. 1752.

54. Pope Benedict XVI, "La legge canonica si interpreta nella Chiesa," in *Osservatore Romano* 152 (2012) n. 18, 8.

55. Concerning this, see Gadamer, *Truth and Method*, 30–34.

56. Ibid., 312–13.

57. Thomas Aquinas, *Summa theologiae*, pt. II/II, q. 47. Cf. Josef Pieper, *Prudence*, trans. Richard and Clara Winston (New York: Pantheon, 1959); Martin Rhonheimer, *Praktische Vernunft und Vernünftigkeit der Praxis: Handlungstheorie bei Thomas von Aquin in ihrer Entstehung aus dem Problemkontext der aristotelischen Ethik* (Berlin: Akademie Verlag, 1994); E. Schockenhoff, "Klugheit I," *Lexikon für Theologie und Kirche*, 3rd ed., 6:151f.

58. Thomas Aquinas, *Summa theologiae*, pt. II/II, q. 47, a. 2, ad 1: "Clearly prudence is wisdom in human affairs, yet it is not wisdom pure and simple, because it is not about the utterly ultimate, but about the good-for-man, which is not the most ultimate and best of goods that exist. And so Scripture pointedly says that prudence is wisdom for a man, not wisdom absolutely." St. Thomas Aquinas, *Summa Theologiae*, vol. 36: *Prudence*, trans. Thomas Gilby, OP (New York: McGraw-Hill, 1974), 11.

59. Cf. the beautiful remarks by Gadamer concerning the bond of friendship as the presupposition for giving advice: *Truth and Method*, 323.

60. Heinrich Mussinghoff, "Nobile est munus ius dicere iustitiam adhibens aequitate coniunctam," in *Theologia et ius canonicum*, ed. Heinrich J. F. Reinhardt, (Essen: Ludgerus-Verlag, 1995), 21–37.

VIII

1. See *Lumen Gentium*, sect. 36f.; *Gaudium et Spes*, sec. 36, 42, 56, and 76; *Apostolicam Actuositatem*, sec. 7.

2. See the *Compendium of the Social Doctrine of the Church*, issued by the Pontifical Council for Justice and Peace. Available at: http://www.vatican.va/roman_curia/pontifical_councils/justpeace/doc uments/rc_pc_justpeace_doc_20060526_compendio-dott-soc_cn.html. Cf. classic presentations: Oswald von Nell-Breuning, *Gerechtigkeit und Freiheit: Grundzüge katholischer Soziallehre* (Vienna: Europaverlag, 1980); Joseph Höffner, *Christian Social Teaching*, trans. Stephen Wentworth and Gerald Finan Arndt (Cologne: Ordo Socialis, 1996). More recent presentations from the perspective of the anthropological turn: W. Korff, "Sozialethik," *Lexikon für Theologie und Kirche*, 3rd ed., ed. Walter Kasper et al. (Freiburg: Herder, 1993–2001), 9:767–77; Reinhard Marx, *Das Kapital: Ein Plädoyer für den Menschen* (Munich: Pattloch, 2008).

3. Cicero, *De legibus*, 1, 6, 19. Cf. Thomas Aquinas, *Summa theologiae*, pt. II/II, q. 58 a. 1. Concerning the set of issues involved in the concept of justice, see n. 42 following.

4. Augustine, *City of God*, IV, 4.

5. Concerning this, see G. Wingren, "Barmherzigkeit IV," *Theologische Realenzyklopädie*, ed. Gerhard Müller, Horst Balz, and Gerhard Krause (Berlin: Walter de Gruyter, 1977–2007), 5:233–38.

6. Cf. See Marx, *Das Kapital*, 72f.

7. Franz-Xaver Kaufmann, *Herausforderungen des Sozialstaates* (Frankfurt a. M.: Suhrkamp, 1997); Kaufmann, *Varianten des Wohlfahrtsstaates: Der deutsche Sozialstaat im internationalen Vergleich* (Frankfurt a. M.: Suhrkamp, 2003); Kaufmann, *Sozialpolitik und Sozialstaat: Soziologische Analysen* (Wiesbaden: Verlag für Sozialwissenschaften, 2005).

8. Authoritative theoreticians: W. Eucken, W. Röpke, A. Rüstow, A. Müller-Armack, L. Erhard, among others. Cf. A. Anzenbacher, "Soziale Marktwirtschaft," *Lexikon für Theologie und Kirche*, 3rd. ed., 9:759–61.

9. Cf. chap. III, 6.

10. Jürgen Habermas, "Die Krise des Wohlfahrtsstaates und die Erschöpfung utopischer Energien," in *Zeitdiagnosen: Zwölf Essays* (Frankfurt a.M.: Suhrkamp, 2003), 27–49; also his "Glauben und

Wissen," in the same volume, 249–62; Wolfgang Ockenfels, *Was kommt nach dem Kapitalismus?* (Augsburg: Bay Sankt Ulrich, 2011).

11. Marx, *Das Kapital*, 16ff.

12. This contested and, indeed, unrealistic demand was raised by the Pontifical Council for Justice and Peace in its document, "Towards Reforming the International Financial and Monetary Systems in the Context of Global Public Authority" (2011). The text is available at: http://www.vatican.va/roman_curia/pontifical_councils/justpeace/doc uments/rc_pc_justpeace_doc_20111024_nota_en.html.

13. Oswald von Nell-Breuning and Johannes Schasching, eds., *Texte zur katholischen Soziallehre: Die sozialen Rundschreiben der Päpste und andere kirchliche Dokumente* (Kevelaer: Butzon & Bercker, 1989); K. Hilpert, "Sozialenzykliken," *Lexikon für Theologie und Kirche*, 3rd ed., 9:763–65.

14. Oswald von Nell-Breuning, "Integralismus," *Lexikon für Theologie und Kirche*, 2nd ed., ed. Josef Höfer and Karl Rahner (Freiburg: Herder, 1957–68), 5:717f.

15. *Gaudium et Spes*, sec. 36. Cf. n. 1 previously.

16. *Gaudium et Spes*, sec. 73f.

17. Pope Leo XIII, *Rerum Novarum* (1891), 45; Pope Pius XI, *Quadragesimo Anno* (1931), 88; 137.

18. Pope John Paul II, *Dives in Misericordia* (1980), 12. This is the official Vatican translation from: http://www.vatican.va/holy_father/ john_paul_ii/encyclicals/documents/hf_jp-ii_enc_30111980_dives-in- misericordia_en.html.

19. Pope Paul VI, "Closing Comments for the Jubilee Year 1975," 145; "Message for the Celebration of the Day of Peace, If You Want Peace, Defend Life" (1977); Pope John Paul II, *Dives in Misericordia* (1980), 14; *Centesimus Annus* (1991), 10; "Message for the Celebration of the World Day of Peace, An Ever Timely Commitment: Teaching Peace" (2004); Pope Benedict XVI, *Caritas in Veritate* (2009), 33.

20. Pope Benedict XVI, *Deus Caritas Est* (2005), part 2.

21. Pope Benedict XVI, *Caritas in Veritate* (2009), 2; 6.

22. Ibid., 34; 37.

23. See chap. II, 1.

24. See *Gaudium et Spes*, sec. 77–84; *Compendium of the Social Doctrine of the Church*, n. 500f.

25. *Gaudium et Spes*, sec. 80.

26. Pope Benedict XV, *Pacem, Dei Munus Pulcherrimum* (1920); Pope Pius XII, *Ad Petri Cathedram* (1959); Pope John XXIII, *Pacem in Terris* (1963); Pope Paul VI, *Populorum Progressio* (1967); Pope John Paul II among others, their messages for the celebration of the World Day of Peace.

27. *Gaudium et Spes*, sec. 81. This is the official Vatican translation. See: http://www.vatican.va/archive/hist_councils/ii_vatican_council/doc uments/vat-ii_const_19651207_gaudium-et-spes_en.html.

28. Ibid., sec. 42f.

29. Marx, *Das Kapital*, 143.

30. Pope Benedict XVI, *Deus Caritas Est* (2005), 28b. This is the official Vatican translation. See: http://www.vatican.va/holy_father/benedict_xvi/encyclicals/documents/hf_ben-xvi_enc_20051225_deus-caritas-est_en.html.

31. Habermas, "Die Krise des Wohlfahrtsstaates und die Erschöpfung utopischer Energien;" Habermas, "Glauben und Wissen"; Ockenfels, *Was kommt nach dem Kapitalismus?*

32. Paul M. Zulehner, *Gott ist größer als unser Herz* (1 John 3, 20): *Eine Pastoral des Erbarmens* (Ostfildern: Schwabenverlag, 2006), 74.

33. Pope John Paul II, *Dives in Misericordia* (1980), 14.

34. Cf. n. 19.

35. Cf. chap. VI, 3.

36. For a detailed exploration of this issue, see Zulehner, *Gott ist größer als unser Herz*, 70–152.

37. *Gaudium et Spes*, sec. 76.

38. Walter Kasper, *Katholische Kirche: Wesen-Wirklichkeit-Sendung* (Freiburg i. B.: Herder, 2011), 65f., 482f.

39. Kasper, *Katholische Kirche*, 65f.

40. Concerning the theological problem of the institution, see: Medard Kehl, *Kirche als Institution: Zur theologischen Begründung des institutionellen Charakters der Kirche in der neueren deutschsprachigen katholischen Ekklesiologie* (Frankfurt a. M.: Knecht, 1976).

41. Aristotle, *Nicomachean Ethics*, V, 1229a ff.

42. Josef Pieper, *Über die Tugenden: Klugheit, Gerechtigkeit, Tapferkeit, Maß* (Munich: Kösel, 2004); John Rawls, *A Theory of Justice* (Cambridge, MA: Belknap, 1971); Rawls, *Justice as Fairness: A Restatement* (Cambridge, MA: Harvard University, 2001); Otfried Höffe, *Gerechtigkeit: Eine philosophische Einführung* (Munich: Beck, 2007).

43. Fyodor Dostoevsky, *The Brothers Karamazov*, trans. Richard Pevear and Larissa Volokhonsky (New York: Vintage Classics, 1991), 253.

44. Pope John Paul II, *Centesimus Annus* (1991), 46. Cf. Pope Benedict XVI's "Address to the German Bundestag" on September 22, 2011. Text available at: http://www.vatican.va/holy_father/benedict_xvi/speeches/2011/september/documents/hf_ben-xvi_spe_20110922_reichstag-berlin_en.html.

45. Ernst Wolfgang Böckenförde, "Die Entstehung des Staates als Vorgang der Säkularisation," in *Recht, Staat, Freiheit: Studien zur Rechtsphilosophie, Staatstheorie und Verfassungsgeschichte* (Frankfurt a. M.: Suhrkamp, 1991), 112.

46. Concerning the problem of relativism, see Kasper, *Katholische Kirche*, 42, 494.

47. Drawing upon Pope Paul VI and Pope John Paul II, Pope Benedict XVI makes this point in *Caritas in Veritate* (2009), 6.

48. See chap. II, 1.

49. See chap. II, 1.

50. See chap. II, 1.

51. Zulehner, *Gott ist größer als unser Herz*, 22–30.

52. Concerning serenity, see chap. V, 7.

IX

1. For a detailed discussion, including bibliography, see Walter Kasper, *Katholische Kirche: Wesen-Wirklichkeit-Sendung* (Freiburg i. Br.: Herder, 2011), 215–22.

2. Walter Tappolet and Albert Ebneter, *Das Marienlob der Reformatoren: Martin Luther, Johannes Calvin, Huldrych Zwingli, Heinrich Bullinger* (Tübingen: Katzman Verlag, 1962); Heinrich Petri, "Maria in der Sicht evangelischer Christen," in *Handbuch der Marienkunde*, Bd.1: *Theologische Grundlegung-geistliches Leben*, eds. Wolfgang Beinert and Heinrich Petri (Regensburg: Pustet, 1996), 382–419; Thomas A. Seidel and Ulrich Schacht, eds., *Maria, Evangelisch* (Leipzig: Evangelische Verlagsanstalt, 2011).

3. See chap. IV.

4. Martin Luther explained this point impressively in his exegesis of the Magnificat from 1521, "The Magnificat." See *Luther's Works*, general eds. Jaroslav Pelikan and Helmut T. Lehmann, 55 vols. (Philadelphia: Muhlenberg Press, 1955–86), 21:295–355.

5. Heinz Schürmann, *Das Lukasevangelium* (Freiburg i. Br.: Herder, 1969), 58.

6. Thomas Aquinas, *Summa theologiae*, pt. III, q. 30 a. 1.

7. Irenaeus of Lyons, *Against Heresies*, III, 22, 4.

8. *Gotteslob*, n. 594.

9. Concerning this point of view in feminist theology, see R. Radlbeck-Ossmann, "Maria in der Feministischen Theologie," in Beinert and Petri, *Handbuch der Marienkunde*, 1:438–41. This essay shows that there are other, and more positive approaches that take as their starting point Mary as our sister in faith, however much one has to proceed from the Bible's testimony on this topic and has to speak of Mary as the Mother of God and as our mother. Cf. 461–65 in this same volume.

10. That is not only a medieval interpretation, according to Rudolf Schnackenburg, *Das Johannesevangelium* (Freiburg i.Br.: Herder, 1975), 326. It is an interpretation that is also represented among more recent exegetes: Ulrich Wilckens, *Das Evangelium nach Johannes* (Göttingen: Vandenhoeck & Ruprecht, 1998), 296f.

11. Heinz Schürmann, "Jesu letzte Weisung," in *Ursprung und Gestalt: Erörterungen und Besinnungen zum Neuen Testament* (Düsseldorf: Patmos Verlag, 1970), 13–28; Schnackenburg, *Das Johannesevangelium*, 323–25.

12. Augustine, *In evangelium Ioannis*, 119, 3.

13. Heinrich Denzinger, *Enchiridion symbolorum, definitionum et declarationum de rebus fidei et morum* (Freiburg i. B.: Herder, 1963), 250f.; 252f.

14. See. S. de Fiores, "Maria in der Geschichte von Theologie und Frömmigkeit," in *Handbuch der Marienkunde*, eds. Beinert and Petri, 1:99–266.

15. See n. 2 previously.

16. Cf. Christoph von Schönborn, *We Have Found Mercy*, trans. Michael J. Miller (San Francisco: Ignatius, 2012), 119.

17. *Gotteslob*, n. 596; 578.

18. Well known is the painting in the pilgrimage church of St. Peter am Perlach in Augsburg (1700).

19. For some delightful examples of this type, see M.-E. Lüdde, "Unter dem Mantel ihrer Barmherzigkeit," in Seidel and Schacht, *Maria, Evangelisch*, 153.

20. See the historical overview in K. Kolb, "Typologie der Gnadenbilder," in *Handbuch der Marienkunde*, Bd. 2: *Gestaltetes Zeugnis–Gläubigen Lobpreis*, eds. Wolfgang Beinert and Heinrich Petri (Regensburg: Pustet, 1997), 449–82.

21. Such a representation of Mary can be found in the pilgrimage church, Weggental bei Rottenburg am Neckar.

22. *Gotteslob*, n. 595.

23. Ambrose, *Commentary on St. Luke's Gospel*, II, 7.

24. *Lumen Gentium*, sec. 63.

25. Ibid., sec. 61.

26. Ibid., sec. 62, which is quoted by Pope John Paul II in *Dives in Misericordia* (1980), 9. Translator's note: I have used the official English translation of this passage in Pope John Paul II's encyclical, rather than the official translation in *Lumen Gentium* because it conforms more exactly to the official German version of both *Lumen Gentium* and *Dives in Misericordia*, which Cardinal Kasper cites. The translation of the passage in *Dives in Misericordia* can be found at: http://www.vatican.va/holy _father/john_paul_ii/encyclicals/documents/hf_jp-ii_enc_30111980 _dives-in-misericordia_en.html.

27. Denzinger, *Enchiridion*, 2803. Cf. Gerhard Lohfink and Ludwig Weimer, *Maria-Nicht ohne Israel: Eine neue Sicht der Lehre von der Unbefleckten Empfängnis* (Freiburg i. Br.: Herder, 2008).

28. Schönborn, *We Have Found Mercy*, 125.

29. Ulrich Schacht, "'Meerstern, wir dich grüßen…:' Eine literarisch-theologische Exkursion in die deutsche Marien-Dichtung," in Seidel and Schacht, *Maria, Evangelisch*, 117–36.

30. A. Heinz, "Ave Maria," *Lexikon für Theologie und Kirche*, 3rd ed., ed. Walter Kasper et al. (Freiburg: Herder, 1993–2001), 1:1306f.

31. Luther, "The Magnificat," 329.

32. Ibid., 355.

33. *Lumen Gentium*, sec. 62.

34. Ibid., sec. 66.

35. Ibid. sec. 65.

INDEX OF NAMES